"Josie RavenWing's groundbreaking guide is a wonderful, supportive tool for understanding, restoring and marshaling our inner power. Her nurturing and practical exercises will help readers recognize their own spiritual essence, realize their dreams, live with greater vitality and transform our communities, person by person."

Susan Skog
author, *Embracing Our Essence: Spiritual Conversations with Prominent Women*

"Solidly grounded in Mother Earth, Josie moves in Spirit with power and focus. I found her book inspiriting and empowering. It is based on the premise that the Great Spirit is alive in all things and that our human challenge is to awaken into spiritual action through self-responsibility and practice."

Brooke Medicine Eagle
author, *Buffalo Woman Come Singing*

"This book is a gift to those who hunger for a deeper connection with the natural world. It provides hope that human beings can mature to a new level of wholeness, wisdom and compassion. It provides tools that make this growth accessible to all of us. Josie RavenWing brings a depth and wealth of experience to her insights. She is bona fide, for real, to be trusted."

Joan Skinner
professor emeritus, University of Washington Dance Department, creator of the Skinner Releasing Technique

"The future is held in the balance between our headlong rush to planetary destruction and the rebirth of a grounded spirituality that promises personal and global healing. Josie RavenWing has written a rare and beautiful book that speaks to this crisis in our culture. *The Return of Spirit* especially speaks to the hidden power within women in this culture—but not only women. The book provides practical strategies for calling forth the Spirit within each of us and for channeling this energy toward personal healing and cultural transformation. RavenWing's wisdom is rooted in stories from her own remarkable spiritual odyssey, and she writes with luminous clarity. Her writing is a richly textured tapestry woven of the shared experience, tough-minded knowledge and personal communal rituals of a gifted teacher and healer. *The Return of Spirit: A Woman's Call to Spiritual Action* is a wondrous gift to a culture in need of just such gifts."

Dean Elias
Dean of the School for Transformative Living,
California Institute of Integral Studies

THE RETURN OF SPIRIT

A Woman's Call to Spiritual Action

JOSIE RAVENWING

Health Communications, Inc.
Deerfield Beach, Florida

Library of Congress Cataloging-in-Publication Data

Cataloging-in-Publication data is
available from the Library of
Congress.

Publisher: Health Communications, Inc.
            3201 S.W. 15th Street
            Deerfield Beach, Florida 33442-8190

Cover design and cover illustration by Andrea Perrine Brower

With much love and hope,
I especially dedicate this book to
my daughter Sara
and to the future generations,
that they may delight in mystery and
the joy of spiritual action.

Contents

Acknowledgments

There are many people who contributed knowingly and unknowingly to the creation of this book. Students, clients, teachers and friends number among them. My special gratitude goes to creative writing teacher Sally Bryan, who gave the gift of her attention and expertise to my early writing efforts in high school; to Joan Skinner and the profound impact her "Releasing" work had on my awareness of energy; to "Dawn Boy," who helped me make room for mystery; to my family for their encouragement; and to Timothy Casady, Deb Felton, Julie Gammack, Julie Janss, Joyce Renwick and Pam Schoffner for their invaluable input and editorial support.

Additional thanks and blessings go to the HCI staff for their help and belief in this book, particularly to Christine Belleris and her role as a liaison, to artist Andrea Perrine Brower who gave inspired form to my vision for the book cover, and especially to publicist Kim Weiss, who originally encouraged me to send my manuscript to HCI and who has supported my work in many ways. I also extend warm appreciation to my editor, Nancy Burke, who helped polish away the last rough edges and bring the book's inner glow to the outer eye.

Finally, I give my enduring love and gratitude to Mother Earth for her endless presence, creativity and beauty. She has been a source of wonder and solace since my youth, an arena for spiritual action in my adulthood, and a wellspring of inspiration for this book. May her circle be unbroken.

Introduction

Until recently, many Westerners regarded spirit as a mysterious and unwieldy prisoner. It appeared to dwell only within the confines of man-made structures, a captive fed by the guardian clergy and at their beck and call. The rest of us had visitation rights. We spoke to spirit within the prison walls and then returned to our secular lives, content we had done our virtuous duty for the day or week or year. Our streets were safe from spirit's unpredictable nature. It might reach a ghostly arm through the prison walls from time to time, and touch us through a night's dream or a sudden, unsatisfied longing of the heart, but for the most part, our homes and businesses were sanctuaries removed from spirit's untamed presence.

But the return of spirit is now upon us. It has escaped from the churches and temples and is running wild through the forests and fields, playing its Pied Piper songs through the city streets, even slipping into our homes, beds and bodies on an increasingly regular basis. What are we going to do? How shall we treat this presence among us? What does spirit want from us and what do we want from spirit?

Of course, in reality spirit was never captive nor is it suddenly more present in nature, our houses or our bodies. The shift taking place is simply one of human awareness. Our imprisoned concepts about the potentials for spiritual contact and experience are being loosened and freed.

What catalyzed this change in Western attitudes about spirit? One factor is the increase in global human communication: a greater ability to travel and be in touch with people from other cultures. We have greater access to viewpoints that encompass more immediate and intimate contact with spiritual forces. And we are integrating these viewpoints. Principles from the East, from shamanistic cultures, and now even from quantum physics are subtly blending and creatively reforming into new shapes as we quicken with the return of spirit to the West. Psychotherapists are writing about soul and using spiritual rituals. Nurses are treating patients with Reiki. Businesswomen are going on vision quests and coming back with glowing revelations.

There are several other major forces changing our attitudes toward spirit. Western women have made a definite impact. Weary of relying on male clergy and patriarchal biases for their own spiritual experiences, increasing numbers of women are both creating spiritual rituals and including the feminine aspects of spirit in their cosmologies. Some are becoming clergy or spirituality teachers themselves. And one of the strongest elements affecting current spiritual attitudes is the Earth. As the ecologically destructive impact of Western technology loudly confronts us, a rebirth of respect and reverence for the material and spiritual treasures of Mother Earth is finally dawning.

Our spiritual awakening—this state of human flux and opened mental doors—is cause to rejoice. There is also a great need to redefine ourselves in the midst of these changes. If the clergy are not the sole keepers and intermediaries of spirit, if spirit is within and around each one of us, then we have to change our views about ourselves and spirit. For many of us, this is a baffling endeavor. How do we go about living a spiritual life? Are there things we can actually do to increase our spiritual contact or enhance our awareness of spiritual connectedness with other humans and the natural universe? Can we be practical and methodical in our approach to the mysterious realm of spirit? As we acknowledge our longing for a more spiritual life, that longing demands a workable response.

The Return of Spirit is one woman's response. After decades of spiritual experiences and accumulated learning, I decided it was time to share what I knew with more than friends or the students in my spirituality retreats. The need for practical solutions to human psychological, physical and spiritual challenges grows as we approach the millennium. From my observations as a psychotherapist, spirituality teacher and world citizen, I see the human race struggling to mature and enter a new developmental stage which is more egalitarian and spiritually fulfilled. Maturity demands responsibility, and responsibility encompasses knowledge and increased options for action. The themes of spiritual knowledge, responsibility, choice and action are the unifying strands of this book, themes aimed at broadening and further freeing the readers' concepts of what spirit and a spiritual life can be.

From the infinite archives of spirit, I selected 10 major subjects—one per chapter—to develop these themes. I felt each subject would be relevant to and easily understood by most Westerners and would be of specific interest to women. I also decided to include exercises so the readers could more quickly ground the concepts into spiritual action. I initially thought this would be primarily a woman's book, but in the process of writing I realized most of the material also had equal relevance or importance to men. I feel even the chapter on menopause is useful to men because it gives them a unique spiritual perspective on women's cycles and may increase harmony and understanding between the sexes. I decided to use "she" or "her" as the generic third person to counterbalance the volumes of past literature that use "he," "him," "man" or "mankind" to refer to both genders, but men's spiritual well-being is equally considered throughout.

The first section of this book deals with gaining knowledge and taking actions than can develop and enhance our own spirits. "Gathering Power" lays out the principles of spiritual energy and awareness, and offers methods for gathering such energy to increase personal strength, vitality and enjoyment. "'Mother' and the Quest for Awareness" expands the options for spiritual awareness and action into the rich and broad domain of nature. And the chapter on "Meaning, Art and Menopause" explores the spiritual potentials of women's cycles and their link to creativity. This chapter also encourages women to use the time of menopause to dismantle culturally imposed definitions about their own social meaning and to redefine themselves, for themselves.

The second section of the book focuses on tapping into spiritual resources and energies for healing of self and others. The "Opening the Way" first chapter in that section introduces the ways our culture is incorporating more holistic and non-Western healing approaches. In "An Underground Spiritual Revolution in Western Medicine," I highlight an energy-based spiritual healing revolution that is being quietly and methodically spearheaded by nurses—primarily women. My goal in including the subject is to bring this inspiring spiritual revolution—with its many publicly available healing trainings—to a greater audience. "Carrying the Weight of the World in Our Bodies" looks at ways in which many Western women are "disembodied spirits," how media images and male attention to their bodies cause many women to feel outside themselves and become preoccupied with their appearance. This chapter encourages women to reenter their bodies and claim their own value from within as a particular kind of spiritual healing. "Cutting Free of the Past" elucidates the spiritual and energetic nature of human sexual exchanges. It offers a powerful healing process through which people can disconnect draining energetic ties to biological parents, siblings, children and past sexual partners.

The last section opens the vista for spiritual awareness and action to the larger global community. The chapter on spiritual ritual gives an overview of existing spiritual rituals and religious beliefs, shedding light on both their positive and negative effects. It outlines the elements of effective spiritual ritual and encourages people, especially women, to courageously create their own rituals. In the "Our Spiritual Teachers: Danger or Delight" chapter, I focus on the power dynamics between spirituality teachers/leaders and their students/followers in order to help both maintain their spiritual balance. The final chapter ties together the previously mentioned themes of spiritual knowledge, responsibility, choice and action into the subject of possession. I point out our human tendency to be spiritually passive, hoping and waiting for outside forces to "possess" and save us, thinking that spiritual enlightenment will come to us magically rather than through efforts we each can and need to make. I offer more empowering attitudes and suggest alternative spiritual actions that capitalize on our innate spiritual gifts.

Many Westerners are weary of a life based solely on materialism and complex social interactions. In our hidden dreams burns hope for a love affair with life and an enduring fulfillment of heart. We won't be satisfied with a one-night stand or a teasing glance. But the love of our life—spirit—is here! All we need to fulfill our private longing is some relationship counseling and a long-term commitment. The return of spirit need not be a temporary and ephemeral visitation. For each of us it can be a permanent and passionate embrace.

PART ONE

The Individual in Motion with Spirit

*Be like a spider. Pick up the first thread
of meaning in the opening chapter, follow it with
patience and perseverance through the pages
that unfold, and by the end of the book you
will have netted rich spiritual nourishment
in your new and shining web of
manifest power.*

1

Gathering Power: Increased Vitality for Everyone

I stand on the Earth, repeatedly pulling power up through my feet and bringing it in rolling waves to my belly. The wind circles around as if it too is offering me its power. When I feel my body pulsing with energy I begin walking down the country road, heading west with the flock of ravens above me. I continue pulling energy up with every step. After a few minutes my efforts seem almost superfluous. The Earth meets my small efforts with her own massive ones, sending up such powerful rushes of energy that I feel I'll be lifted off the ground. Walking is an effortless glide, as if I were a weightless balloon skimming just above the Earth's surface. . . .

In recent years a quiet revolution has slowly and inexorably cracked the traditional Western worldview. It is a spiritual revolution, its nature partly masked by more neutral concepts of energy or power. Physicists, artists, environmentalists, healers and New Age seekers alike are taking part and being affected.

What is this revolution and how does it contrast with the former worldview?

3

For much of human history, particularly Western history, our concepts of power have been unbalanced. We often equated power with domination; power is there to be taken by conquering other humans or nature. The core of the model is: someone wins and someone loses.

Frequently women have raised objections or become uncomfortable when I've said I was going to teach them methods of gathering power. This discomfort arises from their negative associations with the word "power": associations from patriarchal models of conflict/domination, abuse of power and the win/lose model. Women have often been subjected to male abuses of power, so some discomfort with the term is understandable, but not insurmountable. An alternative definition and a fresh model for uses of power are needed.

We might want to consider *power as a spiritual essence, a cosmic flow of energy that creates, sustains and transforms moment by moment the universe of which we are a part.* That essence is abundant and free. Spiritual power is both outside and within each of us. We all have the need and ability to experience and exercise it responsibly in positive, enjoyable and productive ways.

The revolution I allude to is an *awareness of the spiritual nature of the universe.* The revolutionary knowledge that spiritual power is freely available to everyone—not just the priesthood—shatters the former Western models of scarcity, struggle and limitation. This bounty is actually the foundation of all religions. But despite the enriching potentials of Judeo-Christian traditions, the West has been cut off from the sacred heart and power of nature, from dreams, healing abilities and other forms of spiritual communion and experience. Women particularly are discouraged from becoming spiritually powerful. But most men are equally bereft. We are all thirsty voyagers in an illusory desert.

As varieties of spiritual knowledge pass from culture to culture, many Westerners are taking advantage of the opportunity to explore the benefits of spiritual practices in their own lives. Conscious contact with and awareness of spiritual power are changing individuals and systems *from within*.

Spiritual Ecology

One of the most dominant and compelling concerns of our time is ecology, the proper use of global resources. We have been spending our material resources like children gone wild in a candy shop. Only recently have we considered that we might come to the end of our pennies, or that the shop might run out of supplies.

What is true for the macrocosm of the planet is true for the microcosm of every human being's daily life. The idea of conserving personal energy, or of gathering and storing power, occurs rarely to most individuals. But many people operate on a deficit of energy, overextending themselves for others, for their jobs and even, at times, in pursuit of their own enjoyment. Eventually this deficit shows up as chronic fatigue, as stress symptoms and as other forms of imbalance or "dis-ease." And occasionally, a crisis or some other event occurs which places an unusually large demand on our available energy. If we are already running on a low tank, we may find ourselves unable to meet the demands of the situation. Or, we may scrape through only to find ourselves in a state of extended collapse, unable to face even the simpler challenges of daily living. We are burnt out, without adequate reserves and ignorant of potential resources to remedy the situation or prevent it from happening again.

Like many people, I sought solutions to this pattern only after first exhausting myself more than once. Shortly after my divorce and as a single mother, I began a full-time graduate program while working simultaneously 30 hours a week as a counselor. After several years of this routine, I was burnt out, running on caffeine and sheer will. I finally collapsed with a bronchial infection that lingered for months. No great surprise, given my lifestyle. I was depleted on every level, and in that state could serve no one, including myself.

However, I learned something: this was not a wise way to live! I began looking more seriously at the various spiritual and holistic practices I was already investigating and applying them a little more diligently to myself. "Physician, heal thyself" was a good motto for me at that time. Slowly, my life began taking on a more balanced rhythm. I started eating better, dropped the heavy caffeine habit and took more time to charge up my spiritual batteries. In later years, various teachings and teachers added the missing piece of knowledge: that it was actually possible and intelligent to store extra reserves of power and avoid the kind of serious depletion I'd experienced.

Taking care of ourselves by understanding energy flows, keeping an eye on the balance of our own input and output and gathering power are keys to increased vitality and better overall health. These practices can minimize the possibility of being caught on "empty" as we travel down the path of life, with its many challenges and side-roads.

Awareness of Energy

Spiritual awareness is the backbone of spiritual action. We can develop awareness through a variety of practices until we crawl, then walk and finally leap into the infinite realm of spiritual action.

As with all things, before we can change a pattern, we must first become aware of it. And in order to gather power or energy, we must be able to feel or perceive it in some way. Here is a simple four-part exercise for developing awareness of energy. After completing the first part, the others may be done immediately after or at later times.

GAINING AWARENESS OF ENERGY

1. The first goal is to use your hands to feel the energy of your own body, which extends past your skin into what people call the aura or luminous cocoon. This energy is usually felt in the palms as either a tingling, heat, pressure or pulsing.

    Sit or stand comfortably. Spend a few moments rubbing the palms of your hands briskly together until they feel hot. This will help you focus your attention into your hands and bring extra energy to them. Once they are hot, hold them two feet apart, palms facing. Pay utmost attention to any sensation, particularly at the center of your palms, a place that is particularly sensitive to feeling energy. Begin bringing your palms toward each other very slowly. Continue to focus your awareness on any sensations, such as tingling, heat or pressure. Notice whether the sensations intensify as you bring your hands closer together. Once you have brought them to within an inch of one another, slowly move them apart, increasing the distance as far as you can while still feeling some sensation. The intensity of sensation usually diminishes as you increase the distance between your palms. Play with this exercise a few times by increasing and decreasing the distance between your hands until you gain confidence in your ability to feel energy. Don't worry if you don't feel much sensation the first time. Like anything else, the more you do this, the sharper your perceptions will become.

2. If you enjoy this exercise and would like to expand your experience, do it with a partner. To begin, rub your own palms together and have your partner do likewise. Once they're hot, turn them so your palms are facing your partner's. Move several feet apart, then go through the same sequence of slowly approaching and distancing yourself from your partner's hands. Notice whether your partner's energy field has a different quality than your own. If so, in what ways? Most hands-on healing techniques that are energy-based are developed from this simple foundation of awareness. Healers become adept at perceiving imbalances in their patients' energy fields by sensitizing their hands to disruptions in the normal energy flows.

3. The third part of this exercise is a learning experience that can be incorporated as a diagnostic tool by healers. Have your partner stand up. Then slowly run your hands about two to six inches away from your partner's body from the head down to the feet. Start with the front of her body, then go to the back, and then to the sides. As you get a sense of her overall energy, notice if there are places where you feel anything out of the ordinary, such as more intense heat or pulsing, areas that feel cold or empty of sensation, or areas that pull at you in some manner. These are often signs of disruption in the normal energy flow. They may signify an old or recent injury, a stressed organ or some other imbalance. If you find such disruptions, ask your partner if she's aware of ever having any problems in that area. Don't be concerned about being "wrong" in your perceptions. Sometimes problems are felt in the energy field before they are registered in the physical body. Or you may be picking up a temporary energy fluctuation that may disappear without your partner's ever being aware of it. Again, the more you practice and the more partners you work with, the more

sensitive you will become. If you have a strong interest in healing, there are many books and courses to help you develop your skills and expand your methodologies.

4. Finally, expand your awareness of energy to the natural world. The principles are exactly the same: first warm your hands and focus your attention in the center of your palms. Then "scan" the energy field of your choice: stones, small plants, trees, animals, insects and the four elements of earth, water, air and fire. If you are aware that a plant or animal is sick, dying or dead, scan its energy field. Then compare it to one that is alive and healthy. Once again, the more you practice, the more sensitive you will become, and the greater your knowledge will be about the energetic nature of the world around you.

Basics of Energy Exchange

Although energy cannot be created or destroyed, it is in a constant dance of cosmic motion and transformation, even in solid objects. And energy is always being exchanged between humans and their surroundings.

Historically, many students and masters of awareness have learned that energy moves through the human body in certain ongoing patterns unless disrupted by injury or ill health. With training, some people can "see" the flows. Others can feel them through their hands. Eventually they see that these patterns extend past the skin into the auric field. The energy body is actually larger than the physical body, its surface typically 18 inches out from the skin.

This energy body is a semipermeable luminous egg or cocoon perceived as such by healers, Eastern yogis and Western shamans alike. The outer "shell" partly shields us from the constant buffeting of cosmic and earthly forces swirling around us. It enables us to feel a sense of autonomy and stability of form. The healthier and more vital we are, the more strongly our cocoons can fend off destabilizing energies that can cause weakness and illness.

But even a strong energy body has a necessary degree of permeability that lets in nourishing energies and lets out energies that are harmful or no longer needed. These energy exchanges with our environment include the more obvious functions of breathing, drinking, eating and eliminating. There are also less tangible exchanges of energy. These include human thoughts, emotions, sexual feelings and spiritual power. Such energies can travel between and affect people both close to one another and at great distances. And though Western scientists have documented that thoughts travel within an individual's nervous system as racing impulses, it is only recently that some have discovered that these impulses can be transmitted between people.

Since Westerners don't often consider thoughts as energy, neither do they consider the possibility that unexpressed thoughts and emotions can affect others. Having worked for many years in the field of psychology, I can confirm with great assurance that this is indeed true. Many times, whether in my private practice or in mental health facilities, I have encountered people in extreme emotional states of depression, anger or grief, and I've felt the impact of these energies as tangibly as any physical sensation.

I once experienced the power of another's unexpressed emotion in an intense moment while working at a substance abuse program. A resident made a suicide threat just before I arrived at the facility one afternoon, after he'd somehow snuck in a bottle of wine and become quite drunk. The program director brought the man to my office, knowing I would be there shortly to deal with him. When I arrived, the director filled me in on the situation as we stood just outside in the hall. Then he left me on my own.

As I entered my office, beyond the stink of alcohol fumes and stale vomit that first assaulted my senses was the even more palpable stench of despair emanating from my client. It hit my psyche like a black and overpowering tsunami. I felt like I'd stepped into hell. Misery dripped from the ceiling, demon phantoms of anguish rippled on the walls, failure oozed up from the carpet and psychic agony poured out of every inch of this man's skin. I immediately felt completely depressed and hopeless myself. I had to take a number of centering breaths and remind myself that what I was experiencing—as if from within—was actually coming from outside me. From my client. Then I was able to separate myself from the man's torment so that I could begin helping him, rather than collapsing with him into despair.

Everyone, upon reflection, will realize that others' mental, emotional, physical and spiritual energies affect them. We know that being around a joyful, loving person has a very different impact on us than being confronted with a hostile person or group, even if not a word is exchanged between us. A sexually charged glance from someone we are attracted to can get our heart and hormones racing. A touch from a gifted healer can mobilize our own healing energies. Being in the presence of someone who is spiritually developed can set our own spirit in motion. And in the 1960s, there was even an expression coined to describe the effect of being "straight" around a person who was "stoned." It was called getting a "contact high."

Most of the effects of energy exchanges between people could be called accidental. Carl "bad-vibes" John with angry, jealous thoughts as John walks by. A few seconds later John stumbles over his own feet. A stranger on a bus listens with compassion to an older woman's story about a recent loss in her life. The older woman leaves the bus feeling oddly comforted. In both situations, the people were oblivious to cause and effect. The outcome of the first was mildly negative, the second positive. If we're not really aware of the principles of energy in our daily lives, we don't consider how our unconscious use of energy might affect others. This is what I mean by accidental. Nonetheless, conscious or not, there is a constant invisible exchange between ourselves and others. It is as if we are all subtly interconnected in a vast web of energy strands extending around the entire planet.

If such is the case, and I believe it is, then every one of us matters, every one of us contributes energetically in some way to the greater global community. The more personal power and energy a person has, the greater her impact when she either consciously or blindly throws her own energies out into the planetary web. That reality is something to wear with grace, awareness and responsibility. If we regularly gather power, we heighten our own vitality and have extra reserves at our disposal. What we do with that power is a very individual matter, inextricably intertwined with goals, ethics and awareness.

Within the cosmic power dance are other humans who we affect and are affected by. But we often forget the interplay between ourselves and nature. Westerners rarely recognize nature as a spiritual or energetic dance partner. We need to be more responsible toward our natural environment, for physical resources *can* be depleted. We can, however, take advantage of nature's limitless supply of spiritual energies and gather power from them. The Earth and sun, flowers and wind can all be sources of spiritual exchange. Goals and focus are the determining factor: *energy follows our intention and attention*. It is through acting on this principle that we can learn to gather power from nature, store it and direct it with awareness back out into the greater environment in a dance of spiritual action.

Gathering Power

Earlier an exercise was given for expanding awareness of energy. Now we'll look at some basic principles for gathering, directing and storing energy. Our tools are our own body, breath, mental concentration and intention.

The best all-purpose place to store energy in the body is the belly, specifically from the navel down about four inches, the area some Eastern martial arts call the *hara* or *tan tien*. Some spiritual disciplines say that women store power best in the womb. This makes sense as the womb is both physically and energetically designed for expanding to accommodate and nourish one of the most potent forces in the universe, the power of life itself. Many spiritual paths acknowledge the belly as our natural center of power. Power coils in the human belly, waiting to be recognized, fed and exercised through consciously unfolding it into spiritual action. Therefore we will work with the intention to gather and direct power into our belly.

Breath is one of our greatest spiritual tools and is intimately linked to sustaining life. The deeper we breathe into the belly, the more vibrant and alive we feel. When we add our mental concentration or *attention* to breathing and a mental *intention* to gather even more energy, the mind becomes a second powerful tool.

Here is a simple starting point for power-gathering activities. With practice, it can be done in several minutes. If you really want to get "pumped up with power," the exercise can be extended for an hour!

GATHERING POWER FROM THE EARTH

This exercise is best done outdoors with bare feet, but it can also be done indoors and with shoes on. Stand with your feet about hip width apart, feet either pointed straight ahead or slightly turned out. Bend your knees slightly, and maintain that stance. Center your head in a relaxed way over your neck, shoulders relaxed and spine as straight as possible without being rigid. Relax your abdomen so that each time you inhale, your belly expands slightly. Take several deep, slow breaths into your belly and focus on your power center there. Imagine that your belly is an empty container, perhaps a bowl, created to hold and store power. A small glowing ball of light floats in its center. You will soon feed that ball with more energy so that it can grow and expand to fill the container.

Once you have a solid connection to your belly, and your mind is relatively calm, shift your focus to the soles of your feet. They are the transmitting surfaces for an exchange of power with Mother Earth. Allow your weight to drop toward the soles of your feet, feeling your muscles relax from head to toe as your energy flows downward with the pull of gravity. Let your breathing deepen. Notice how your bones allow you to remain upright even as your muscles give in to gravity. Experiment with what part of your feet best supports your weight, finding the place of balance that is the most effortless for your muscles. Focus through the soles of your feet as tension drains from your body to be absorbed by Mother Earth.

As your muscle relaxation deepens, you may notice that another force is in motion. Not only does Mother Earth pull on us, but she also emanates energy. See if you can sense some of this energy moving up to meet you as it travels through the soles of your feet, particularly through the bones. Focus especially on sensations or images of energy flowing upward through the large bones of the legs and up the spine. When the muscles are relaxed, the Earth's energy can cause the body to vibrate. If this happens, welcome the movement and simply allow it to happen.

After experiencing this energy rising from the Earth, begin to focus on storing some of it in your belly. Inhale, and imagine that you are pulling up energy through the soles of your feet. You may visualize it as streams of light. Feel it flow through your legs, up your spine and around the back and top of your skull. Exhale, and direct the energy downward through your throat and upper torso, until it reaches the small, glowing ball of light floating in your belly. Let the energy expand the ball slightly. Continue breathing and with each inhalation pull energy up through your feet, your legs and spine, and around your skull. With each exhalation, send it down to your belly, expanding the ball of power there with every breath.

When the entire container in your belly is filled with a large ball of glowing power, spend a few moments simply breathing deeply into your belly and feeling the energy there. Know that you have filled yourself with a reserve of energy that can be drawn upon as needed. You can repeat this exercise whenever you wish to charge yourself up. You don't need to wait until you feel tired and depleted to fill up with power. Instead, begin moving into a consciousness of abundance. Make energy-gathering a regular practice so that you always have reserves to draw on.

Although this exercise focused on drawing energy into the body through the feet, our hands are equally fine receptors for gathering power. Using the same principles of breath, mental focus and the belly-as-storage-area, experiment with gathering different kinds of energy in through the hands. An excellent source of power is any plant at the flowering stage. Flowers exude huge amounts of free-floating sexual energy. Since sex and life are so intimately connected, this potent energy is wonderful for enhancing our own vitality. We can simply place both hands near a flower or flowers, inhale the energy through the fingertips and palms, up through the arms, and send it down to the belly.

I gather power in a variety of ways on an almost daily basis. This supplies me with reserves of energy that I can depend on for emotional, physical, creative and spiritual support. If I know in advance I'm going to need extra energy for teaching a weekend seminar or doing a healing session, I try to gather even more power ahead of time. If you are going to have an important business meeting, a critical confrontation or a strenuous workout, you have good reason to spend extra time gathering power beforehand. You will go into the situation more centered, energized and confident. And if you do regular power-gathering as a daily practice, you will benefit by having a healthier, more vital physical and spiritual life.

As we experiment with various power sources, we may discover how the elements of water, air, fire and earth affect our overall vitality and balance. We are made of all four elements. Much of our body is water. The air we take in sustains life. Minerals form our bones and teeth and contribute to our physical health; even various metals—like iron and copper—play their parts. And we burn the calories from fuel—food—for energy and heat. Systems such as shamanism, Chinese medicine and geomancy—*feng shui*—all take into account the elements' effects on us, both the elements inside us and the elements outside us in nature. Each element is energetically and spiritually unique. As we become increasingly sensitive, we too may notice subtle differences in their effects on us. And it can be fun! The whole world is our playground.

READER/CUSTOMER CARE SURVEY

If you are enjoying this book, please help us serve you better and meet your changing needs by taking a few minutes to complete this survey. Please fold it & drop it in the mail. **As a thank you, we will send you a gift.**

Name: _____

Address: _____

_____

Tel. # _____

(1) Gender: 1) ____ Female 2) ____ Male

(2) Age: 1)____ 18-25 4)____ 46-55
2)____ 26-35 5)____ 56-65
3)____ 36-45 6)____ 65+

(3) Marital status:

1)____ Married 3)____ Single 5)____ Widowed
2)____ Divorced 4)____ Partner

(4) Is this book: 1)____ Purchased for self?
2)____ Purchased for others?
3)____ Received as gift?

(5) How did you find out about this book?

1)____ Catalog 2)____ Store Display
Newspaper
3)____ Best Seller List
4)____ Article/Book Review
5)____ Advertisement
Magazine
6)____ Feature Article
7)____ Book Review
8)____ Advertisement
9)____ Word of Mouth
A)____ T.V./Talk Show (Specify) _____
B)____ Radio/Talk Show (Specify) _____
C)____ Professional Referral _____
D)____ Other (Specify) _____

(6) What subject areas do you enjoy reading most? (Rank in order of enjoyment)

1)____ Women's Issues/ 5)____ New Age/
Relationships Altern. Healing
2)____ Business Self Help 6)____ Aging
3)____ Soul/Spirituality/ 7)____ Parenting
Inspiration 8)____ Diet/Nutrition/
4)____ Recovery Exercise/Health

(14) What do you look for when choosing a personal growth book?
(Rank in order of importance)

1)____ Subject 3)____ Author
2)____ Title 4)____ Price
Cover Design 5)____ In Store Location

(19) When do you buy books?
(Rank in order of importance)

1)____ Christmas
2)____ Valentine's Day
3)____ Birthday
4)____ Mother's Day
5)____ Other (Specify _____

(23) Where do you buy your books?
(Rank in order of frequency of purchases)

1)____ Bookstore 6)____ Gift Store
2)____ Price Club 7)____ Book Club
3)____ Department Store 8)____ Mail Order
4)____ Supermarket/ 9)____ T.V. Shopping
Drug Store A)____ Airport
5)____ Health Food Store

Which book are you currently reading? _____

Additional comments you would like to make to help us serve you better.

_____

_____

Thank You !!

ELEMENTAL ATTUNEMENT

Here are some suggestions for attuning to the energetic effects of the four elements. During and after spending time with each element, pay attention to the state of your emotions, mind, body and overall energy level. Notice how the experience feels: soothing, calming, centering, grounding, invigorating, irritating, stimulating, warming, cooling. Be aware of any results, such as: dreaminess, nervousness, diffuse focus, alertness, grogginess, clarity, lightness, heaviness, constriction, expansiveness. None of the four elements is negative, but we may feel more spiritual affinity for some than for others. Or an element that affects us in ways we enjoy one day may have a different effect on us the next. It is only by spending time and attention with each element that we become sensitive enough to learn how they can contribute to our well-being at any point in our lives.

Water: Take a long shower, hot tub or bath; go swimming; meditate on the ocean, a lake or river; take a walk in the rain or a rainforest; drink several glasses of water over the course of an hour. Notice the contrast between this and experiencing a drought or being mildly dehydrated.

Air: Spend five minutes doing slow, deep breathing while sitting indoors; take a five-minute walk outside, breathing slowly and deeply; chase a whirlwind; stand or walk outdoors when there is a light wind and when there are heavy winds. Notice the contrast between this and shallow breathing or being in an "airless," stuffy room for a period of time.

Fire: Spend 20 minutes sunbathing (if weather permits) or walking outdoors on a sunny day; do a sauna or sweat lodge;

meditate on a candle flame; make a fire—indoors or outdoors—
and gaze at it for 20 minutes while warming your body with its
heat; eat something strongly spiced with capsicum (cayenne
pepper). Notice the contrast between this and being chilled or
experiencing a period of grey, sunless weather.

Earth: Spend time gardening, especially the hands-in-the-dirt
variety of planting and weeding; meditate on a crystal; lie on the
earth (weather permitting) for at least 20 minutes; go to the
beach and bury yourself in sand, spending at least 20 minutes
there; spend time in a cave or dirt cellar; lie on your back with a
stone over your navel for a half hour; mold and sculpt real clay;
go on a long hike and sleep on the ground overnight; take a mud
bath! Notice the contrast between this and spending hours in an
airplane or indoors or in the city, without touching your feet to
real earth.

Here are some examples of how I work with the four elements
to gather power. If I am preparing to do hands-on healing, I may
repeatedly place my hands over a fire and pull some of its energy
into my palms with each inhalation until they feel suffused with
power. If I need clear and creative mental energy, a brisk walk
pulling power from the fresh air does wonders. If I need some
power to calm or cleanse away an internal storm of emotions, I
pull on the soothing water energy of a long shower. And if I need
grounded strength in my body for any variety of physical activities, I may lie belly down on the earth and pull energy into my
body, or I may eat grounding food from the earth such as brown
rice and potatoes.

Another energy-gathering exercise that has an almost immediately powerful effect—one that demonstrates how we can draw
power out of "thin air"—comes from the Taoist tradition of *nei
kung*. The exercise is based on the importance of bone marrow to

our overall vitality, health and longevity. The Taoists noted long ago that although a baby's bones are entirely filled with red marrow and abundant blood vessels, the older we get, the more the red marrow is replaced with yellow fat and blood cell production decreases. By pulling in energy from the air around us through the fingers and toes, spiraling it around the bones and then compressing and packing it into the bone marrow, the amount of fat is gradually reduced and the amount of red marrow increases. These exercises are thoroughly described in *Bone Marrow Nei Kung* by Mantak and Maneewan Chia, an excellent book for those who are intrigued by the idea of slowing or reversing the aging process through this kind of power-gathering.

In *Cultivating Female Sexual Energy*, another book by the Chias, an exercise is given for drawing power from the ovaries— which are chock full of *chi*, or life force. The ovarian power is circulated up the spine and through the body for increased vitality. Even though ovarian energy cycling is primarily for premenopausal women, residues of power may remain in and around the ovaries for many years after the cessation of menstruation. Postmenopausal women may therefore wish to practice it as well.

Wind and Fire Power from the East

A variety of Eastern disciplines have recognized the calming and restorative benefits of utilizing the air or wind elements to gather energy and power. *Qigong* or *chi kung*, which means "breath training," is one Eastern practice which uses the air element for a variety of energy-gathering goals. Deep qigong belly breathing with an inner affirmation such as "I am well" is a calming and energizing practice used for healing purposes. It is considered part of the "soft style" of qigong. Qigong "hard" style is a martial art form. Hard style qigong and other systems of martial arts incorporate aspects of power gathering. The deepest spiritual core of martial arts is awareness of energy. Part of martial artists' training includes gathering power in the belly—through meditations and breathing exercises—to be used both for vitality and for directing out through the limbs toward one's opponent. Another way this gathered power is focused from the belly outward is in the use of the "*ki'ai*," a loud vocalization familiar to us from Bruce Lee films.

Some Western martial arts instructors have sadly abandoned teaching their students the meditative, healing and other energy-based principles of knowledge at the core of these Eastern disciplines. Instead, they favor a purely physical approach. By doing so, they sever the spiritual art or soul by focusing only on the martial aspect. I advise anyone interested in studying the martial arts to seek out instructors who offer the spiritual/energetic knowledge as well as physical self-defense. And for those who wish to read more on qigong, I recommend *Quigong for Health* by Masaru Takahashi and Stephen Brown, *The Root of Chinese Chi Kung* and *The Essence of Tai Chi Chi Kung* by Dr. Yang Jwing-Ming and *The Way of Energy* by Master Lain Kam Chuen.

At the opposite end of the Eastern spectrum from calm *yin* qigong belly breathing are the *yang* yoga styles of "fire breathing." Fire breathing is very rapid. It draws much more oxygen and energy into the body in a given period than normal breathing and quickly heats up the entire system. This is a fast way of gathering power. But it shouldn't be overused, as some symptoms of spiritual imbalance, hyperventilation and dizziness can occur. Occasionally I'll do fire breathing for a few minutes just before a physical workout or a meeting where I know I'm going to need to be energetic, intense and fierce!

Some Westerners have learned a variation of fire breathing through a therapeutic process called "rebirthing." Like yogic fire breathing, the overbreathing of rebirthing provides extra energy.

As in yoga, that power can be applied to specific healing processes or spiritual awakenings, or can be stored for future use. Through qigong, yoga and rebirthing, the wind and fire of the East are spreading around the planet, providing new means for healing, gathering power and increasing vitality.

Self-Inventory for Energy Leaks and Loss

Since awareness is key to all aspects of self-knowledge, it is important to apply it to the arena of personal power. Although I encourage energy-gathering as a regular practice, sometimes life demands more of it than usual. We may also need to change certain habits, patterns, attitudes or even environments if they are causing us to lose power faster than we can replace it.

Stress is a far-reaching term which covers many aspects of life and can either be empowering or debilitating in its effects. Some daily stresses are so constant we don't even consider them as such unless circumstances render us less able to cope with them than usual. Gravity is one such example, an invisible daily stress that both strengthens and weakens us. As we age, depending on our overall muscle tone and health, the pull of gravity eventually takes its toll on our skin, connective tissue, and sometimes our bones. And yet, dealing with gravity also teaches us many things and up to a certain point is strengthening. Learning to get from the stage of crawling to the mastery of walking is very stressful, but in the process we discover a great deal about both our bodies and about gravity, and our bones and leg muscles become stronger. This experience of persisting through stress—while gaining strength, skills and knowledge—is heady stuff, clearly expressed by toddlers in their gleeful and triumphant first march. The stress of gravity hasn't ended, but the benefits of walking are ample reward for our efforts. However, if we have ever injured any part of our legs, spine or torso, we know that gravity once again becomes a more formidable stressor.

Almost everything we do stresses or challenges some part of our being. Yet we rise again and again to these daily challenges, often without thought or appreciation for the adaptability of the human organism. Sometimes, however, certain stresses add up and we can no longer adapt without a debilitating loss of energy. Following are some of the stresses that might warrant changing our circumstances or gathering more power to successfully deal with them.

Physical stresses: inadequate rest, chronic muscle tension, poor posture, injuries and ill health, substance abuse, extremely demanding physical jobs or, conversely, lack of adequate exercise.

Mental stresses: degree programs or other demanding studies, learning a new job or ongoing workload demands, confusion about goals and moving to a new location—especially to another culture that demands learning a new language and customs.

Emotional stresses: all variety of social pressures and expectations, social isolation, new or difficult relationships (including with oneself) and the loss of someone important.

Mental/emotional stresses: environmental, interpersonal, hormonal/developmental, occupational and financial stresses.

Spiritual stresses: crises of belief/faith, lack of belief in spiritual power, lack of knowledge of spiritual connectedness.

How many of these stresses can you identify in your recent or present life? Are there others I didn't mention? Sit down and make a list of the stresses in your life and then do an honest assessment of your overall energy. Are you scraping the bottom of your energy tank, or are you "topped off" and barreling down life's freeway with plenty of reserves for the road?

Stress is an ongoing aspect of everyone's life, but we can choose how we deal with it. Awareness, practical spiritual and secular tools or options, proper attitude and means for gathering power can make the difference between balance and imbalance. Adequate sleep and dreaming can be as powerful a source for gathering energy as bone marrow nei kung, depending on the circumstance. We must first know our condition and then explore our choices. Personal inventory alone is an act of power. Acting upon the knowledge we gain is living the spiritual journey.

Energy and Goals

Since energy follows our intention and attention, understanding the role of goals is a critical one for gathering power and preventing its loss. Confusion of goals was listed earlier as one form of mental stress. When our goals are confused, our energy can be dispersed in too many directions at once, without a clear channel in which to flow. Having no goals at all is equally debilitating, and the mechanics of that dilemma will be explained by first explaining its opposite.

Consider the image that a goal is like bait on the end of an invisible fishing line. We fling this bait out into the future, however near or far, and then our energy moves toward it like a fish moves toward a fat and tantalizing worm. People who have strong, clear goals often exude a certain vitality. Their energy has a direction. It's mobilized toward the realization of those goals—whether they are attainable or not.

When a person has no goals, her energy collapses or dissipates. An example of this is the person who worked hard all her adult life and finally retires. If she has no goals for retirement, often her health will decline, depression may set in and an unnecessarily early death may result. Sometimes this same sequence occurs with women whose goals are centered around childrearing. When their youngest chick leaves the nest, these women often sink into clinical depression, a condition that fresh goals can often reverse.

Some people may have numerous goals in one area of their lives, and inadequate goals in others. This makes them vulnerable. Should that one area become disrupted for some reason, their energies suddenly have no direction. I learned this lesson in my early 20s. During that period I was a dedicated dancer. I often spent eight hours a day or more in dance classes, as a dancer and a choreographer, and in dance company rehearsals or performances. I was considering making this my life's work. Then one day I was out on a leisurely drive and someone ran a red light, crashed into my car and I was thrown close to a hundred feet through the air before landing like a strange large cat on my hands and knees.

That brush with death was quite sobering and life changing. I realized the rather precarious nature of my physical well-being and goals as a dancer. I decided shortly after that to continue dancing but also to begin exploring other career options that wouldn't depend quite so heavily on peak physical performance. I expanded my goals into new areas and developed a more balanced platform for my energies to leap from. I believe the close encounter with death advised me well.

In your self-inventory of energy leaks, look for areas where your goals are limited, weak or nonexistent. Then become a hunter. Hunt for power and for new places to aim it.

The Quick Fix

We enjoy the feeling of going through our day with a high level of energy, just as we enjoy the ability to relax and rest when we need to. But we have also become accustomed to the quick fix. Many who seek a high energy state become dependent on various substances that induce it. The downside is that those same substances often make relaxation difficult and deplete our energies. We can then get trapped into needing increasingly more of the substance just to get through life's daily demands, as I did with coffee while in graduate school.

Power-gathering practices also can supply us with energy fairly quickly, sometimes immediately, and don't have the downside of depletion that caffeine, white sugar and other substances do. As with many endeavors, the broader effect of power-gathering is seen most clearly over the long term. As we practice, our spirit, vitality, overall health and ability to meet life's challenges with greater energy grow subtly stronger day by day. Occasionally, the quick fix substance may be useful in an emergency, but it is not a solid foundation for a lively and resilient energy body.

Certain foods and herbs also provide us with concentrated and nourishing power, and eating them can be part of our power-gathering practices. Bee pollen is a good source of pure energy. It is the manifest life force from plants and eating it increases our own *chi*. Wheatgrass or its juice has concentrated chlorophyll and enriches the blood. Many foods and herbs are natural, non-caffeine stimulants. They increase physical energy, drive the circulation and warm the body. These are yang, or warming foods, as opposed to yin, or cooling foods. Many yang foods can be found in our kitchens, including garlic, onion, ginger, cayenne, black pepper, cinnamon, anise and rosemary, to name a few. Ginseng, known to herbalists as the "king tonic," and its milder counterpart, *don shen*, are also potent herbal stimulants.

In addition to bee pollen and herbal stimulants, fresh-picked organic produce is still humming with life and chi, and for that reason fits the bill of excellent power food. If you need a boost and want to get it through eating, these foods and herbs can strengthen your system while enhancing your energy level. They are a safer bet then the quick fix menu.

Protection and Transcendence

Gathering power also is valuable as a form of self-defense or protection. We know now that thoughts and emotions are energy forms that can affect not only the person having them but others. We are constantly bombarded with these energies. Short of living alone in a cave, this is almost impossible to avoid.

However, we can defend ourselves against energies that may not be beneficial to our mental, emotional, physical and spiritual health. Gathering power consistently is one of the best ways. To understand its protective function, we'll use the image of a volleyball. If a volleyball is well-filled with air, punches to its surface bounce off with no ill effects. If the ball is not completely filled, however, a blow to the surface will penetrate toward the center of the ball. If there is little or no air inside, the ball can be flattened with minimal pressure.

Our energy body is very similar. If our luminous cocoon is resilient and filled to the brim from gathering power, harmful energies are more easily repelled and bounce off with little or no effect. But the lower our energy reserves, the deeper into our cocoon these outside forces can intrude, and the greater the risk to our overall health.

When we expand our energy field with power, we also transcend our normal boundaries. As a counterbalance to the narrower fixations of daily life, people have long desired and sought out experiences of spiritual transcendence via many methods: yoga, extended prayer, meditation, ecstatic dance, vision questing and other practices. The more power we gather, the more our energy can expand toward transcendental vistas. From the ancient scriptures to modern times, stories abound of such efforts and their various "out-of-body" results. They offer a legacy and a lure of what is within the realm of spiritual possibilities.

Gathering power on a consistent basis is responsible spiritual action. Doing so increases our choices, our strength and our vitality, and is good for our mental, emotional, physical and spiritual health. It reduces the potential of being victimized by a variety of forces. Finally, gathering power can be part of the great spiritual journey of transcending our normal routines and identities, of exploring the interconnecting webs of abundant universal energies.

2

"Mother" and the Quest for Awareness

As the rising sun bathes the red canyon in first light, the sounds of drumming ricochet off the high, glowing walls with a steady pulse. One by one, slowly and silently, 12 grimy but radiant women follow the echoing beat to the small fire nestled on the earth. They emerge through the juniper trees, straggle in from up the arroyo, or crawl down like spiders from their high cliff ledges. When all are assembled in a circle around the burning cottonwood, I stop drumming. While sprinkling a handful of fragrant cedar onto the glowing coals, I begin a prayer of thanksgiving to the powers that were with these women during the three days of their vision quest. Each woman joins in softly. Our voices drift up with the pungent smoke, up toward the azure heavens where a hawk spirals lazily in the warming desert air.

For some years I have taken groups of women to the Southwest for week-long spiritual retreats. During those life-changing days, I share a wealth of options for spiritual action. It is a time for the women to renew their connection to spirit. They learn ways to increase awareness of spirit in their bodies, in nature and in the energetic flow between the two.

On the retreat we are often outdoors, and it is there I encourage the women to thoroughly explore the domain of "Mother." Mother is the term I use to refer to the spiritual energies of Mother Earth and of all that is natural upon her body and within her atmosphere. The term Creator would also be a valid one. However, just as a human mother is generally available to us through physical proximity as we grow up, the spiritual forces with us on Earth are readily available as well. Mother seems appropriate to describe what is in easy reach of human experience as we grow up here on Earth, while Creator includes what is also much farther away.

The women's explorations of Mother build steadily during the week until the three-day vision quest ceremony. Then, in the tradition of spiritual seekers of many cultures, the women each set off alone into the wilderness to search for even deeper connections with—and revelations from—the sacred realms. All they have learned both culminates and expands during those vision quest days in the desert landscape. Each woman finds herself, spirit and Mother.

For city dwellers, a sustained focus on Mother is quite unusual and greatly shifts the balance of attention. Most of our daily focus is confined to human activities, urban environments and modern technology. All are so absorbing we rarely notice that a sole focus on these elements is also narrow and limiting. Except for the occasional moments when we stop to smell a flower, enjoy a day at the beach, or are inconvenienced by extreme weather conditions, we tend to forget there is much more out there beyond our human activities and relationships. We forget that we are an intimate part of Mother. Even city people with spiritual interests and pursuits forget. We often focus more on our internal experiences and those of other people than on our bond to Mother. As retreat participants spend most of their time outdoors and shift the balance of their attention more toward Mother, they rediscover their connection to her and to the rest of life.

This natural union with Mother has always been there, waiting to be revealed through direct experience. It blossoms through a spirit-to-spirit connection rather than through man-made objects or philosophical theories. Former religious concepts and representations of Mother become irrelevant in the face of personal contact. Mother represents and offers herself for what she is. And because we are part of her, making room for Mother also makes room for the spiritual expressions of our own beings. The week of retreat is a solid reminder that there are many treasures in Mother's realm, but in order to perceive them we must dismantle certain habits.

Every woman arrives the first day of retreat with quite a bit of baggage. Not all of it is physical. The majority is a weighty mass of habits accumulated over the years. Usually this burden was acquired so unconsciously that even if the bearer's spirit is being crushed by it, the effects of the excess weight are rarely understood. Much of the baggage takes the form of entrenched patterns of thinking and emotional response. Some of the other patterns that are soon revealed include preoccupations with appearance, food and schedules.

Our habits tend to put us to sleep. They lull us into spiritual oblivion with their monotonous and repetitious tones. As a remedy, from the beginning of the retreat I point out the dulling effect of habits and then systematically disrupt them. The shamans of old knew well that every time even a modest habit is broken, a breathing space is provided for our spirit to flex its muscles and see the world in a new way. As their patterns are interrupted repeatedly throughout the retreat, the women's awareness is heightened and purposefully shifts to several key elements and practices. The women begin focusing on feeling the power flows within themselves and in nature rather than fixating on their external appearance. They exchange normal social conversation for the spiritual value of silence. They eat light, primarily vegetarian meals, and gather more energy from other sources. And finally they spend several days without eating and without human company. Throughout a week of breaking deadening habits, each woman attains more spiritual awareness and freedom.

The results are magnificent. An inner experience of renewal is only the beginning of these results. Each woman gains a real sense of intimacy with Mother. Many have visions, powerful dreams and personal healings. All awaken to a feeling of wonder at their own beings and the larger universe.

Power and Silence

How can old habits be dismantled and replaced by spiritual actions so we can directly touch spiritual mystery? Gathering power, stopping energy leaks and cultivating the benefits of silence are all effective for achieving this transformation.

As the women come together for the retreat, they form a new social group with a variety of potential benefits and hazards. The most common hazard the group dynamic presents to each participant is the draining of energy through unnecessary social chitchat. In a new group, we tend to fall back on everyday conversation. We gather information on each other's family background, work history, significant other, astrological birth sign, etc. The uncomfortable unknown is thus conquered and we settle into our social niches within the group. The presence of mystery is talked away. And that is one of the first things I discourage! Becoming accustomed to the presence of the unknown is one of my greatest goals for the women. It shakes up their old habits and wakes them from their inertia. And often, the domain of spirit is most directly experienced within the unknown.

Instead of indulging in normal conversation and information-gathering, I ask the women to allow each other space to be more mysterious, both to themselves and to one another. I describe the advantages of this habit-breaking maneuver, which include the freedom to behave in new ways and create more room for spirit. I also point out the unusual quality of being in an all-women's group that has as its primary goal spiritual development and awakening. This circumstance in itself is a shift from normal patterns. Since they only come together for a week, the women make choices about their interactions. Instead of engaging in idle and draining chitchat, they can honor one another spiritually with silence and become a powerful and unique support group!

To help them in their efforts to break normal talking habits, I offer them a practical exercise. Throughout the week, retreat participants commonly have a variety of unusual spiritual experiences as a result of our activities. After such extraordinary encounters, most people rush to share the event with others. We are story-tellers, after all, with a common fascination for hearing a good tale. My suggestion, however, is that the women don't speak of their spiritual experiences for at least a few days after they've occurred. I explain that this new behavior benefits them by again breaking an old pattern. In addition, the power of their experiences is contained by silence, which allows it to gestate, grow and deepen. Every time we talk about an event, especially one that recently occurred, we dissipate some of its energy. This is considered good therapy for diffusing intense emotions. But one of the goals of the retreat is teaching women how to gather and hold increasing amounts of power, and not speaking about their spiritual experiences furthers this goal.

BREAKING (CHATTER) FOR POWER

Here are some suggestions for breaking typical conversation patterns in your daily life. All of these practices will help you increase your spiritual awareness and power.

1. Should you have an unusual spiritual experience or dream, wait at least several days before deciding if and with whom you want to share it.

2. If other people try to share such an experience with you, stop them and ask how long it's been since the event occurred. If it's been less than several days, tell them you don't want to hear about it for at least a few days. If you wish, you can explain your understanding of why it would be better for them to wait. Or you can tell them that you'll explain at a later point. Observe their responses to being interrupted and note your own feelings when interrupting them.

3. Go for a walk with a friend. Make a mutual agreement in advance that neither of you will speak the entire time. You can add to your experience by including the power-gathering exercise 1 outline on the next page. Or simply take a normal walk, but without speaking. Observe the responses of yourself and your friend to this prolonged silence. Don't share your observations for several days.

4. Leave the tip of your tongue curled slightly back and touching the roof of your mouth—the palate—at all times during the day except when you need to eat, drink or

speak. This is an Eastern centering technique practiced by Hindus and Taoists alike. It will also make you more aware of when and if you really need to talk.

5. Do less than your share in a group conversation. Observe the possible tendency to one-upmanship storytelling in yourself and others.

Breaking the habit of normal conversation is one of the many challenges the retreat women face, and one of the most difficult. We are not very comfortable with either silence or the unknown. We've been conditioned to fill the spaces in our lives with constant noise, objects and activities. Even when we're alone, most of us deny ourselves external silence, preferring some background sound from the television, radio or stereo. And when we're with others, we often feel compelled to keep up a steady flow of conversation. If too many moments pass without talk, we begin feeling uncomfortable and embarrassed, as if we were party hosts failing to keep everyone entertained.

Beyond the social conditioning of our culture, there are other factors that create this discomfort with silence. Whether we are alone or with others, when there are no external distractions we are more intensely aware of our own internal state. As this is not always a peaceful experience, we tend to avoid it.

Why is going within rarely a calming exercise? Perhaps because we have thoroughly bought—and paid for with our peace of mind—the philosophy, "I think, therefore I am." Children of the Age of Reason, we have so deeply accepted this dictum that if we are not constantly thinking, we are consumed with the anxiety that our very existence, our raison d'etre, might disappear. We *must* think. Constantly. We review past actions or events: what is already known to us. Or, we try to find various means for navigating what is still disconcertingly unknown to us: the future. These are the primary activities of our ongoing internal dialogue. The waters of our inner being are not calm. Our thoughts are like myriad restless minnows always darting here and there, disturbing the surface with their frantic motion. And because these activities focus on either the past or the future, when we are thinking we are never fully present in the moment.

The internal dialogue is a major handicap to developing spiritual awareness. Only by concentrating our attention in the "now" can we directly experience spirit. The present moment is an eternal river full of endless spiritual potentials, potentials never to be repeated in exactly the same way the next moment. Every time we miss the present, we pass up its gifts. Fortunately, the universe is benevolent in that we are constantly given fresh opportunities. However, the question we might ask is, "How many gifts do I really want to pass up?" If spirit offers itself to us only in the present, and if thinking keeps us trapped in the past and the future, then the sincere spiritual quester will want to escape the trap and take up spirit's offer. When we silence the internal dialogue, we can both escape the trap and immerse ourselves in endless spiritual possibilities.

Meditation is one of the most practical means for mesmerizing those restless minnows of thought into temporary inactivity. Its effectiveness is acclaimed by yogis and Christian saints alike. Every reliable form of meditation I've ever tried provides a constant, non-thinking focus such as the breath, a candle flame or a mantra, to keep the mind occupied until it finally accepts stillness. Once our thoughts are still, we enter the world of spirit and the unknown. For those reasons, I teach the women in my groups several forms of meditation throughout the retreat, including a Taoist-based cycling breath, *tai chi* moving meditations, and some I've created myself. During the first few hours we're together, I usually start the women with a simple focus on their own breath. As they strengthen their powers of concentration, I help them expand on that focus with other meditative processes.

BREATHING TOWARD INNER SILENCE

Here is a simple breath meditation, a tried and true method of many spiritual disciplines for calming the mind and bringing awareness into the present. Try it for five minutes daily for a few days. Then gradually increase the length of time until you can do it for at least 15 minutes. You may enjoy the benefits so much that occasionally you will expand the practice to an hour.

Sit or lie down comfortably and relax your body. Then start paying attention to each breath without trying to alter your normal breathing in any way. Listen to the sounds of every inhalation and exhalation. Also notice that each breath has its own unique rhythm. Follow those rhythms with your attention. As you meditate, your breathing may become slower and deeper of its own accord. Allow it these changes. Next, notice the qualities of the air you are breathing. Become aware of its softness and buoyancy. Notice how the air you exhale is warmer and more humid than the air you inhale. Feel these differences inside your nose and throat. Now try to be aware of as many of those elements simultaneously as possible: the sounds and rhythms of your breath and the qualities of the air. Absorb your awareness deeper and more fully with each passing breath. If you become distracted by thoughts, simply and calmly bring your attention back to focusing on your breath. You may need to do this again and again, but if you persist, your mind will eventually accept inner silence for increasing lengths of time. And spirit will reward you in a variety of ways.

Silencing the internal dialogue is the first new behavior the women learn in order to deepen awareness of spiritual mystery. Gathering power is the second. In chapter 1, I recommended gathering power as a method for preventing depletion of energy. I bring this benefit up to the women during their retreat, and teach them the exercises presented in that chapter. I then give them additional motivation for continuing such practices: *power follows power*. If we sincerely wish to have powerful spiritual encounters and experiences, the more personal power we carry within us, the more we will attract spiritual power from outside ourselves. Since the culmination of the retreat is the vision quest, a time when the women involved most determinedly court spirit, I advise them to gather as much power beforehand as possible. One of the most consistent ways we do this is on our many walks in the desert. After I teach the women the second exercise for gathering power from the earth, I expand it into a walking exercise.

THE BELLY WALK

You might want to review "Gathering Power From the Earth" (p. 14) before proceeding. Once you are confident about the process, begin practicing it while walking. I suggest taking extremely slow steps at first until you get everything coordinated. Even though you are still pulling energy up from the Earth and storing it in your belly exactly as you did before, doing so while moving may be an initial challenge. As you walk, remember to pull energy up through both feet simultaneously like you did when standing. You will improve with practice, so don't get discouraged.

When you feel you can concentrate reasonably well while walking, set a rhythm for your steps and breath. This has several benefits. It will increase your ability to focus, and during long or otherwise challenging walks, like hiking uphill, it will increase your endurance. Begin with a rhythm of eight: four steps to inhale and gather power, four steps to exhale and store the power in your belly. Remember to breathe through your nose if at all possible. Again, start slowly and then pick up speed as you practice this eight-count process.

The specific rhythm is arbitrary. Depending on your stamina and the terrain, you may need slower or faster breaths. If the walk is easy and you are in good shape, you may be comfortable with a 10- or even 12-count rhythm, where each in and out breath takes five or six counts. If you are hiking up a steep incline, you may need to shift gears into shorter and shorter breaths, and your exhalation may need to be even shorter than your inhalation. For example, on some steep hikes a shift into two counts (or steps) to inhale deeply and one count to quickly and fully exhale may be necessary. This type of rhythm allows you to get rid of the depleted air quickly so you can gulp in your next dose of fresh and welcome oxygen. Once the terrain levels off again you can gradually shift back to longer and more even breaths.

The main elements to remember are to keep gathering and storing power, and to find a pace at the beginning of your walk that you can maintain throughout, even if the length of your breaths change. If this sounds contradictory, I will clarify with an example. Imagine the regular sound of a clock ticking or a metronome beating. The pace of your steps matches the rhythm of the sounds, and stays consistent during your entire walk. However, the length of your breath, or number of steps per breath, can change depending on the terrain. Maintaining this steady pace for walking is important. An even pace allows your body to sink into a predictable rhythm around which it can adapt its needs for energy, thus making its job easier. Initially you may be tempted to slow down on inclines, but I have found it is actually more fatiguing to do so.

Gathering power, setting a steady walking pace and establishing breathing rhythms that adapt to various terrains will increase your energy and endurance. And because the belly walk is a moving meditation containing several focuses for the mind, you may also discover the added benefits of internal silence and enhanced spiritual awareness.

During one of my desert retreats, a participant went through a brief period of rebellion on a particularly challenging "belly walk." She followed my guidelines for several days of walking, but this particular day she found herself in the midst of a real uphill battle. Our group was hiking up a mile-long trail which took us from the bottom to the top of a deep canyon. Part way up, Greta met an internal wall of resistance to the belly walk exercise. She slowed down and let her breathing and pace become irregular. She told herself she didn't think the exercise was helping anyway, and she was going to do things her own way this time.

Greta was the last person to reach the top of the canyon—and the most fatigued! After recovering, she made her way over to me for a brief conversation. She said she'd had her moment of rebellion and had learned a lesson the hard way. Shortly after walking in her old way, Greta realized she was losing energy. She stubbornly persisted for most of the remainder of the trail nonetheless. Near the end, as an "experiment," she returned to the exercise I'd given her. Less than a minute later, her stamina improved and walking became much easier. As the result of her uphill battle, she understood that the suggestions I gave the group day by day had practical and beneficial results, and that she had come on this journey to learn something new. We both laughed over the stubborn quality of old habits and continued on in good humor.

The women in my retreat groups struggle daily to overcome the inertia of the draining social and mental habits that keep them distracted from spiritual awareness. They each have moment-to-moment choices to make about their use of energy, and grow more perceptive about the results of their choices. I encourage them to keep coming back to their goals, to the reasons they are at the retreat, so their choices will be made on the basis of internal motivations and not because "teacher said so." And I remind them that the more grounded they become in any spiritual practice and awareness during our week together, the more likely they are to continue after the retreat ends. Everything these women learn can be applied in "normal life." And that is where most of the human journey takes place.

Unfolding the Spiritual Will

A few hours before one of these Southwest retreats began, I stood in the warm sun gathering energy for what I knew would be both an exciting and demanding week. Maria, one of the participants who'd arrived early, relaxed nearby in a lounge chair. As I grounded myself on the desert soil, something pulled my gaze upward and I saw a red-tail hawk circling high in the distance. With a deep breath of appreciation and anticipation, I immediately pulled a strand of energy from my belly up through my torso, moved the strand through my right arm, and sent it out my fingertips in the direction of the hawk. Several moments later I felt it connect with the regal bird, and then, like a fisherman, I began slowly and gently pulling my "fishing line" back in toward my body. As I did so, I mimicked the spiralling motion of the hawk's flight with my right arm, the arm the energy-strand was attached to. Slowly and steadily, the hawk circled closer until it flew directly over my head. I continued moving my arm while I sang one of my "power songs" to the bird. After about five minutes of mutual and sustained delight, I stopped singing, let go of my connection to the red-tail, dropped my arm and pulled my "fishing line" entirely back into my body. The hawk immediately bobbed slightly downward in its circle, and then flew straight away toward the area from which it came. I murmured a "thank you" and then lowered my eyes. When my gaze lit upon Maria, I struggled not to burst into hilarious laughter. Her jaw was dropped about as far as it could go, and her eyes were wide in amazement.

"How, what—what did you do?" she finally stammered.

"I was dancing," I replied with a grin. "I was dancing with Mother by unfolding my spiritual will. She and I are old dancing partners from way back."

Maria did not appear particularly enlightened by this statement.

"Don't worry," I assured her. "It's one of the main things I'm going to be teaching you all to do this week. And I know you're going to enjoy it just as much as I do."

The phrase "spiritual will" is the term I use to describe a spiritual organ that is every bit as real as the human brain or heart. It is most concentrated in the belly, which is why I refer to that area as our power center. However, the will also composes and holds together the entire energy field that we call a human being and that makes each of us unique in the universe.

The will is not as dense as the physical body it helps hold together and it is not totally contained within the body. Some of it hovers around us, forming the aura or luminous cocoon. When we sleep and dream, strands of the will automatically escape their usual confines. They form our "dreaming body" so that we may travel to other realms where, unrestricted by the laws of the physical universe, we may experience more freedom, including the freedom to fly. But for most people, the activity of the will in dreaming takes place without the kind of guidance and awareness we have while awake. Very few of us are trained to be "lucid dreamers" and gain more conscious control over the will's nocturnal activities. In fact, few of us use the will consciously when we are awake. But with enough awareness and strength, we can intentionally direct the will out from our physical bodies and send it in search of spiritual knowledge, adventure and new "dancing" partners. Maria witnessed my own waking dance of will in my interaction with the hawk.

In order to accomplish such feats again and again, I've needed to strengthen my will by nourishing and exercising it. Every time I gather power and store it in the belly, I am feeding my will. Every time I engage in a spiritual practice such as meditation, energy-based healing or creating a spiritual ritual, I am exercising my will. This is what I teach others who are interested in expanding their repertoire of spiritual actions. And because the physical body houses a great deal of the will's energy, the stronger and healthier the body, the more robust and lively the will. That is one reason I not only encourage the women to prepare for the retreat by exercising regularly for at least a month in advance (and to continue to do so afterwards), but also include spiritually directed physical activity as a major part of the retreat itself.

If we have developed a strong and vital will, how do we then consciously direct it out of the body? If you have studied martial arts with good teachers, you may be familiar with some of the dynamics of sending energy out from the belly, or of pulling it from the belly and moving it out through the arms, legs or voice while punching, kicking or yelling a *ki'ai*. Even though the concept of will may still be new and a bit difficult to grasp, remember that it is basically energy. And as we learned in the first chapter, energy follows our intention and attention. That principle is key to the unfolding of will. Just as in gathering power, setting a goal—the unfolding of will—and then applying a strong mental focus coordinated with breathing provides the elements needed to accomplish the goal.

UNFOLDING THE WILL

Here is a beginning exercise to help you integrate this new information about the spiritual will. If you practice it regularly, maintain a strong body and gather power, in time your will can become a very responsive instrument for a variety of spiritual endeavors.

Sit or stand comfortably with a straight spine. Your goal or intention will be the unfolding of will. Spend a few minutes breathing slowly and deeply into your belly. As you do so, form a mental image of a ball of light sitting in your belly. This ball becomes larger and brighter with each inhalation. Once the ball is strong and glowing, visualize a strand or vine of its energy beginning to unfold from the ball and emerging out of your navel. With each exhalation, push the vine a little further out, directly in front of you. Just like the ball, this vine glows with light. Keep directing it forward until it extends at least five feet in front of you.

Once this is accomplished, shift your intention to bringing the vine back into your belly. With each inhalation, pull both your abdominal muscles and the vine inward. Continue to do so until the entire vine of will has been gathered back into the ball of power in your belly. Then relax. You have just completed your first exercise for the unfolding of will.

Unfolding the vine of will can be used to contact and then learn from various spiritual sources in our universe. One of the main ways I use it is to communicate and interact—to "dance"— with Mother. These may be rather foreign concepts for some Westerners. We are quite accustomed to manipulating and taking from nature on physical levels, but spiritual interactions with her are rarely considered, let alone engaged in. And yet this is not only possible but within relatively easy reach of most people.

In chapter 1, I introduced Mother as an endless source of power and gave examples of how to gather some of her energy. Try to shift perspective now and see her as a future dance partner for your spiritual will. Rather than pulling energy from her, this section focuses on exploring the potentials of unfolding the will outward—touching, interacting with and learning from Mother. The will is not only a means of making contact. It is also a kind of spiritual telephone cord. Information can flow both ways, between you and whatever you touch with your will.

This potential of will was one of the most exciting spiritual discoveries I ever made. As I practiced unfolding my will to contact plants, animals, minerals and the Earth herself, I was quiet and "listened" with my will. Everything I touched gave me various kinds and qualities of feedback about its nature. The knowledge came in one or more forms on any given occasion: sensations, images and occasionally emotions. At first I doubted my experiences, concerned they might be my own fantasies, but over time these doubts slowly dissipated. I began trusting that when my own internal dialogue was silenced first through meditation, whatever came to me was from the outside sources my will was touching. This was exciting not only because of the novelty of the situation. I was also increasingly aware that we are not alone in this world. There are numerous other beings available for spiritual interactions. And I was thrilled to find I was not completely dependent on books or other people for information about them. I now had the means for direct access to knowledge of an herb's properties, the wind or a butterfly's nature: my will!

This kind of spiritual involvement with nature is essentially shamanistic. Western traditions tend to view the physical universe as a secular environment, and Creator as a distant force whose spiritual nature is separate from creation. Shamanism is a bridge between those dualistic views. It acknowledges the spiritual nature of the physical universe and encourages full exploration of the sacred within everything. The will is a deluxe vehicle for such explorations.

Coming to an intimate relationship with Mother Earth is a cherished result of my willful contacts with her, and one whose development I encourage in my retreat participants. I teach them several ways to go about forging such a bond through the exercise of will. One of the simplest and most accessible ways is to lie belly-down on the Earth and unfold the will into her precisely as described in the last exercise. Silence your internal dialogue and then wait in a state of trusting receptivity for whatever might come through the spiritual telephone cord. Once the will is unfolded, communication is possible. If you have questions, it is best if they are appropriate to the situation. The Earth doesn't tell us who our next president will be or how to pick a winning lottery number. More practical is to ask her about herself, her needs, her nature, or about possible future actions you can take to deepen your relationship with her. Again, be receptive to her responses in whatever form they come. You may receive only subtle impressions. However, your own spirit and will may "translate" some of the Earth's knowledge into words your mind can understand. With time and practice, the ability to perceive and interpret this kind of information grows stronger and clearer.

I've found that surrounding myself with the Earth's physical/spiritual presence intensifies my will's connection to her. There are three ways I've accomplished this, each a bit different but all quite effective. I recommend all of them to the reader.

1.   Find a cave, preferably one where you won't be disturbed by other people, and spend hours or even an entire day and night within it.

2.   If you don't have access to a cave or want to try another approach, dig yourself a pit in the earth. Again, a secluded environment is preferable. Make the pit a good foot longer and wider than your body, and try digging it deep enough so that when you lie down on your back with a blanket or two beneath you, the top is at least a foot above you. Once you have everything arranged for your stay (and I recommend you stay at least overnight if possible) cover the top of your pit with a large blanket or tarp, or have a friend do it for you. Anchoring the edges of the covering with some large stones is also practical. Then you won't have to worry about it sagging down or collapsing partway through your sojourn. If you are alone, simply anchor the blanket on three sides before you climb into the pit. Then slide carefully in through the open end, reach up from inside the pit and anchor the loose end of the blanket with a few more stones. It's slightly tricky but manageable.

3.   The third way to surround yourself with the Earth's presence requires building or having access to a sweat lodge. The sweat lodge is an outdoor ceremonial structure resembling an inverted basket. (It's described in detail in chapter 4.) Spending extended periods of time on its earthen floor will provide similar benefits as a cave or pit. If the weather is cool, you can even bring some fire-heated stones into the lodge to keep you warm.

I have tried all three of these environments for anywhere from overnight to a full two days. I've loved every experience for the sense of intimacy with the Earth that I gained. Being enclosed in Mother Earth's embrace is very sheltering. For that reason, yogis and shamans and others of serious spiritual intent have retreated to caves from time to time to deepen their pursuits. When you are in a cave, earth pit or sweat lodge, all the energies constantly zooming around on the Earth's surface—especially those from man-made machinery—energies that impinge on us day and night, are blocked or at least seriously muffled. Protected from those disturbances, your experience is more and more womblike. When I spend hours in sheltered earth seclusion, my unfolded will becomes increasingly sensitive to the subtle vibrations of the Earth's body and our connection grows stronger. I have composed many new songs in such circumstances, listening to Mother Earth's heartbeat and subterranean melodies for sources of inspiration. And since my first journey into Mother Earth's domain, I have never doubted that she is indeed alive.

There is a fourth and powerful condition for willfully connecting to the Earth. This is the vision quest ceremony, involving days alone sitting, standing or sleeping and dreaming on Mother Earth's surface. I've completed numerous such ceremonies myself for periods ranging from one to seven days at a time, and have instructed and sent close to a hundred others out on vision quests. The potentials and results of such ceremonies are vast and highly individual, but the Earth and all of Mother make essential spiritual contributions.

The Earth is a mysterious being, one whose spiritual energies extend out from her body just as ours do. And just as we can use the will and all our senses to perceive human energies, we can do the same to increase our awareness of the Earth's emanations. How do we expand this awareness? You must first spend as much time as possible outdoors, exploring the vast and varied geographies of Mother Earth. While walking with the will unfolded, stop periodically, listen and feel. Notice how thoughts, emotions and energy may change from place to place. During these inventories, pay attention to clues like increased or diminished strength in the body, alertness or drowsiness, feelings of calm, restlessness or irritability. If possible, explore varied environments such as mountains, deserts, forests, beaches and jungles. Keep tuning in.

As awareness and sensitivity increase, you will find a great deal of diversity from place to place. Traditional Chinese geomancers—*feng shui* masters—are trained to both notice and utilize the Earth's many vibrations. Knowing the different vibrations' effects on human energies, feng shui masters use their expertise to advise others on the most ideal locations for building houses, temples, gardens and healing centers. Feng shui encourages harmonizing with rather than disrupting nature in any building process. The geomancers help find the sites whose energies are most conducive to daily living, meditation, healing and even business.

The masters of feng shui are not alone in their search for specific kinds of energies on the Earth. Many cultures acknowledge the existence of natural "power spots." These are highly energized places—like ocean beaches or mountaintops—conducive to varied spiritual states of awareness. Whether stumbled upon accidently or sought out by seers and shamans, these places are then utilized for meditation, healing, vision questing, dreaming and other spiritual ceremonies and practices.

When I send women out on vision quests, I first have them go on a scouting expedition to find a power spot for their ceremony. They walk slowly through the area, stopping periodically to unfold their will and gather energetic information, until they find a site that suits their individual needs. Usually they tell me the place they've chosen simply feels "right" to them, but some specifically search for locations in which they feel energized, alert and safe, or dreamy and slightly out-of-body.

You don't need to be preparing for a vision quest to seek out power spots. Finding them can also be the goal for more modest endeavors, and can be done close to home. Simply explore the yard or local parks for sites that feel conducive to meditation, healing, heightened energy, dreaming or writing, for example. You can end up with a detailed map of easily accessible power spots for personal spiritual purposes and enjoyment.

Before I began doing the Southwest women's retreats, a friend and I spent a great deal of time there exploring and searching for unusual power spots. We walked for hours in the desert, wills unfolded, stopping here and there to sample the energetic "scent" of each place. In this manner we found a hidden cave, a crystal mound, an ancient and powerful tree, and several other unique sites we used later for ceremonies with the women on retreat.

Besides exploring and deepening our connections to the Earth herself, there are other opportunities for us to willfully dance with Mother. These include dance partners such as plants, minerals, animals, other people and what we call forces of nature.

The easiest way to use the will to connect with plants or minerals is to place them in direct physical contact with your belly and then unfold your will into them as described earlier. The process works with the smallest plant and the greatest redwood, the tiniest crystal or the most massive boulder. If you are especially interested in discovering the properties of herbs or various minerals and their healing or spiritual effects, you'll particularly enjoy these explorations. Once willful contact is made, you must allow enough time to feel the results before pulling your will back into the body. As you become proficient with this method, you can begin trying the same exercise but from increasingly greater distances from the object of attention. This strengthens the will further while allowing you to discover that physical distance need not diminish the connection. Regular energy-gathering and silencing the internal dialogue increase our personal power and concentration. This enables us to unfold the will greater distances without weakening the results.

It is a bit more difficult to find animals that allow direct contact with our belly for these exercises, unless one has pets. But once you are able to throw the will a good distance from your body, you can begin seeking out dance partners from the wild animal kingdom as well as from the strange and fascinating world of insects. These creatures are more challenging to deal with than plants and minerals, since they may not remain immobile during willful contact. Nonetheless, they are highly entertaining dance partners.

Because we so rarely focus our spiritual attention and will on them, animals are often acutely aware when we do make such contacts. Once they become aware of our will's touch, they often respond with rather unique and unusual behaviors. I've frequently had birds put on rather startling airborne displays, and occasionally have had deer approach me or butterflies alight on my body in response to my will's contact. After dancing with animals, insects or anything else, we should remember to pull the will back in so it doesn't remain attached to them. This is a good habit, especially when we move on to dance with our energetically challenging human partners. We humans are also expressions of Mother, even though city dwellers sometimes forget this in their isolation from the rest of nature.

Consciously unfolding the will toward humans is a unique and powerful way to learn about individual and group energies. Through the invisible cord, we can discern whether others' energies are harmonious with our own. We can sense their unspoken moods. We can gather information about their state of health and level of spiritual awareness. This exercise of will is a wonderful tool for public speakers, for healers of any kind or for those wishing to be more sensitive to friends and family. I often unfold my will toward groups I am teaching in order to take the energetic and spiritual "temperature" of those individuals present. This helps me know what to expect and how to best orient the pace, exercises and teachings during the seminar or workshop. On a more active level, I may also choose to send energy through my will out among the participants, giving them a temporary "power boost" and creating a climate of group unity and spiritual harmony.

When I use my will to dance with other humans, I take special care to pull it back in when its purpose is fulfilled. The will connection allows energies to flow back and forth between the persons at each end. For as long as it remains attached to someone else, our energies are going to be partly mixed, opening the door to a variety of potential effects on one another. My own thoughts, emotions and spirit are challenging enough. I prefer not to have to sort through someone else's due to a sustained mixing of our wills! Therefore, I withdraw my will after each contact as a very practical and real exercise of detachment.

I believe consciously pulling back the will is an especially important spiritual action for healers. Even if they haven't consciously engaged their will with their clients, because of the intimate nature of healing and the compassion of most healers, some of their will's energy usually unfolds automatically to assist them in their work. If they remain thus entangled with every client, they run the risk of becoming drained and of taking on their clients' problems. I know too many counselors and hands-on healers who become ill or depleted because of such energetic embroilments. Gathering power before healing sessions and consciously pulling in the will afterwards (in addition to any other energy-clearing techniques) are positive and helpful means by which healers can stay balanced and healthy.

Somewhere on the road of life, most of us will encounter other individuals or groups that are hostile to our well-being. If you should ever have this experience, it is very practical not only to abstain from unfolding your will toward them, but also to pull your belly in hard and keep your will tightly contained. In this way, your energies are effectively sealed off from contact with negative forces. You have protected yourself through conscious spiritual self-defense. If you have been regularly gathering power, your luminous cocoon will be vital and resilient and will provide additional energetic shielding against those forces.

As I described in the first chapter, we are semipermeable energy fields. We can both affect and be affected by other energy fields. The conscious exercise of will increases our awareness of these fields and expands our range of choice for varied interactions. Mother is the immense, immediate spiritual university in which we can use will to amass knowledge and experience of our energetic options and surroundings. Besides teaching us about human, mineral, plant and animal interactions, her course of studies also includes forces of nature such as the wind, lightning and rain. These forces are known for their impact not only on our physical beings but on our psyches. Storms, Santa Ana winds and the full moon are well-known mood influencers. Their diverse energies penetrate the membrane of our luminous cocoon and permeate our cells and souls.

Although these aspects of Mother are more ephemeral than a boulder or an oak tree, it is still possible to unfold the will and dance with them. Since the wind is often accessible when we step outdoors, I highly recommend it as one of our more steady dance partners. There is nothing quite like the exhilaration of facing a high wind, unfurling the will into it, and feeling one's spirit sailing about in the wind's embrace!

When I'm in the desert with the retreat participants, I encourage this activity of will, enticing the women with stories of moody west winds, ferocious north winds, seductive south winds, enchanting east winds and the wonderfully challenging whirl-winds. Women derive unique spiritual benefits and power through establishing deep connections to the winds. Without going into great detail about the potentials of these connections, I simply send the women out to face the winds again and again, unfolding their wills and learning from their own direct experiences.

During one of the retreats, on the day before setting out on vision quest, we sat in a circle across from White House Ruins in Canyon de Chelly, Arizona. Everyone was gathering power, preparing for a demanding spiritual exploration of the ancestral energies of the ancient Anasazi who once populated the canyon. As we sat immersed in Mother's power, I heard a telltale distinc-tive sound approaching through the desert brush, one I'd heard many times before. I readied myself, sat up straight and unfolded my will to catch the moment. A human-size whirlwind burst suddenly into our circle! We were all electrified by its wild but determined presence which remained with us for several startling moments before dashing down the canyon and disappearing. "Power follows power," I reminded the women quietly a few min-utes later, after basking in the energized silence of the wind's aftermath. The whirlwind was drawn to the power we'd amassed throughout the week and the power we were gathering there in our circle. It had then confronted us with its own challenging power before continuing on its way. I took this as an omen that more power awaited the women in their approaching vision quest.

The women had prepared for their quest since the first moment of the retreat. They'd eaten increasingly lighter foods: fruit, nuts, vegetables and whole grains. (The diet enhances spiritual alertness and eases their bodies into the three days of fasting on the quest.) They'd practiced the exercise of will in a variety of ways, including gathering power and dancing with Mother. Their bodies exuded vitality from all of these practices and from hours of daily desert walks in the invigorating high-altitude air. Each day they tried silencing the internal dialogue through meditation and breaking their normal conversation habits. Many of the patterns of their usual lives were disrupted. They were in a new environment away from home, work and friends, and they had been following the numerous guidelines for spiritual awareness and development I'd offered them. They devoted less time to outer appearance as they discovered deeper and deeper levels of inner beauty. The way they experienced themselves and each other was changing. They were more focused on supporting one another spiritually in the present than on the details of each others' pasts or possible futures. Each woman was becoming a witness to and dance partner of spirit. As they looked out into nature or each others' eyes, they saw Mystery endlessly unfolding.

Finally, after spending time hunting for their power spots, the women were ready for the vision quest. After a special send-off ceremony, each woman strode purposefully away toward her chosen site, carrying with her the basic necessities: sleeping bag or blankets; tent or tarp for nighttime warmth and daytime protection from the searing desert sun; extra clothing and water. Some also took paper for recording thoughts or images, or ceremonial objects like a special crystal or drum. Although undercurrents of nervousness about this journey into the unknown swirled among them—familiar anxieties like those I'd experienced before embarking on my own vision quests—I was satisfied that the women were well prepared. They were grounded enough in the spiritual practices I'd taught them that they could continue without me during the vision quest. Some women couldn't imagine being without human company for three days, but I knew they wouldn't be alone. Mother was waiting to welcome them deeply into her embrace.

Yes, the women are back, empty of physical food but filled with power, with new songs and dreams, with revelations and visions, restored to Mother and themselves and filled with Mother's spiritual nourishment. One by one, I turn them to face the rising sun, to face the east. It is to the east that they, like the beloved Changing Woman of the Navajo creation story, may return again and again throughout their lives for renewal of body and spirit. I bless each woman with the smoky incense from cedar, the holy plant for new beginnings. After every woman has been blessed and has eaten some light food, we gather our material and spiritual belongings and prepare to walk out of the canyon, to continue the journey and the vision quest that is life.

3

Meaning, Art and Menopause

The spiritual quest engages the seeker in weaving a unique tapestry. The raw material is the seeker's hidden and unfinished self. On this journey, the artist is the art form, her life the threads of the tapestry. Every breath and event are strands of color that can be arranged and rearranged on the loom of her creativity. Menopause affords the questing weaver an opportunity to become more original, to imbue her art—her Self—with fresh meaning that delights her own soul first.

My recent transition through menopause was one of the most intense periods of my life, similar to a sustained vision quest. I found myself confronted with many of the issues I address in this chapter. Through a tumultuous period of change, I was catalyzed into sorting through the tangled skein of personal and social values on which I had based my meaning in the world. For inner balance, I drew deeply on my many spiritual practices, including gathering power and exercising my will in nature. I also read some of the available literature on menopause for helpful information and suggestions for appropriate herbs and other nutritional supplements.

Although it was a difficult time, I learned a great deal more about myself and about the society that helped shape my values. I had recently moved to a new city, and although the books I read on menopause provided some welcome perspective and companionship, I had no women friends nearby to share my struggles with. I was on a solitary journey, a deep rite of passage. In the process, I recreated myself. I reshuffled my values, choosing those that were currently relevant and supportive of my spirit to become the loom for my new tapestry. And then I quite literally used art to weave the new images of my being: I began writing books and I composed more songs in a two-year period than I had over my entire life.

These artistic ventures were immensely therapeutic. Even in my darkest moods, if I successfully wheedled myself into sitting down and writing, my day regained purpose and value. As the words poured out of me, sometimes the joyful recognition of an ongoing personal adventure drove away the gloomier clouds. I was creating beauty, coaxing it out of my mind, heart, cells and all its other secret hiding places. Sometimes this beauty emerged as a song or poem, other times as the next part of a chapter I was working on. The process of recreating myself through art—of choosing to bring the intrinsic beauty and power of my own nature out into the light of day—was the spiritual core of my rite of passage.

For me, menopause was both an important part of the journey of awareness and an ongoing demand for spiritual action toward my own Self. I share with you now some of my insights and reflections from this rite of passage. The images on the tapestry are derived from personal experience, but like all art, they are intended to have a more universal relevance.

Meaning from Outside

Every one of us has a deep need to perceive our life as meaningful. No matter how large or small the event or experience, we thrive when we can say, "Yes! That meant something to me."

What are the sources and symbolic wellsprings that provide meaning to life?

During my journey through menopause, I reflected on this a great deal. As I watched the seasons turn and shift over the months, I saw an ongoing source of meaning inherent in many events of nature. When a heavy cloud cover gathers, this usually "means" impending rain or snow. When a young woman first menstruates, this "means" she is now capable of becoming pregnant and bringing forth life. Although we can find symbolism in natural events, nature also contains its own meaning, independent from our psyches.

Within the human landscape, the groups we form are a source of meaning as well. The "group mind" of families, cultures or the entire human race may agree on the meaning of events or trends. These meanings can powerfully shape the quality of life for both individuals and groups and are often intricately attached to our belief systems.

Astrology is one example of a popular system that is meaningful to many. A person is born at a specific moment in time and, according to astrologers, that moment defines much of her life. Astrologers believe the movements of the planets shape the person's temperament, talents and preferences. Many successes and difficulties in a person's life likewise have meaning ascribed to them by the astrologers' complex charts.

Westerners are quite conditioned toward the external. We base the meaning of our lives on what others think and feel. We women have been particularly constrained, valued for our youthful appearance or our ability to make babies. After menopause, our bodies are *devalued*, even to the point of unnecessary hysterectomies to remove the now "useless" and meaningless womb. But the revolution is on. We're talking and writing about the once hush-hush topic of menopause, flaunting our hot flashes and holding on harder to our wombs. We're shaking off the past and looking to redefine the future with more freedom. The exploration of spirit and creativity can serve us even further as we recraft our lives with new and original meaning.

From the Womb of Creation

Personal creativity imbues the fabric of our lives with meaning, whether at menopause or any other time. Creativity pulls on deep resources and spiritual power within us, and brings to the surface hidden facets of our nature so we can know ourselves as an ever-unfolding mystery. The often joyful expression of our deep creative power is best known in the arts. Most artists attest to the great satisfaction of extracting a word, a glance, a gesture from the flow of daily events, and then fleshing it out with music, color or dance to create a rich expression of symbolic meaning.

At menopause and after, creative acts become increasingly important. We no longer ovulate, which is one kind of creative act, and we no longer have the option to bring human life out of our wombs. Many of us, whether we've born children or not, experience a profound sense of loss—a loss of personal meaning and potential—at the closing of this door. If that is the case, we must allow ourselves to grieve and then move on. Just as one area of the brain can take over the function of another if need be, so can we replace reproductive function with other creative actions.

We can be creative in almost any area of life, whether it be relationships, work, domestic chores or recreation. Artistic creativity is a deeply integrative act, a worthy replacement for retiring ovaries, and can deeply engage the spirit. Artists throughout history have felt that their creativity aligns them with the creative, cosmic Source and forces of the universe.

We may want to seriously consider using the pause of menopause for our spiritual revolution by exploring the domain of beauty through artistic creativity. Classes in the arts can be helpful, but some of us may prefer to simply embark on artistic adventures completely on our own. Whatever our choice, we need to remember that we are bringing power, beauty and meaning from our womb of creation for ourselves first and foremost.

Magic and spirit are often closely associated with art. Many artists credit some invisible muse or spiritual force as their source of inspiration. Such artists feel their mastery of technique enables them to become better vessels of spirit. The fact that a great work of art often has universal appeal attests partly to the brilliance of the artist. But its appeal also suggests that spirit speaks through both the artist and the finished product, and is finally heard by the audience.

Art is not only magical, but revolutionary and spiritual in its ability to bypass the thinking mind. Our first response to art—as artist or audience—is usually from the gut, is nonmental and is full of beauty and individual meaning. Beauty touches the human spirit at a profound level. It can elevate us from the mundane, can heal, inspire and fill an otherwise seemingly empty moment with hidden meaning, even rapture. These qualities hold true both with beauty in nature and beauty shaped by human hands or minds.

Shamans are magicians who create ceremonies rich with mythic beauty and meaning. These ceremonies mark seasons of nature and human rites of passage. In addition to having personal spiritual power, shamans are often artists who add symbolic creativity to ceremonial details. These ceremonies, enhanced through the power of spirit and beauty, help ground the individual and community in meaning. Women at menopause might wish to take inspiration from the shamans to create their own ceremonies and ceremonial objects of beauty.

The Navajo are a people who recognize the spiritual meaning and power of *hozhone:* beauty and harmony. Their culture incorporates both references to beauty and actual artistry in prayers and healing ceremonies. Intricate and colorful sand "paintings" are created for a single "sing," as some of their rituals are called. These spiritual creations take many hours to draw and are actually fine lines of dyed sand carefully trickled onto the earth. These sand paintings represent holy figures and events from the Navajo creation story (the "Dineh Bahane") and every sing tells some part of the story. When the purpose is a healing, the medicine men choose the sing that is most appropriate to the patient's situation, and the mythic content of the story becomes the subject of one or more sand paintings created during the event. The goal of a Navajo healing ceremony is to restore the patient to hozhone within herself and in relation to her external environment. Part of this goal is accomplished by having her sit on the sand painting, identifying and becoming one with its meaning and beauty. She becomes the sacred hero or heroine of the story, takes the journey, rallies human and divine resources, overcomes the obstacles and is changed and healed. Once she internalizes its meaning and beauty, the sand painting is then "erased." Its purpose has been fulfilled and its elements return to nature.

Primitive cultures often imbue artistic creations with magical qualities and the artists with unique spiritual powers. Some artists of contemporary "primitive" cultures, who work with natural materials, feel they must first look for the inner spirit of the piece of soapstone, amber or cedar wood, and then strip away all that hides the spirit. The form of the spirit is what remains intact.

Whether beauty is mirrored directly through nature or is reshaped through human art, the human spirit is similarly affected. As we witness beauty, our entire being harmonizes with itself and the universe. Beauty is meaning. Beauty holds its own truth and passes from Spirit to spirit through nature and art.

Rite of Passage: Interface Between Two Worlds

Many "baby-boomer" women are going through menopause. Some treat it as a purely physiological process. Others try to find or create spiritual significance and practices that make menopause a deep and true rite of transformation. For those who regard menopause as a spiritual opportunity and act on its potentials, the results reverberate with power through the remainder of their lives.

We have a great deal of room for both choice and creativity in the ways we imbue this transitional period with meaning and weave it into our tapestry. We don't have choice about the actual occurrence of menopause—it happens to every woman who lives long enough—but we can choose our attitudes and what kind of personal meaning we wish menopause to have. We can be responsible and even spiritual toward this process.

Menopause and life after menopause have more than one meaning. The simplest is biological. Moving through menopause means women can no longer conceive a child. This is probably the only clear and universally agreed upon biological meaning of this process, besides the fact that hormone levels change. What else menopause means or "should" mean to a woman is less clear.

Traditional Western medicine tends to treat most female functions as problems to be attacked, much the same as it treats illness. Whether it is menstruation, childbirth or menopause, the "illness model" for these natural events puts a strange warp into the fabric of our lives. Sometimes there *are* specific challenges and very real problems with all three processes. But we fare better with a more holistic approach that includes prevention and supports our inherent strengths. Such a holistic approach does not regard menstruation, childbirth and menopause as illnesses, as enemies to be conquered, but as opportunities we can learn from on every level.

We face other problems of meaning around our sexuality. We are valued if our appearance is youthful, thin and sexually alluring in the eyes of our beholders. We are all under scrutiny—both from men, other women and finally ourselves. Are we meeting Society's criteria or not? Is a wrinkle or grey hair threatening doom? Are we losing our culturally-defined beauty and thus our meaning to ourselves and others? Is our real beauty, which is within, ignored both by society and by ourselves?

When we incorporate current cultural attitudes about physical appearance and sex appeal, then menopause means something quite ominous and depressing. Rather than looking forward to a time of increased status, we may feel victimized, seeing menopause and its aftermath as a time of diminishing respect and desirability. Unfortunately, in our society, these fears have often been based on an all-too-real foundation. Many men do abandon their aging wives for younger women or have affairs with other women on the side. And many elderly women are subject to the scorn of the young rather than being valued for their life experiences.

This devaluing of post-menopausal women has not always been the case. In many tribal cultures, women were traditionally viewed as having a new status and increased power and wisdom after passing through menopause and moving into the "elder cycle." Since life expectancy was shorter then, a woman might well be approaching the last decade of her life if she survived past menopause, so she could properly claim elder status. Having her final cycle of life treated with respect and being regarded as a person of wisdom held great meaning for the woman and benefitted her tribe.

We can both use and take heart from this positive model of aging. We needn't feel victimized or accept social invisibility simply because of our diminishing sexual hormones and changing appearance. We can accept and take advantage of the menopausal season by gathering energy, creating beauty and redefining ourselves according to our own inner values and spirit. By doing so, we attain a tangible aura of power that is more than an adequate substitute for lessened physical and sexual allure. Those people who value such spiritual power will be drawn to us and will make good companions on our journey.

Rituals are a unique link between meaning imposed by society and meaning created from within. They have special value for menopausal women. Rituals and ceremony promote healing and balance. They allow us to arrive at a new sense of identity, molded in part by our own spiritual nature. If we want to be spiritual revolutionaries, we can create our own menopausal rituals. Indeed, the entire process of menopause can be a ritual that every woman shapes for herself, an opportunity to choose which cultural symbols and meanings she wishes to add to her ongoing tapestry and which she wishes to discard. Later, in chapter 8, the specifics of ritual-making are described.

Reflections from the Past

Our relationship to our own life is the most consistent and continuous relationship we have. Strengthening the meaning of this relationship in a creative, affirming manner is the great challenge menopause presents to women. And as with all relationships, such strength grows partly from an understanding of the past. It is there we can see the naked fabric and textures of all the cultural attitudes and values we have assimilated.

At least half of this cultural fabric was woven by men. And often close to a hundred percent was woven by people other than ourselves. We need to unravel and reweave this fabric in a fashion closer to the deeper meaning and beauty of our true self. This act of power is the other pause of menopause. Here is a series of exercises for that pause.

THE MIRROR OF TRUE REFLECTIONS

You will notice that the term "mental body" is italicized throughout. This is done so that when you go through this exercise the second time, you can substitute "emotional body" for mental body, and can see clearly where to change the term in the text. The third time you go through the process, substitute "physical body," and the last time use "spiritual body." I don't recommend doing all four in a row, as it is a demanding process. One per week for four weeks should give you time to integrate the results of each exercise before moving on to the next. In the text of the exercise, you will also notice an asterisk in the 10th paragraph where the term "mental body" is first used. The sentence it marks will need to be changed slightly for the other three processes, and the appropriate substitutions are given in a footnote at the bottom of the page.

I'd like to encourage you now to prepare yourself for a look into the mirror of your past. No matter what your age, this kind of self-reflection is always a valuable process. Settle comfortably into a chair or lay down on your back if you prefer, and begin with some simple relaxation so that your body won't distract you from your goals. Close your eyes and take four slow, deep breaths down into your belly, your center of spiritual strength and power, your center of creativity.

Now begin to imagine you are floating in warm water, perhaps salt water, so that you are completely supported and need make no physical effort whatsoever. Try to feel the water cradling your head, and as you do, allow all the muscles in your scalp, forehead, eyes, jaw and lips to completely let go, melting and relaxing into the warm, buoyant water. Then feel the water under the back of your neck, gently lapping around your throat, and let go of all the muscles of your neck and throat and be supported by the water you are floating on.

Now become aware of the water supporting your shoulders and arms, and allow the muscles all the way down to the wrists and then fingers of both hands to melt and be completely supported by the soothing, warm water.

Next, bring your awareness to your torso. Feel the water under your back and even lapping across the front of your chest, your breasts and abdomen. Let go of all the muscles in your back, the entire spinal column, the muscles around the breasts and rib cage. Let the surface and deep muscles within the abdomen melt and relax. Don't forget the powerful muscles of the buttocks in this process. Feel your entire torso being supported by the warm and buoyant water.

Finally, send your awareness all the way down through your legs. Feel the water beneath your thighs, calves and heels. Allow every muscle to melt and let go, from the hip joint, inner thighs, around the knees and calves to the small muscles in your feet and toes.

Take four more deep belly breaths, and as you do, send your awareness in a long wave from the top of your head to the tips of your fingers and toes, letting go even more deeply with each exhalation until you are completely relaxed and supported by the gentle embrace of the water. Enjoy this state for a few moments, luxuriating in the peace and tranquility of relaxation. Adjust your body if need be for even greater comfort.

As your body maintains its relaxed state, with your mind's eye, your imagination, create a large mirror in your field of vision. If you have difficulty visualizing it, simply intend a mirror to be there whether you can see it or not.

This mirror is a magic mirror, a mirror of true reflection. The more frequently you use it, the more your mirror will be polished and cleaned, and the clearer the reflections will become.

You are going to ask the mirror to reveal the impact on you of past messages you have received from your family, friends, enemies, coworkers and your culture. The mirror will help you focus specifically on the messages you consciously or unconsciously accepted and see their effects on your own self-definition. Once you can see them, you can choose which meanings you want to keep and which you want to discard.

Now ask the mirror to give your *mental body* a form that you can perceive. The form might be an abstract symbol, an animal, a machine or even a person. Once the image is clear, ask the mirror to reflect what kind of shape it's in. Has the meaning of your mind, your intelligence, your mental body, taken any blows in the past?* Who has attacked or insulted it, or put limitations on how you might use it? Ask the mirror to briefly reflect their names or faces, whether they be family, friends, teachers or the media. Each time you see someone who has influenced your mental body in negative ways, simply say within your own mind, "I see you, I acknowledge your influence, and from now on I'll choose more clearly whether or not to accept your meaning."

Once you are done with this review, scan the image of your mental body for dents, cracks or bruises. If you see any, you can choose to continue this process of awareness and healing by taking some deep belly breaths, and with each exhale send healing

---

* When doing this process for the emotional body, substitute the following sentence: Has the meaning of your emotions, your expressive heart, your emotional body, taken any blows?

When doing this process for the physical body, substitute the following sentence: Has the meaning of your body, your earthly form, your physical self, taken any blows?

When doing this process for the spiritual body, substitute the following sentence: Has the meaning of your spirit, your divine nature, your spiritual body, taken any blows?

light and energy to your mental body and watch it begin to change.

Now ask the mirror to reflect those people from your past who had a positive, nurturing affect on your mental body. Again, with each image, simply tell them "I see you and acknowledge your influence, and from now on I'll choose more clearly whether or not to accept your meaning." Acknowledging positive influences is as important as acknowledging negative influences. To make clear choices in defining our own meaning to ourselves, we must gain awareness of all the forces which have shaped us.

When you have completed this part of the process, create a positive statement about the value, meaning and/or potential of your own mental body. Take a few moments to carefully choose your statement, perhaps looking for something that will allow you maximum freedom and creativity. Then tell the mirror you wish to see this statement reflected in it, either in words or in some symbolic image. Once you perceive it, inhale and pull the power of the reflection out of the mirror. Then exhale and send it down into your belly where it can continue to grow. Take a few moments to feel this new energy within you.

Before releasing the mirror, ask it to reflect, from your innermost being, a whole and "meaning-full" image of your total self, one which includes all four bodies: mental, emotional, physical and spiritual. Once again, pull the power of this image into your belly with several deep inhales. Then let the mirror fade from your inner vision. In the future, if you feel you are losing your center, your self-defined meaning, send your attention into your belly for a while, and renew your contact with this powerful image.

To finish for now, take several deep belly-breaths and as you exhale, sigh audibly. That will help you return to this time and space. Gently wiggle your fingers and toes, and take a long luxurious stretch. If you have been lying down, turn onto your side and curl into the fetal position for a moment. Then roll onto your knees. Use your hands to push yourself to your feet. Keep your head, neck and back hanging over toward the ground and your knees bent. Then uncoil your vertebrae from the bottom up, slowly uncurling upward, head dropped over until the rest of your spine is upright. Bring your head up last and straighten your knees. Now you may wish to walk around for a few moments till you have your "land legs" back again.

Taking this kind of personal inventory can help us gain self-awareness and self-definition, and become more responsible toward the self. If we seek empowerment during "the change," other inventories of past patterns may be needed. Let us consider three different expressions of the past that may demand spiritual action at menopause: depression, physical problems and stress.

Depression is often rooted in unresolved past experiences. It is also one of the most common symptoms experienced by menopausal women. In its extreme state it can be destructive to personal growth and require therapeutic interventions and support. But if it is not severely incapacitating, we may want to shift our perspective on depression. We can see its self-absorptive quality as the inner spirit's summons to deep introspection and examination of past values. By doing so, we can then use depression as an opportunity for positive personal transformation.

Most women discover that stress exacerbates depression and other menopausal symptoms. The sources of stress are sometimes immediate, but many may be rooted in the past, including the people in our lives. At menopause we may need to scrutinize our relationships. Is stress the dominant dynamic in any of them? Who nourishes, stimulates and encourages our growth and well-being? And who drains, oppresses or demeans us? What is the balance between people who are positive influences in our life and people who are negative influences? How long has this been true?

If we see a relationship has more stressful, negative qualities than positive ones, we might ask ourselves what we're getting out of such negativity. Is the other person reinforcing negative concepts we have about ourselves? Even though that may seem like a strange reason to stay in a relationship, people tend to be most comfortable with the familiar and known. And if we've incorporated negative messages about ourselves from early in life, we may stay around people who support those destructive but familiar self-concepts. Strange creatures that we are, we often prefer our known pain to the potentially more joyful unknown. When the degree of pain or the desire for more pleasure becomes unbearable, we may finally get off our behinds and risk the temporary discomfort of the unknown to search for more positive relationships!

Change during "the change" may be called for in other areas besides our relationships. We may heed the messages of menopausal depression, stress or feelings of personal restriction by making job or career changes. Or we may decide at that point in our lives that we are tired of working for other people, and go into business for ourselves. If we have have spent most of our adulthood raising children, we may seek a job outside the home for the first time. Cherished dreams from the past—long tucked away in our psychic attic—may suddenly emerge from the introspective reveries of a gloomy depression, leap into the light of day, shake off the dust and demand fulfillment posthaste.

And what about physical symptoms? Many men and women turn a deaf ear to the body's messages until a crisis erupts. From time to time we may receive internal signals that we are not living in harmony with ourselves, that we are making too many social and professional compromises, or giving energy to others while neglecting our own needs. But in the momentum of daily habit, we often ignore the signals until they are quite loud. The clamor usually manifests itself as a physical illness, "accidental" injury or psychological distress—like depression or anxiety—that won't disappear. Powerful inner voices of knowledge and authority, the voices we've ignored, rejected and dethroned, rise up from anonymity and demand their place as temporary rulers. Their purpose is to stop us in our tracks and command our attention.

When we listen, our "symptoms" may give us information about how we arrived at our state of disharmony or "dis-ease." After decades of turning a deaf ear to some of our inner voices, problems can mount up. Menopausal depression or physical distress may be a strong call to acknowledge both the voices and unresolved problems from the past.

The body is a poet and speaks to us in symbols, exclaiming with surges of delight when we treat ourselves especially well, maintaining a quiet hum when all systems are balanced, and grumbling with metaphors of danger when our lifestyle is toxic to any aspect our well-being. Like learning any language, we learn the language of the body by listening. And to most clearly hear the body's poetry, we must silence our usual mental chatter. We can use the "Breathing Toward Inner Silence" exercise in chapter 2, and in the silence more clearly hear the body's messages. Here are some possible "interpretations" of body-language meanings to help you orient yourself to body poetry.

1. Upper back and shoulder tension: unnecessary psychological burdens needing release.
2. Chronically stiff neck: bullheadedness, rigid outlook. We may need to open to new perspectives.
3. Pain or constriction in the chest, particularly around the heart: imprisoned emotions seeking release and expression.
4. Chronic digestion and elimination problems: what we've been taking in is "hard to swallow," digest or get rid of. We may need a new diet of more nourishing food and relationships.

As we take time to listen to our bodies, we increase our understanding. Usually we know we're on the right track when an interpretation of a "symptom symbol" results in an inner "aha!"—a feeling that the pieces of a puzzle are finally fitting into place. Once the source of a problem is identified, we can enter into a dialogue with the body and find out what actions to take toward inner harmony and resolution.

Regular physical exercise also relieves and helps manage menopausal depression, stress and some physical symptoms. But none of these symptoms are enemies to flee from or conquer. They are nudges to go within and reexamine the effects of past actions, attitudes and patterns so we can shape the present and future with creativity and power.

Reflections Toward the Future

Although we may have been unconsciously molded by influences from the past, we can use the menopausal rite of passage to enter the present and future with heightened awareness. It is never too late to make positive changes. And at the midpoint of life, a potent image from the future can inspire us to do so: death's beckoning motion from the end of our earthly dance.

In her book, *The Change*, Germaine Greer comments on how women may experience an intense awakening to their mortality at menopause. She says we are brushed by the wings of death at this time. The transition of "the change" is a crossroad that can be either terrifying or exhilarating for women, depending partly on how well we make use of death as an advisor.

Modern culture expends a great deal of energy denying death. We are fixated on youth. We hide our elderly away someplace where they won't remind us too strongly of the passage of time and our own eventual fate. We give the dying over to hospitals, doctors and life-support machines; we prefer not to have the presence of death tainting our homes. And even though we repeatedly see death on television or in films, both real or fictitious, it still has an unreal quality. The denial marches on.

If we were on more intimate terms with death, we might well live our lives differently. A daily awareness of death brings wisdom and a heightened appreciation of life. Women going through "the change" should take advantage of death's sudden whisper and listen to the advice it brings to us, the living. Rather than running from its shadowy reflection in the future, why not embrace its existence as a reminder of the gift of life? Menopause can quicken our awareness of life's potentials and of the fact that we don't have forever to accomplish them. We can use the opportunity to fill the future with meaning and spiritual action.

My own awareness of death and of life's fleeting qualities began long before menopause. When I was about nine, my friend Ralphie and his father Big Ralph were killed by a drunk driver in an automobile accident. Death was a presence that apparently obeyed its own rules and timing. When I was 21, death was my initiation to formal adulthood. Shortly after my birthday, a careless driver ran a red light and crashed into my car. My physical injuries were relatively mild, given the circumstances, but the blow to my psyche was profound. Once again I felt the tenuous and ephemeral quality of life, like a small flame in a large and windy cosmos. I was acutely conscious that there was no guarantee I'd live to old age. A brick could land on my head. I could choke on my food. Lightning could strike me. Or another irresponsible driver could snuff out my existence.

Despite some anxiety for a period after my accident, there was also a positive outcome for my psyche. I now appreciated each day of my life with greater enthusiasm, knowing it could be my last. Death became a strange ally and advisor. And just as Ms. Greer described, at menopause its whisper alerted me once again to the passage of time and to the relentlessly approaching end of my physical existence. I seized the opportunity this renewed awareness afforded me, and began writing. I didn't want to die before returning the gifts of spiritual knowledge to the world that provided them and that would continue on without me.

From our first bleeding through our last and beyond—from the womb to the tomb—women have certain spiritual advantages in their relationship with both life and death. The functions of our bodies are a blessing, not the "curse" so deeply imprinted on many women's minds. There are spiritual attributes common to both menstruation and menopause. In order for women to take advantage of these attributes from menopause on, we first need to go back and understand the spiritual dynamics and potentials of menstruation.

Our first menses dramatically brings our attention to the power of life within us: our new ability to conceive. At the same time, the blood tells us in a blunt and straightforward way that conception has not yet taken place. The potential is there but the egg, unfertilized, has died and is being flushed from the body in a crimson stream headed back toward Mother Earth.

The potent juxtapositions of life and death at menstruation are deeply spiritual, despite our culture's tendency to deny women this knowledge and celebration of self. And our culture is not the only one that tries to either hide women's truths or give us negative messages about our bodies. Many religions deem women unclean at menstruation, to the point where women are not allowed near ceremonies, altars, religious objects, food preparations or even men. Some religions mask this negative attitude by saying menstruating women are very powerful and their power could overwhelm the purpose of a ceremony or its leader. And there may be a grain of truth in this.

Despite these religious and social problems for women, we still hold deep spiritual advantages through being made just the way we are. We are blessed with monthly reminders of life and death that connect us with the larger cycles of nature. And we are resilient with the knowledge of change as a constant force.

Besides the reminder of life and death, another spiritual factor is common to both menstruation and menopause. A shaman and seer shared the following information with me, and its impact was so profound and illuminating I've been sharing it with other women ever since.

When we menstruate, our luminous cocoon is effected in a manner unique to women. Sometime within the week preceding bleeding, the cocoon cracks open slightly, and stays open for several days. Consequently, women are spiritually receptive to a great deal more input than usual. Although our sensitivity and irritability are often blamed on fluctuating hormones at this time, they are also partly due to our energetic vulnerability. More energies affect us than during the rest of our cycle. If we understand the dynamics of this, we can take spiritual advantage of the situation. It is prime time, power time, a time to partly withdraw from worldly activities and concerns and to focus on using the spiritual opening for spiritual pursuits. As the universe rushes in more strongly through the crack in the cocoon, we can familiarize ourselves more intimately with the forces we normally ignore.

During one menstrual cycle shortly after learning the teachings of the opened cocoon, I spent an afternoon outdoors perceiving the crack and taking advantage of it. I focused my attention in front of me where the split in the cocoon was supposedly located, and observed that everything directly before me had an unusually heightened clarity. As I continued my focus, I noticed something else. In a very visceral sense, I experienced a startling contact with whatever I saw. If I looked at a rock a few feet away, I felt I was touching the rock directly and was somehow present in its energy field. Whether I looked at a tree a block away, clouds miles away or the distant sun, I was there! Physical proximity was irrelevant as my spiritual will rushed out of my eyes and directly contacted one energy after another. The effects of the wind also intensified. Each time I faced the wind I felt its motion blowing through my cocoon and entering my belly and womb. The result was mysterious and highly energizing. During subsequent menstrual cycles I explored further, always weaving the results into the rest of my life.

Menstruation is an unusual and richly spiritual opening that women can take advantage of by spending time in nature, meditating, dreaming and embarking on various creative projects. Nature is a source for a variety of spiritual interactions, and its potentials can be perceived and experienced more deeply during the period around menstruation. Meditation is another vehicle of spiritual awareness. It provides a calming balance during the increased influx of energies. Dreaming, whether awake or asleep, always allows the will to unfold with unusual freedom, to explore spiritual terrains unavailable in normal consciousness. During menstruation we can pay special attention to our dreams, for we may receive significant guidance and revelations from them. And any art project will both enhance and ground our opened awareness into physical expressions of spirit.

Spending time away from other people may be a relief during menstruation. Because our cocoon is less shielding than usual, others' energies might effect us more intensely. We might be easily irritable and off-center as a result, unable to take full spiritual advantage of our "power time." Ideally, several days each month we might retreat from all outside pressures and instead both protect and nurture our spirits. Most women can't do this because of work or family responsibilities. But even if we can only manage a few hours a day, those hours may be invaluable for our balance and provide the extra time we need for spiritual practices. Menstruation needn't be an emotional and physical nuisance to endure once a month. It can be a time of spiritual renewal.

What does this have to do with menopause? In some mysterious fashion, when a woman's bleeding cycles end permanently, the luminous cocoon remains somewhat open in a similar way to menstruation. This openness can be a blessing or bother, depending on how we handle it. Once again, beyond hormonal fluctuations, the increased openness of the energy field could account for the mood swings and emotional sensitivity of menopause. We are adjusting to a spiritual transition, not just a biological one. Every spiritual action recommended for menstruation can be applied to menopause. What once occurred several days a month is now a permanent opportunity, and we can take advantage of its increased potential for spiritual knowledge and power.

However, the openness and vulnerability of menopause can be difficult to adjust to. Unlike menstruation, where we might be able to withdraw from the world for a few days a month, most women do not want to be hermits for the remainder of their postmenopausal lives following menopause. How then do we go about managing this potential spiritual blessing so it doesn't become a curse of over-sensitivity?

Some methods have already been suggested. Doing the personal inventory is a good starting place, particularly to understand and weed out toxic relationships. Any of the power-gathering exercises are especially useful for two reasons. The first is their potential to fill our cocoon with vital energies that can protect us from negative forces. The second is their effect of providing a surplus of energy for dealing with the new challenges menopause presents.

Centering exercises are another valuable balance to our

increased openness. The simple "Breathing Toward Inner Silence" exercise (p. 37) draws our focus and energies toward the center of our bodies, into our breath, and away from external energies. Another centering exercise is to visualize a ball of light in the belly—several inches below the navel at a woman's center of gravity—and simply focus on it for a few minutes several times a day. Grounding exercises are equally important, especially when we feel "over-charged" from increased energies moving into our luminous cocoon. Go back and look at the suggestions for the earth element in the "Elemental Attunement" exercise (p. 17). The earth is a powerful grounding ally, and women may wish to spend extra time with it as they move through menopause. It is also a very receptive element. We can literally shake extra and unwanted energies from our hands, feet or other parts of our bodies directly into Mother Earth, who will simply use or transform them.

The stress inventory outlined in chapter 1 is also particularly useful during "the change." Identifying current stressors gives us the option to either eliminate them from our lives or seek better ways of dealing with them so they don't sap us of strength. And if we are consistently more open to energies, why not consciously surround ourselves with as many positive ones as possible? Our favorite music, friends and the vast realm of "Mother" are all especially beneficial.

Since the cocoon may be more open at menopause and menstruation, women may want to counteract this situation for a while if it becomes overwhelming. Protective visualizations are an excellent method for temporarily sealing ourselves up.

PROTECTIVE VISUALIZATIONS

Close your eyes and calm your mind through the "Breathing Toward Inner Silence" technique. Then use your mind's eye to see yourself surrounded by the glow of your aura, your luminous cocoon, which is slightly open directly in front of you.

Visualization #1: With each exhalation, direct the will's energy to unfold from your navel area. See it first as a vine of light extending forward and moving to the crack or opening in the cocoon. Once it reaches the opening, with each exhalation fill your vine of will with increasing energy until it expands to fill and seal up the entire opening in the cocoon with its light and power. Sit in meditation in your sealed, quiet space for as long as you need to.

Visualization #2: Use the same process as in Visualization #1 until the opening in the cocoon is filled with your will's light. Then ask your will to act as an energetic "bouncer": letting energies through that are beneficial to you and keeping out those that are not. As you sit in meditation, observe and/or feel what kinds of energies are allowed in, and what they give you, share with you or teach you. Stay in this space as long as you like.

Visualization #3: Unfold the vine of will in the same way as in Visualization #1 until it reaches the opening in the cocoon. Rather than stopping it there, let it continue through the opening. Then see the vine expanding in all directions, curving around the outside of the cocoon until it completely surrounds it like an outer shell of light. Now visualize the shell becoming mirror-like on the outside, so that any energy coming toward your cocoon simply bounces off the mirror, reflected back out into the universe from which it came. This is a particularly effective method for fending off negative or destructive energies. Again, sit in quiet meditation for as long as you like.

After completing your meditative process in any of these three exercises, pull your will back into your belly with several strong inhalations. Once it is all back, move your fingers and toes a bit, stretch, sigh, open your eyes and return yourself to normal awareness.

Now that we have various ways to manage the more constant openness of menopause, let's look at one more similarity between menstruation and menopause. When the cocoon cracks open at menstruation, one of the many forces that can impinge more strongly upon our awareness is the presence of death. At menopause, the more permanent energetic openness allows our awareness of death to become keen, and our love of life can grow to match it. Menstruation gives us a chance to re-create ourselves monthly through a death/rebirth cycle. That opportunity is present throughout and after menopause: a daily adventure of confronting life and death with increasing awareness.

One menopausal woman's comment on the potential for such an ongoing confrontation was: "This is no fun!" Again, many of our attitudes toward our own mortality are conditioned by culture or religion. For those who believe in an afterlife or reincarnation, death doesn't present the finality that others dread. Most religions and spiritual paths claim the soul and its awareness move on in their journey after the body's last breath. So do the growing number of "life-after-death" and "near-death-experience" accounts. But we are usually so attached to the physical aspect of existence that we have great difficulty contemplating its end: death and detachment of the spirit from the physical body. Beyond trying to appreciate death's reminder that every moment of life is precious, menopause can be used as a time to also practice detachment and letting-go meditations. Here is one possibility.

MEDITATION IN DETACHMENT

Either lie down or sit comfortably and "Breathe Toward Inner Silence." When your mind is quiet, focus down into your belly and unfold your vine of will. Place your awareness in your will and allow it to travel out of your body and begin to float upward. When you are at some distance above your body, look down at it. Tell it you are preparing to say good-bye to it. Then allow any images or memories from your past to pass before you. Thank each one for whatever it shows you. When you are ready to move on, thank your body for having served you throughout your life. Then turn your attention upward once again. See a tunnel of light begin to form. Enter it and travel down its center until you emerge into a realm of light. Allow yourself to bathe in that light until you feel completely sated. Perhaps there are luminous beings in that realm that have something to communicate to you. When you feel content and are ready to leave—knowing you can return again to this realm whenever you so desire—re-enter the tunnel and follow it back until you emerge out the other side above where your physical body awaits you. Follow the vine of will down, traveling through it with your awareness until you enter your belly and your awareness is back inside your body. Pull the remainder of your will back in with a few inhalations. Feel your body from inside. Then slowly move fingers, toes, stretch, sigh, open your eyes and return to normal awareness.

By seeing the past clearly, we have more freedom to shape our future and fill it with power and meaning. And by accepting the inevitable presence of death in our future, we can choose to live more fully in the ever-changing present.

The Journey to Freedom

Menopause can be a revolution of increased self-knowledge, self-definition, creativity and freedom. Rather than see ourselves as helpless victims of biological circumstance—caught in a trap of negative meaning or overwhelming challenges—we can look forward to actually being sprung free from the traps or challenges of our pre-menopausal past.

Here are various benefits to anticipate during our spiritual journey of change.

Freedom from birth control. This is a big one for most women, since there are still no worry-free methods. Energies bound up in monthly birth control concerns are now liberated and directed for other purposes.

Freedom from child care. Although there are a few exceptions, by the time most women reach menopause any children they have are grown or past the stage of major dependency. This means more free time and energy.

Freedom from the weight and beauty game. Women of "the change" may decide that it is finally time to take a permanent break from obsessing about their appearance and look forward to future relationships based on mutual appreciation of inner beauty. (This whole area is explored in more detail in chapter 6.)

Freedom from social game-playing. Women who use menopause to come more fully into their power, who redefine their own meaning and value from within, will be increasingly independent from the impact of others' opinions and judgments. They are also less vulnerable to social intimidation tactics, less influenced by male approval, and more free from social stress. There may be other freedoms as well for women. We need but look for them, value them, and fill our newly spacious world with them.

Mothering Ourselves

Menopause and life after menopause can be a time to more freely and specifically direct our mothering, nurturing instincts toward ourselves as an expression of spiritual self-care.

And such nurturing may be very much needed. There are many uncomfortable and sometimes unnerving symptoms that menopausal women experience. Some women only have a few mild ones and sail through this transition relatively easily. Others have more severe symptoms. The following list of possible symptoms is not given to provoke anxiety, but to help women identify them and take actions that can relieve them.

Possible menopausal symptoms include: hot flashes; hot or cold sweats; dizziness; weight gain; headache; difficulty breathing; shortness of breath; heart palpitations; vaginal dryness; generally dryer skin, mouth or eyes; increased or decreased sexual libido; joint pains; cold hands and feet; fatigue; chest or breast pains; insomnia; emotional irritability or "mood swings;" fear of insanity or anxieties about physical health; inability to concentrate; increased forgetfulness; loss of strength or sensation in the extremities; and vision problems, including blind spots before the eyes, increased astigmatism or far-sightedness.

Some of these symptoms appear directly related to the hormonal changes of menopause, and clusters of these symptoms may be interrelated. For example, if a woman is suffering from insomnia, it is possible that she will also feel more irritable, fatigued, unfocused, and be more disposed to headaches and dizziness. Some symptoms may not be related to hormonal shifts, but rather to processes of aging that men also experience. These include dryness of skin, eye problems, changes in sexual libido and more difficulty with mental concentration. Clusters of psychological symptoms may be hormonally related and/or reflective of our attitudes toward menopause and aging. A final consideration is that some symptoms may be messages that destructive aspects of our past lifestyle are catching up with us, demanding we take notice and change; or that habits which were fine for us at an earlier time are not good for our present circumstances.

Knowing about all aspects of the menopausal process can short-circuit our victim-like feelings and bring us the power to act. The following are just a few of the growing number of books on menopause that can expand both our understanding and options for action.

The Menopausal Years, by Susan Weed. Lists many potential symptoms and offers a variety of therapeutic actions for each, including emotional, herbal and ritual suggestions. I highly recommend this one.

Secrets of a Natural Menopause, by Edna C. Ryneveld. Straightforward suggestions for a variety of natural remedies.

Menopause, Naturally, Updated, by Sadja Greenwood, M.D. Good general perspective with suggestions for diet and exercise.

Women and Hormones, by Alice T. MacMahon. Focuses specifically on hormones: what they affect and what affects them.

A Change for the Better, by Patricia Davis. A positive perspective.

Sister Moon Lodge, by Kisma Stepanich. A more mystical, shamanistic focus on menopause with many suggestions for rituals.

Women of the 14th Moon, edited by Dena Taylor and Amber C. Sumrall. For those who enjoy descriptions of other women's menopausal experiences through essay, story and poem. A few dietary and herbal suggestions are also included.

The Change, by Germaine Greer. Extensively covers many aspects of menopause, including social, medical, psychological. Champions self-empowerment.

The Fountain of Age, by Betty Friedan. Covers many aspects of aging, preparing reader to meet not only menopause but the rest of one's life with power and understanding.

The Silent Passage: Menopause, by Gail Sheehy. One of the first of its kind and highly recommended.

Besides exploring the available literature, what else can we do to nurture ourselves?

While our hormones are going through massive changes and sometimes pulling our emotions along in a turbulent wake, exercise can be a great salvation. Maintaining a strong healthy body through regular exercise is always important—and there is nothing like the welcome release of exercise-related endorphins for a woman who is thrashing about in a menopausal squall of difficult emotions. I find dancing, walking and biking great salvation during those storms. There are so many forms of exercise, that I'm confident every woman can find at least one that is reasonably enjoyable.

The issue of various hormone replacement therapies is not

addressed in depth here. There is increasing literature on the subject, but there is still much public debate about the risk of dangerous side effects. We must be as well-informed as possible, and may want to investigate other alternatives which are known to be safe. Western medicine, largely dominated by men, has tried to wrest the control of women's bodies away from women, whether through unnatural childbirth procedures, unnecessary hysterectomies and other surgeries, or through prescribing harmful drugs. We need to educate ourselves about our own bodies. We also need to take back more control over what is done with and to our bodies, particularly in the area of health. Learning about hormone therapies and their alternatives is one important exercise of our self-care process.

Contact with the earth and the life force of plants is a wonderful therapy for many people. Gardening can be particularly satisfying, both grounding and spiritually fulfilling for menopausal women. It puts us in touch with the changing, cyclical aspect of life and nature of which we are a part. And it gives us a balanced perspective about our own seasonal change. The creative, generative qualities of life and growth in the garden may ease the sorrows of women grieving their inability to bear children in the future. By drawing us outdoors, gardening also provides opportunities for various interactions with "Mother"— such as unfolding the will into the wind, into passing birds, the earth and the plants themselves. Gardening also gives us the chance to grow our favorite flowers as well as fresh organic "power food" and herbs that are both pleasurable and healthful.

A healthy, balanced diet is increasingly important during and after menopause. We need energy to deal with the ongoing changes, and we need to keep our bones strong and all systems well-nourished. Our growing spirit needs a sturdy home. There are even some foods and herbs that compensate for decreased estrogen. Having observed that many Asian women have fewer menopausal symptoms and better overall health than Westerners, researchers looked at their diet for clues. Their plant-based diet is abundant in phytoestrogens, compounds converted in the gut to hormonelike substances that the body can mistake for estrogen. These phytoestrogens come in two forms: isoflavones—found primarily in soy foods like tofu and soy milk—and lignans, found most concentrated in whole grains and flax seed, and in lesser amounts in fruits and vegetables. One or two 4-ounce servings of soy foods each day is a healthful addition to the diet and soy has another plus: calcium for ongoing bone strength.

In addition to a healthy diet, there are a variety of helpful nutritional supplements and herbs that can balance some of the effects of menopause. Again, try to be as well-informed as possible about them before using any, and be aware that the effects of herbs and other nutrients may take longer to notice than the effects of hormone replacement therapies.

Here is a short list of some herbs and supplements that either I've personally found useful or have been consistently recommended in the literature.

Herbs

Dong quai: useful antispasmodic for treating insomnia, hypertension and cramps, and a valuable blood purifier. Relieves menopausal symptoms as well as most female gynecological ailments.

False unicorn root, red clover, black and blue cohosh, marigold, sage, wild yam and licorice root: for estrogen support.

Ginseng: another valuable herb, one that is also energizing and excellent for relieving depression.

Vitex (chaste berry): for progesterone support. Also renowned for decreasing the number and intensity of hot flashes.

Sarsaparilla, damiana: for androgen support.

Combination of marigold and lady's mantle: to diminish vaginal dryness.

Marigold, red clover and melissa (taken internally): to diminish dry skin.

Other nutritional supplements:

Calcium: 1500 mg recommended daily to improve bone health.

Magnesium: 750 mg recommended daily in conjunction with calcium.

Boron: 3 mg—and no more—recommended daily to increase calcium absorption for bone strength and stimulate some estrogen production.

Vitamin D: 400 IU (international units) recommended daily, also to support calcium absorption.

Silica: a homeopathic remedy recommended for improved bone health. Follow instructions on the label.

For alleviating hot flashes:
  Vitamin E: 400-1200 IU daily
  Bioflavinoid hesperidin: 1,000 mg daily
  Evening of primrose oil: 500-1,000 mg daily
  Gamma oryzanol: 300 mg daily
  Lachesis: a homeopathic remedy
  Progesterone cream: ointment made from extract of wild Mexican yams (for topical use)

Explore this area of health care. It's fun and interesting, and helps us take back responsibility for our own well-being. Make sure you read up on each herb or supplement before embarking on a program. Three books that I've found quite helpful in this regard are: *Super Nutrition for Menopause* by Ann Louise Gittleman; *The Way of Herbs* by Michael Tierra; and *Prescription for Nutritional Healing* by James F. Balch, M.D. and Phyllis A. Balch, C.N.C.

All the suggestions for spiritual action and empowerment from chapters 1 and 2 can be increasingly helpful to menopausal women. More will be offered in the following healing section. They also can be helpful, even if they're not described specifically for menopausal women. For now, a suggested daily regimen of spiritual exercise for women going through "the change" might include:

1. a morning meditation ("Breathing Toward Inner Silence")
2. "Gathering Power from the Earth" or bone marrow nei kung at midmorning
3. a midday minimum 20 minutes of brisk exercise (earlier or later if midday is impossible)
4. a "Protective Visualization" period in late afternoon
5. some time for creative art in the evening
6. an evening meditation just before bed to clear away any stress from the day and to promote deep and restful sleep

One of my last recommendations for self-care is to form or join a support group with other women moving through the transition of menopause. This can be a wonderful place to exchange information, alleviate social isolation, and learn that there is both variety and commonality in the ways women experience this process. These groups can also be a place to be creative and spiritual together. Women's theater groups, dance or exercise groups, creative writing and spiritual ritual groups are but a few potential offshoots of such a support system.

Menopause is an opportunity for women to see and break free from many of the cultural constraints that affect us during the first half of life. We can also use this time to tap deeper sources of innate creativity, and to decide that the remaining years of life will be an adventure into self-definition and spiritual empowerment. Visibly and invisibly, we are doing more and more in each of these areas. Female "baby boomers" alone are turning out hundreds of wonderful books, teaching about and/or tending to their own spiritual development, making positive career changes and elevating social awareness. All of us are reshaping our own meaning and in the process affecting the global community. Menopause is a sturdy loom waiting for each of us to weave our own tapestry and to applaud ourselves at every phase of its creation.

PART TWO

Spirit in Healing

4

Opening the Way

The domain of healing is a spacious arena for spiritual action toward oneself and others. Within this lively environment, spiritual adventurers can flex and strengthen the will, and become cunning strategists who stalk and confront enemies of health. They can invoke and learn from benevolent healing forces, seek counsel from the messages of pain and illness, and grow to understand human desires for both life and death. And as they circle through and around the arena, those spiritual seekers and adventurers may find themselves redefining healing. Rather than only being a "cure" of symptoms, they may discover healing is a process of "higher education" in the understanding of self, energy and harmonious living.

My interest in health and healing began when I was a young girl. Oldest of four children, I was enlisted early on in the care of my younger siblings. By the time I was eight, my parents would occasionally have me baby-sit the younger ones for a few hours at a time. I was proud of my parents' trust in me. I was also frequently and secretly anxious a sibling might get injured or ill while in my care and I would be unable to meet the crisis.

To better prepare myself for such an event, I frequently curled up in a chair, my scholarly glasses endlessly slipping down my nose, and pored through Dr. Spock. I repeatedly read through that well-worn, thick paperback, stumbling over medical terminology and braving descriptions of all variety of terrifying possibilities. In the process, I suffered what medical students frequently go through: the certainty that every disease I read about lurked within me. Every little birthmark, ache and twinge, cough and upset stomach heralded potential disaster and was subject to my intense scrutiny. I imagined the possibility of my own premature and tragic death countless times, and even wept for myself and my bereft family. For variety, I imagined losing each and every one of them to some sudden horror, with all the accompanying anguish. Despite this self-inflicted emotional turmoil, I became quite educated in the field of human disease for an eight-year-old, confident I could at least diagnose a variety of ailments in my siblings, even if I couldn't cure them.

This childhood interest led me toward further explorations of health and healing as I grew older. Several decades later, I've concluded that true healing involves a realignment of the total person and her energies. Spirit cannot be left out of the process, for it is the invisible but unifying force which helps guide us to wholeness and wellness.

A growing number of Westerners are reaching similar conclusions. Without rejecting what is valid in traditional or allopathic medicine, the trend toward a more holistic, body-mind-spirit approach to health is blossoming. In the process, healing practices from many cultures are being used by Westerners looking to more actively participate in their healing. In order to demonstrate what is available to us in this domain, the rest of the

"Spirit in Healing" section of this book will be a travelogue of my own experiences and those of Anima.

Anima, or Ani, as I will call her, is a fictional composite of many friends, students and therapy clients of mine who have set out on their own spiritual journeys of healing. Her name, Anima, is one of several Latin words for spirit that also mean breath or wind—the animating power of life.

Self-Care

In the domain of healing, it is wise to follow the advice of "physician, heal thyself" and begin, as Anima did, with a focus on self-care.

Ani came to me as a recently divorced woman in her early 40s with a variety of complaints. Among them were a drinking problem, frequent tension headaches, backaches and constipation, and bouts of depression and anxiety about her future and self-worth. A workaholic accountant for a large business firm, Ani was chronically fatigued and got through her days on coffee. A full-bodied woman, she constantly worried about her figure, even though she was by no means overweight. The aftermath of her divorce six months earlier left her sexually insecure and anxious about her desirability. As a result, since then she'd alternated between weeks of social isolation and periods of frantic "dating" with men she met at parties, bars or through business connections. Ani was embarrassed to tell me how many men she had been sexually active with. Fortunately, she was sober enough with each to insist on condoms and to her knowledge had contracted no venereal diseases. But anxieties about AIDS and dissatisfaction with these casual relationships were an underlying, nagging source of distress for Ani. The last of her major problems was a sense of spiritual emptiness and lack of clarity about her purpose in life. She was a woman adrift in a baffling universe.

Ani was referred to me by a former therapy client who'd described me as a counselor and holistic healer. Ani was a bit dubious about the "holistic healer" aspect. But she trusted her friend's recommendation and set up an appointment, knowing she needed help if she was to reverse the downward spiral of her life.

During the initial intake session, I told Ani about my holistic approach to therapy. I explained how I look for interconnections between the mental, emotional, physical and spiritual, and then explore interventions in each area. I also made it clear that she had choices about her condition. My role was to help increase her range of positive choices and encourage her to act on them. Ani agreed to do her share and we looked for a starting point.

As she was physically fatigued and stressed from too much coffee, alcohol and a typical American diet of junk food, I suggested she begin with a two-week cleansing diet. The goal was to rid her body of toxins, increase her appreciation for healthier foods, eliminate coffee and allow her overworked adrenal system to recover, and to begin increasing her overall energy level. Then she would have the strength needed to tackle other problems and face life more vigorously.

The cleansing program I suggested was designed by Dr. Randolph Stone. Dr. Stone combined his knowledge of both Western naturopathic and Eastern ayurvedic healing into a new holistic healing system he called polarity therapy. The program also includes polarity yoga and hands-on, energy-based healing. A week of the cleansing is the minimum for noticing results. But the first time it's done, two weeks may be needed to overcome a lifetime of poor eating habits. When the body takes in more toxins than it can release—from environmental pollutants, pesticides, chemicals and antibiotics in our foods, too much dietary fat, alcohol and recreational or prescribed drugs—the liver becomes one of the main warehouses for these excess toxins. Dr. Stone's cleansing program takes this into account and focuses primarily on flushing the liver while correcting the diet.

DR. STONE'S LIVER FLUSH AND PURIFYING DIET

The liver flush drink and liver flush tea are to be drunk each morning before you eat or drink anything else (except water). Both can be consumed on a daily basis for as long as you like— even if you are not doing the cleansing diet—for their tonic, cleansing health benefits. The ingredients for each are readily available in health food stores that sell herbs.

Prepare the tea first so it will be ready for you to drink immediately after you have the liver flush drink.

Liver Flush Tea

    1 teaspoon licorice root
    1 teaspoon fenugreek seed
    1 teaspoon flax seed
    1 teaspoon fennel seed
    1 teaspoon peppermint leaves
    4 slices of peeled ginger root cut ⅛-inch thick

Boil the ginger root three minutes in 1½ pints water. Then remove from burner and add the other ingredients, mix briefly and let steep 10-15 minutes while you prepare the liver flush.

Liver Flush

Mix together well, preferably in a blender:
fresh juice of several oranges and/or grapefruits (minimum 2 cups juice)
2-3 tablespoons of pure, cold pressed olive oil (consult label)
3 crushed cloves of garlic (minimum) and ⅛ teaspoon cayenne pepper
small chunk of fresh ginger root (or more according to personal taste)

After blending the ingredients, you may want to set aside 1-2 ounces of the mixture to mix with 2 teaspoons of crushed psyllium seed to increase intestinal cleansing. Then drink the entire mixture, including the psyllium mix if you made it, and follow it immediately with a cup of still hot liver flush tea. During the day, drink as much of this tea as you like. Try to drink at least four cups of spring water and four cups of other liquids—the above or other herbal teas or fresh vegetable and fruit juices—to facilitate flushing of released toxins.

An hour or two after the liver flush, have some fresh fruit or fresh vegetable juice. From lunch time on, eat plenty of leafy green and other vegetables such as lettuce, carrots, turnips, squash, chard, spinach, onion, leeks, celery, cabbage, broccoli, cauliflower, radishes, cucumbers, beets and their tops, and also lots of sprouts (alfalfa, wheat, mung, soy, lentil, etc.). You may also eat fruits such as apples, pears, grapes, peaches, prunes, figs, raisins and fresh berries. Eat all fruits and vegetables in raw form as much as possible, but they may also be steamed, baked or made into soups for variation. Do not fry them. A moderate amount of raw nuts—preferably almonds—may be eaten. Wheat grass juice, available in many health food stores, is also very beneficial.

Do not eat meat, fish, chicken, eggs, starches (potatoes, rice, bread, cereal), sugar (although very limited amounts of honey or maple syrup are permissible), milk or milk products, coffee, caffeinated tea, alcohol or drugs—not even aspirin. Do not use aluminum cookware, because it releases some toxins into food and liquids when heated.

A good practice each morning before doing the flush is to take a hot-and-cold shower combination. Stay in the hot water for 2-3 minutes and the cold for one minute. Alternate up to three times. Begin this gradually with water that is not too hot or cold and work toward the extreme temperatures slowly over several weeks. The practice improves circulation and elimination.

Some people also suggest doing a coffee enema each day of the flush. Coffee enemas induce both purging of the liver and intestinal motion. This helps relieve problems with the gas, headaches and bad breath associated with detoxification during fasting or cleansing diets such as this one. To make the coffee enema solution, place two quarts of steam-distilled water in a pan and add six heaping tablespoons of ground coffee (don't use instant or decaffeinated). Boil for 15 minutes, cool and strain. Use only one pint of liquid per enema, and save the rest in a jar for the next three days. Do only one enema per day during the program. Don't use petroleum jelly on the tip of the enema. Instead, use a 200 IU capsule of vitamin E to lubricate the end. Stick a pin in the end of the capsule and squeeze the liquid onto the tip. This will also have a healing effect on the anus and the lining of the colon if these areas are inflamed.

If you regularly drink coffee or take in caffeine through teas, soft drinks or chocolate, you may experience caffeine withdrawal headaches the first few days. You might consider beginning your program on a Saturday if you work Monday through Friday. That way you will have gotten over the headache hump by the end of the weekend. You may also experience other symptoms during the first three to four days of the cleansing process, such as muscle aches, periodic fatigue, coughing up phlegm and emotional releases. Some people also taste or briefly reexperience drugs they've used in the past, such as antibiotics or "recreational" drugs. Although some of these symptoms may be temporarily uncomfortable, they are actually good signs that the process is working, so be patient and wait them out. By the second week, many people experience more mental alertness, some weight loss if needed, a more even emotional state and heightened spiritual awareness.

This program can benefit anyone at almost any time. It is especially useful if you are feeling low on energy or are in poor health, or if you have been overloading on junk foods. Some people enjoy cleansing four times each year at the turn of the seasons, to meet changing weather conditions with strength and a healthy, vital body. Of course, as with any new health program, you may wish to check with your doctor before starting.

I saw Ani after her first week on the program and there was a distinct change in her appearance. Her eyes looked clearer, brighter and more serene. Her skin had a fresh glow in contrast to her previous pallor. All of these are typical results of cleansing. When I inquired about her experience with the program, her responses were also typical.

"I definitely had some headaches the first few days and I slept a lot more than usual, including several daytime naps. I guess my body was letting me know how run-down it had gotten, and that it really needed the extra rest. I did feel slightly like I had the flu for a day or two, as well as being a little spacy some of the time. But for the last couple of days I've felt more energetic and light. I like this feeling, so I'm going to go for the second week of this program, even though starting the day with a raw garlic beverage isn't my idea of a gourmet breakfast!"

I laughed and confessed I still plugged my nose while drinking the liver flush so I wouldn't taste the garlic, but told her that some people actually grew to love the flavor of the drink. I supported Ani's plan to continue for a second week. I also told her once she was done, she might consider staying off coffee for good. My own experience was that after cleansing my body for two weeks the first time on the program, I was much more sensitive to what I put into it. One cup of coffee had me so wired and uncomfortable I dropped my own heavy habit and never went back to it. My awareness of what foods were or weren't good for me also increased, a fact I resented at first because a few of my favorites were on the negative list!

As Ani prepared for her second week of cleansing, I suggested an exercise program to raise her energy, counterbalance her sedentary lifestyle and ameliorate some of her depression and anxiety. It turned out she'd been considering an aerobics class at a nearby YWCA. The class was available right after work and she decided to try it three times a week, on the condition that if she didn't like it, she'd consider other options. I also suggested checking out yoga for relief from her back problems and as a more inner-directed form of exercise for her spirit.

I was somewhat concerned that in her typical workaholic style Ani might go overboard with an exercise program. We discussed that possibility and she decided to stop taking on overtime accounting work, so she'd have more free time and energy. And she would guard against excessive exercise.

On the days she wasn't doing aerobics or yoga, both of which she enjoyed and benefited from, Ani did a mile or two of the "Belly Walk" as an extension of the power-gathering exercises I'd begun teaching her. The belly walks also served another purpose besides exercise and power-gathering. They exposed Ani to the healing power of beauty, in this case the beauty of nature. Although she walked in the city, the earth and trees and other plants, the birds and sun and sky, were all readily available sources of beauty. She started gaining a sense of inner serenity and harmony from her contact with nature.

Ani not only benefited spiritually, but found emotional stability, physical toning and reduced stress as a result of her belly walks and exercise classes. At my suggestion, she took up her long-abandoned hobby of oil painting to nurture her own ability to create beauty. She also did "Breathing Toward Inner Silence" for brief periods each day to calm and center herself as needed. Her energy level and physical health continued improving over the weeks, her headaches diminished, and her ability to meet daily work demands increased.

I then familiarized Ani with the concept of energy leaks or loss, and had her do the personal inventory of stresses outlined in chapter 1. We looked over her energy-leaking habits on every level to see which could be eliminated, and then replaced them with power-gathering exercises.

In order to teach Ani power-gathering techniques, I first acquainted her with the basic principles of energy awareness described in chapter 1. I also described some energy-based viewpoints on health and healing and introduced her to the concept of energy blocks—whether mental, emotional, physical or spiritual.

How do we apply energy-based concepts to life and healing? I will give some examples from my own life as well as from Ani's.

When I am writing books or songs, I occasionally come up against a block. Mentally, creatively, I can go no further. Sometimes I butt my head against the block, straining and pushing to find a way through it. Once in a while this works. But a strategy that works better for me is to *temporarily ignore the block and go in an entirely different direction*. My most successful diversionary tactics are "belly walks." I gather power while enjoying the mental benefits of fresh air and the spiritual benefits of contact with "Mother." More often than not, partway through the walk inspiration suddenly strikes. Ideas begin rolling in like thunder.

Other effective tactics I've used are reading a good novel, cleaning the house or continuing to write, but in some entirely different area of the book or song where I am not blocked.

After years of experimenting with these tactics, I've realized there is a fine line between constructive diversion and procrastination. What helps keep me from crossing the line is holding fast to my intention of eventually triumphing over the block.

In working with Ani, I also used a go-a-different-way-for-now approach in dealing with her postdivorce sexual behavior. During our initial interview, it was obvious this issue was highly charged and laden with conflict. She resisted even speaking about it. Rather than deal with her sexuality in the early part of therapy, we simply went in other directions on the healing journey. I had faith that when she gained enough trust in me and herself, we'd address the sexual issue effectively.

In her journey of healing, Ani came upon a healing system that applies the principle of *breaking up energy blocks*. One day she came to her session and asked if I knew anything about reflexology. A friend of hers was going to a Saturday workshop on the subject and was encouraging her to attend. I told her I thought reflexology would be an excellent addition to her self-care program and explained the fundamentals. Reflexology is based on Eastern systems of knowledge about energy points and energy flows in the body. The main theory is that the hands and feet contain numerous "reflex" points that correspond to the entire body. By stimulating a point on the hand, for example, one can simultaneously stimulate and help heal the corresponding body part. This is done by pressing firmly—with a finger or eraser-end of a pencil—on the palm of the hand or sole of the foot. There are reflexology charts illustrating which points correspond to which organs and other body parts. Usually the points that are sore—or feel crunchy, indicating a buildup of little crystalline mineral deposits—correspond to places in the body most needy of attention. The body's available energy is blocked in some way—often by chronic tension, overload of toxins or trauma from past injuries—from adequately supplying those places with the healing energy they need. Applying pressure to the reflex point breaks up the block to the corresponding body part and allows a fresh influx of energy. This technique is also common to Rolfing, Reichian body work, acupressure and shiatsu. In each of these healing methods, the therapist applies direct pressure to tense, blocked muscles until the tension breaks up and the muscles relax, allowing increased blood circulation and energy through those areas.

Ani appeared somewhat mystified about the possibility of alleviating a stomachache or stiff neck through pressing on her foot, but was curious enough to attend the reflexology training. She not only enjoyed it, but also met a few people she liked with whom she formed a bimonthly practice group. They were all thrilled to find that they needed minimal training to use reflexology both for self-care and for the care of others.

Another useful method of dealing with energy blocks is to look for ways to *penetrate a weakness or opening*. Most of us who have ever been determined to win an argument of any kind have done just that: looked for the weakness in the other person's position in order to penetrate her defenses and move on to victory. Looking for weaknesses may not seem like the most exalted of tactics, but it can be effective and appropriate in a variety of situations.

In Ani's case, I had her apply the penetration method to some of her own energy blocks. I suggested she review repeated criticisms or feedback she'd gotten—from friends, family, business associates, her ex-husband—which she had dismissed, refusing to believe they were true. One such message was, "You don't really listen to me." Ani protested again and again that she was a good listener and didn't understand what all these people were talking about. Nor did she grasp why she eventually alienated some of them.

We began looking at her defensiveness from the philosophical stance of "methinks the lady doth protest too much." I suggested Ani start noticing her listening patterns to observe when she was the most attentive, when her mind wandered, and when she entirely shut down her ability to hear. I encouraged her to do this without self-judgment so she could more easily discover her patterns. Over the next few weeks she found several. If a person discussed a subject that both interested her and didn't conflict with her worldview, Ani was an attentive listener. But if the subject seemed to have no relevance to her life or threatened either her self-concept or her worldview, Ani increasingly "tuned out" until her attention was elsewhere.

Observing these patterns without self-blame allowed Ani to get past her own defenses and see them in a new way. As she increased awareness, she discovered more choices. If a friend talked too long about something she had no interest in, Ani decided she would either be forthright and let the person know of her disinterest, or actively try to steer the conversation in a new direction. If a subject was mentally or emotionally unsettling, she again had several options. One was to be frank and tell the other person. A second choice was to listen while silencing the internal dialogue and breathing calmly. This would allow her to stay centered while absorbing the information, and allow her to choose her responses from a place of balance rather than reactivity. As a result of penetrating the weaknesses in her own block, Ani moved on to become a more active, attentive listener who enjoyed the benefits of personal growth and improved interpersonal relationships.

We can also use ritual as part of our spiritual arsenal for dealing with energy blocks. For instance, one day I learned Ani had a major block—or resistance—to cleaning her house. She liked the results whenever she managed to get around to cleaning, but as this happened rarely, her "slothfulness," as she called it, was a frequent source of self-criticism. There were a few clues in her past that explained the possible origins of this resistance.

However, as Ani was long aware of them and the knowledge had not helped in the slightest, I suggested a ritual to *transform the block*.

Ani's mother often told her that cleanliness was next to godliness. Because Ani did desire such spiritual exaltation, we arrived at a way in which housecleaning could be transformed into a spiritual ritual. First, she lit some scented candles and placed several in every room to evoke a spiritual and pleasantly fragrant environment throughout the house. Next, she assembled all the necessary tools for cleaning—broom, mop, dust cloth, vacuum cleaner, bathroom disinfectant, etc.—in one place. Then, with cedar incense, she blessed them as ritual objects and herself as high priestess. Finally, she spent several minutes meditating until she came to inner silence, after which she put on some of her most uplifting music tapes and began cleaning. Every gesture of the cleaning process was regarded as a spiritual caress, as if she were suffusing all she touched with light, energy and beauty. When she finished cleaning, she blessed herself once more with the cedar incense and sat in the afterglow of a ritual well enacted. This is how Ani transformed her block against housecleaning into beauty, satisfaction and spiritual power, and healed an old and troublesome problem.

I've experimented with a variety of ways to incorporate spiritual rituals in therapy. Rituals can be transformative and healing and are sometimes helpful for reaching closure in a variety of ways: to complete the grieving process for a lost relationship; to mark a powerful insight or the end of a certain behavior pattern; or to forgive someone who has intentionally or unconsciously caused pain. Ani and I worked together to create healing rituals for her which served many of these purposes. Sometimes I asked her to make an object that represented a key person in her life she was struggling to come to terms with. I then suggested she take the object somewhere out in nature where she would be undisturbed by other people and do a releasing ritual. She might end up talking, yelling, laughing, crying, dancing, singing or quietly meditating until her process felt complete. Then she usually left the object behind, perhaps burying it in the earth or casting it into a body of water, as a symbolic gesture of closure and letting go. This and other kinds of healing rituals Ani tried were consistently effective, powerful, integrative and often enjoyable, just as they have been for other clients and students of mine.

Ani slowly learned an energy-based approach to healing. Temporarily ignoring the block and going in a different direction, breaking up the block or creatively transforming the block were all practical methods she used in her daily life.

To assist Ani's psychological healing in problem areas, I introduced her to some simple Gestalt therapy techniques and we experienced the transformation of a different kind of energy block. Developed by Fritz Perls, Gestalt is one of several self-empowering therapies that trust the individual to have the best answers to her own problems. Gestalt therapy helps uncover and identify these answers through a process of self-dialogue and being present moment-to-moment. I tried a Gestalt-style exercise with Ani to help her identify what psychological stresses or conflicts might be contributing to her occasional problems with constipation. The cleansing program and ongoing improvement in her diet and exercise had helped a great deal, but the problem still cropped up several times a month. Since she preferred not to be addicted to laxatives, she was open to a safe alternative—Gestalt dialogue.

"Ani, I want you first to ask your colon to talk to you about this problem. As you 'hear' its voice, I want you to verbalize what it is saying in the first person. Start by saying, 'I am Ani's colon. Here is what I have to say.'"

After struggling briefly with some embarrassment and self-consciousness about the subject matter and about role-playing, Ani began. And out of the silence, the somber voice of the colon finally spoke its truth.

"I have trouble letting go, even of what is toxic and what I no longer need."

After this revelation, I encouraged a dialogue between Ani's inner witness—the detached observer within us all—and her colon, in order to learn more and find a healthier resolution between them.

Inner witness: "What is the root of your difficulty in letting go?"

Heavy pause.

Colon: "I'm afraid if I let go, nothing will replace what I eliminate."

Then came some tears. Here was the gestalt, the "aha" of the dilemma. Ani realized the colon's statement was in fact one of her core psychological stances. She saw her basic lack of faith in her own abilities to find nourishing replacements for old, dysfunctional or toxic habits. Gleaning this gem of knowledge from her own depths, she had something new to work with. Over the next round of therapy sessions, we delved into this pattern, looking for its effects in other aspects of her life. We simultaneously explored sources of fresh "nourishment" to replace those elements of her life she was ready to let go of. Her problems with constipation diminished further as understanding transformed the block into guidance for positive action.

Gestalt therapy is a wonderful approach that places the ball of responsibility for change back in the client's own court, where it belongs. The therapist facilitates the process, bringing the client's awareness to unconscious body signals or suggesting formats for playing out the inner drama. The therapist's role is more akin to a midwife's than to a "father" analyst holding all the answers. Gestalt sessions can also be creative, deep, hilarious and dynamic for client and therapist alike.

Whenever we let go of something or give it away, an empty space is created. Energy immediately seeks to fill the vacuum. If we let go of a destructive habit, we must fill the space with something positive or the old habit will try rushing back in. Battling that pattern is familiar to all addicts. A visualization technique called "replacement therapy" is often helpful in dealing with old habits. It helps us fill the empty space with spiritual energy until new, positive behaviors take the place of the old negative ones.

REPLACEMENT THERAPY VISUALIZATION

After "Breathing Toward Inner Silence," look around the inner landscape of your body for the space now empty as a result of letting go of a habit. Its location may or may not seem directly related to what you've let go. Once you find the empty space, visualize an enormous sphere of gold light floating outside your body. Each time you inhale, pull some of its golden light into the empty space until it is filled with light. Feel the warm, healing glow within you. When you are ready, wiggle your fingers and toes, sigh and stretch. Then open your eyes and come back to your physical environment.

Ani found she needed to do this visualization fairly frequently over the course of therapy, for she was letting go of many outmoded or destructive behaviors. However, one persistent habit remained difficult to release: her on-and-off problem with alcohol. I had been using the "flow around" approach to this particular block, not ignoring it but focusing instead on indirectly related issues. I felt timing was important for confronting the issue directly. To do that, Ani needed adequate reserves of strength and energy as well as support. When she seemed strong enough to tackle her alcohol addiction, we looked for clues to the source of the problem. Meanwhile, I suggested she try Alcoholics Anonymous as a source of support.

The Power of the Group Healing Spirit

In the mid-1970s, I worked for four years in an experimental substance abuse program. The center was an intense and confrontational environment. Street heroin addicts, court-referred child molesters with drinking problems and self-referred college dropouts with long-term addictions and identity problems all haunted the residential facility with their pain and hope. I knew of nothing else like that center in its time. The radical director encouraged innovative applications of Gestalt, bioenergetics and encounter groups as well as my own work in dance therapy.

Over time, we found that these many methods were effective to a certain extent. A great deal of real healing and deep insights took place. However, too many residents still, even after several substance-free years of living in the program, returned to their addictions within 6 to 18 months after leaving it. When the program closed, after much introspection I finally concluded that the missing element—a spiritual focus—might have made a significant difference in fostering continued sobriety.

Drugs, alcohol and other addictions provide various kinds of "highs" which appeared to me to be substitutes for deeper spiritual connectedness and ecstasy. Because the quasi-spiritual high wears off as the substance does, addicts seek again and again the lost paradise drugs and alcohol provide. If addicts could turn this natural thirst for spiritual experience to nondestructive and healing practices that accessed various spiritual states, they would have what they truly sought without the negative consequences. And if they had the support of a group doing similar practices, the positive outcome would be even more enhanced and sustained.

Alcoholics Anonymous (AA), and its numerous "recovery" offshoots, are examples of just this type of group. All of the 12-Step recovery programs, which deal with a variety of addictions, have a core reliance on a "Higher Power." The spiritual strength and support of the group itself hold a close second place. Both are potent factors in helping people replace destructive addictions with what are sometimes called positive addictions. For these reasons, I felt Ani might benefit from AA.

And benefit she did. She began substituting AA meetings for evenings at the local bars and admitted her alcoholism. We discussed the energy principles AA was based on and agreed the primary approaches were breaking and transforming energy blocks. The resistance to giving up alcohol was systematically broken by verbally identifying and confronting one's alcoholism repeatedly in front of the group, and the group energy supported this process. The transformative aspect turned the addiction—a block to health and wholeness—into a thirst for and trust in a Higher Power: Spirit.

Recovery groups such as Alcoholics Anonymous, Narcotics Anonymous and Overeaters Anonymous offer both spiritual focus and communal support. But they sometimes don't offer enough tools to support more consistent and sustained day-to-day spiritual experiences. People in recovery, as in the larger community, may need such tools for greater spiritual nourishment and fulfillment. Many people in recovery programs awaken their spiritual thirst and go on to explore other environments. The power of the group and the focus on a Higher Power act as an incubator. Together, they midwife and nurture the natural impulse of the individual to seek spiritual sustenance in nondestructive ways while slowly loosening the grip on the problem habit.

Since Ani was already aware of her spiritual emptiness and thirst when she first came to see me, I supplied her with many spiritual practices from the beginning of therapy. However, until she began AA, she'd had no group support in her healing process. I decided to supplement the welcome group benefits of AA with another group healing process—the Womb Lodge ceremony—which I developed out of my long study of shamanistic healing customs and will describe after giving its background.

I became interested in shamanism in the late 1960s while doing dance therapy research. As I prepared to write my thesis and begin my own pioneering work in this new field, I was inspired by what I read of ancient shamanistic practices. I had already experienced firsthand the interrelatedness of thoughts, emotions and body by applying dance therapy to myself. I learned shamanism not only embraced the same perspective, but also added a focus on ceremony and spirit. These were two important additions to the kind of holistic healing approach I was already moving toward. Since then, I have continued to enthusiastically study the shamanistic approaches of other cultures. After many years, I finally created my own ceremonies, healing songs, dances and other practices based on core shamanistic "technologies."

When a group comes together for a healing ceremony, a great deal of power is generated. One of the shamanic approaches I've used repeatedly and successfully takes place outdoors in a sweat lodge structure. My first contacts with this kind of environment were through Native American practices in the 1970s, and since then the sweat lodge has become more well-known to non-Natives seeking to enjoy its healing or spiritual benefits. I do not lead Native sweat lodge ceremonies. Rather, using creativity and intuition I've developed my own "Womb Lodge" ceremonies for healing and other spiritual purposes. In doing so, I retain certain basic elements from traditional Native sweats. Prayer, song, heat, cleansing herbs and an effort to be sensitive to the motion and timing of spiritual energies are the primary similarities. Womb Lodge ceremonies have a certain intensity and may not be for everyone, but those who choose to participate come away with gifts of spirit and healing.

Many people from recovery programs, as well as other spiritually interested individuals, have attended and benefited from these Womb Lodge ceremonies. I mentioned this to Ani and said I would like to do this ritual for her and any interested acquaintances from her AA group. Although sometimes I hold a Lodge in which the group focuses primarily on the healing of one individual, this was to be for all of them equally. The ceremony's main purpose would be to support the participants' healing and recovery process and to familiarize them with the spiritual qualities of nature. In addition, it would serve to introduce them to another way besides AA where the power of the group can contribute to individual healing: the way of spiritual ritual.

The evening of the ceremony, Ani brought eight curious and mildly apprehensive friends from AA. The fire was already lit, the stones nestled in the fire pit and heating up. A friend of mine was taking care of the fire and was later responsible for bringing the stones into the lodge. Some yards away from the fire pit was the lodge itself, a humble little shelter made of bent willow saplings and covered with blankets, squatting on the ground like a fat mushroom. In the center of the lodge's earthen floor was a smaller pit, empty now and waiting to be filled with the hot stones once the ceremony began. I had Ani and her friends peer inside the lodge so they would be familiar with the pit's location when it was time to file in. Then we spread some blankets on the ground near the fire and I prepared them for the ceremony.

I told the group to consider the lodge as a womb, specifically as Mother Earth's womb, which they would enter, be nourished in and emerge from new and revitalized. Not only would the earth's energies contribute to their nourishment, but the fire's heat (released from the stones that would be brought in) and the water poured on those stones—combining with the air as steam—would provide all four elements in which we would immerse ourselves. I encouraged the group to regard each of the elements as spiritual energies, particularly the fire. The small lodge would get hot once the fire-heated stones were brought in. Rather than resist the heat as this happened, I suggested they actively embrace and pull it into their bodies for healing and spiritual power.

I also told them we would have several periods for prayer. During those times we could call in other spiritual powers to assist and bless us or other people who might need our help. The ceremony would be divided into four parts, with the door flap opened at the end of each one. Following a cooling down period, more stones would be brought in and the door closed once again. I told the group I would periodically sing and/or drum throughout the ceremony to help sustain the necessary energy level and quality. At my suggestion, Ani taught the others the "Breathing Toward Inner Silence" meditation in advance, in case they wanted to use it during the Womb Lodge. Finally, everyone changed out of their street clothes and wrapped themselves in large beach towels as instructed. We filed into the lodge in a circular manner until everyone was seated. The first stones were brought in and the door was closed.

Huddled together on the earth, in total darkness except for the glow of red hot stones, we called out our opening prayers, sang and expressed our hopes for the ceremony. As we did, I poured water on the hot rocks and felt spiritual power gathering and coalescing within the lodge along with the steam. I encouraged everyone to breathe slowly into the belly to deal with the mounting heat and energy. One particularly anxious woman began hyperventilating, but she followed my instructions and soon was calmer. I taught them all a simple chant which they joined me in singing, and the group harmony increased. When I felt the participants were acclimated to the new and unusual spiritual environment of the lodge, I called for the door to be opened by my fire-tending friend, and the first quarter was complete.

The second quarter was the most intense. Its purpose was to identify and release past mental/emotional pain that may have contributed to alcohol dependency. As each participant identified a pain, she internally gave it a symbolic form, a visual image. Then they did a series of exhalations, breathing the pain's "form" out of their bodies and directing it into the earth, where it was composted into fresh, growth-producing energies. As their individual pains emerged, the exhalations began taking the form of yelling, weeping, groaning and sometimes laughter until it seemed the whole lodge vibrated with the intensity of feeling and healing power. Meanwhile I sang and drummed loudly to support the participants and alleviate any self-consciousness they might have about the sounds they made. Then I guided them through the "Replacement Therapy" visualization so the inner spaces once occupied by pain could now be filled with light. The door was then opened again.

Several people were still weeping quietly in the aftermath of release, and those on either side of them reached out spontaneously in gestures of comfort. The power of Spirit and group spirit were coming together in a natural blending of good will and support in the small, contained community within the Womb Lodge.

The third quarter, with its focus on physical healing, was dynamic in a different way than the second. The mood shifted and everyone vigorously and enthusiastically used the fragrant sage I'd given them to cleanse their physical bodies of blocked or disruptive energies. One of the younger participants told me earlier she was recovering from mononucleosis and was still a bit low on energy. I decided to help her more personally with this problem. I took some deep breaths to gather power from the earth and directed my will to align with the fire in the stones. Then I reached out and placed the palms of my hands briefly on the glowing stones, inhaling and drawing the healing, energizing power of fire into my palms. I did this several times until my hands hummed with energy. I then placed my hands on the young woman's belly, exhaled and directed power into her "storage" area. I repeated the process until I sensed she had absorbed as much energy as she could. My hands were not burnt despite the fact they'd touched extremely hot stones again and again.

Our final quarter was mellow and deep. It allowed everyone a quiet, private space with Spirit. Mostly we were silent, devoting this time to meditation or to seeking visions that might help integrate our experiences during the Womb Lodge and guide us forward in our lives. As the door opened the final time and we crawled out into the cool night air, we were reborn into a magical world of glittering stars and glowing coals. We lay belly-down on the earth for a while to ground ourselves, the steam rising from our bodies like dreams set loose into the night. The Womb Lodge and the healing power of the group had nourished us— body, mind, heart and soul—and birthed us back into the world with a new sense of life's spiritual potentials.

The following week, Ani told me her friends felt that the release of pain they'd experienced from one Womb Lodge ceremony was equal to months of counseling. Ani herself felt more optimistic about her own recovery and shared a closer bond with the people she'd brought to the ceremony. She also felt a more real connection to Spirit as a result of the lodge, one that was filling up her former spiritual emptiness.

The Womb Lodge (or other sweat lodge ceremonies) and recovery programs are but a few examples of the power of group healing used in the West. Therapy and support groups of many kinds have blossomed in recent years.

Ani decided to join a monthly support group for divorced women. She found the sharing of experiences a means for increased self-acceptance and a relief from the isolation of her own pain over the failed marriage. She learned from the other women it was possible to move through the pain and come out the other side with more awareness and understanding of the intricacies of human relationships. The group healing spirit was manifested once again.

One-on-One

Powerful as it may be, a group environment is not always the most appropriate for healing. Sometimes an individual may need the entire focus of a healer. There are increasing numbers of holistic approaches available for those healers who work with individuals, including many that recognize spiritual energy as a key element of healing.

Ani came to me because she didn't have the knowledge and resources to solve all her problems. She needed help from another human being. When we were together, I gave her my attention. I also introduced her to a variety of techniques that required my direct guidance at first: visualizations, meditations, Gestalt, physical cleansing, ritual and power-gathering. Over time, however, she was able to practice each of these methods on her own and became more self-reliant and confident in her healing process.

As Ani gained faith and interest in her own healing and in healing practices in general, I suggested resources outside myself. She explored other one-on-one approaches for her own healing and with an increasing interest in the possibilities of helping others. Some of the more well-known methods she found were Reiki, polarity balancing, acupuncture and acupressure, reflexology, energy-sensitive forms of massage and chiropractic adjustments. Except for chiropractic, which primarily adjusts the spine to promote a stronger flow of energy to the entire body, each of these systems is based at least in part on Eastern healing practices. They include a knowledge of the way energy moves through the body, techniques to rebalance blocked or disrupted energy flows, and ways to strengthen and support wellness. Another person's touch is often a healing source of comfort and reassurance, but when that person touches with knowledge of energy and an intention to heal, the power and scope of healing are increased.

Ani found each one-on-one style of healing useful not only for promoting health and ameliorating stress, but for preventing the buildup of stress in the first place. Until recently, we often waited until stress-related problems surfaced as symptoms, and then sought out the ministrations of our medical doctors. Although these sometimes alleviated the tip of the iceberg—the symptom—the causes that lurked below in a sea of poor health habits or ongoing stresses often weren't adequately addressed. It was usually only a matter of time before the same or a new symptom reappeared, and back to the doctor we'd march.

This symptom-focused pattern has not always served us well. Now, increasing numbers of people are turning to alternative holistic practices that encourage self-care and changes in lifestyle, address cause and prevention and eliminate stress and distress. Many physicians are yelling "quackery" and trying to deny the potential of any methods other than their own—sometimes out of self-serving goals, sometimes out of genuine concern. But to categorically dismiss every alternative as primitive hocus-pocus or as dangerous is a great disservice to everyone. While there is definitely a need for our physicians, playing an active part in our *own* health and healing increases respect for our bodies and our lives.

The journey of healing is ideally one of self-empowerment. With adequate information and training, most people have the potential to be healers of self and possibly others, and to experience the mystery and fulfillment of the healing journey. This was the attitude Ani encountered when she went for sessions with a Healing and Therapeutic Touch practitioner who was also a registered nurse. Meeting this nurse opened yet another door for Ani, one that led her to discover a spiritual healing revolution that I'd recently come upon myself. That revolution is the subject of the next chapter.

A holistic approach to healing gives attention to the total person, including her spiritual life, no matter what the identified "problem." It is not surprising that among those who explore holistic healing, many find themselves embarking on a spiritual journey as they discover a new world of energetic and spiritual resources. Such a journey was now becoming a reality for Ani.

5

An Underground Spiritual Revolution in Western Medicine

Although well-defended in its own way, the Western medical system has not been entirely immune to an infiltration of holistic, spiritual healing influences and practices. Not surprisingly, it is primarily women nurses who are the vanguard of this quiet invasion. They are the individuals within the system who have the most intimate and personal contact with patients. And the foundation of their nursing profession is healing, care and love.

The healing practice of laying on of hands is neither a new fad nor a hoax. It is ancient—respected throughout most world cultures and religions. And no matter what her religion or personal beliefs, almost anyone with an interest can the learn basic principles and applications of hands-on healing. Since the 1970s, a growing number of hands-on systems have been available. Reiki, polarity therapy, reflexology, shiatsu and acupressure are some of the more well-known ones.

It is not surprising that nurses, who already have an interest in health, are drawn to explore some of these healing systems. And also not surprising is the fact that some of these nurses then created new healing methods based on their own experiences. Like the women of the early natural childbirth revolution, they encountered resistance in Western hospitals, and like those women, they persevered. Today, these new healing systems are powerful spiritual influences shaping the holistic nursing field and Western medicine alike. I discovered them in my own explorations of healing and shared them with Ani and others also interested in healing.

This spiritual healing revolution has four powerful elements. Rogerian concepts are the theoretical foundation for many holistic nurse practitioners and Therapeutic Touch (TT) and Healing Touch (HT) are practical hands-on healing systems. The American Holistic Nurses' Association (AHNA) offers nurses an in-depth holistic program of self-care and care of others. All but the AHNA programs are available to nurses and non-nurses alike. And like much of the grassroots natural childbirth movement, all of these programs and theories have been spearheaded within the last few decades by women.

Rogerian Theory

The Rogerian Conceptual System was developed by Martha E. Rogers, Sc.D. Because the system is a theoretical foundation for many holistic nurses, I suggested Ani read up on it if she was going to continue her explorations on this spiritual revolution in nursing. As she did, she found many elements in Rogers' system resembled the energy teachings I'd given her.

Dr. Rogers describes people as complex energy fields that constantly interact and exchange energy with the external environment. She sees our physical body as simply a denser form of energy than our mental, emotional and spiritual aspects. Because of the openness of all energy fields in the universe, including our own, Rogers concluded that humans can give and receive life energy to and from many sources. This energy might take the form of physical matter—food—or it might be transmitted in its pure essence. Dr. Rogers' conclusions echo those of many shamans and Eastern spiritual practitioners who have tried to fathom the energetic nature of our universe.

In her efforts to apply her observations about energy to the domain of healing, Rogers compressed the universe into a "diagram" of three spiritual actions or tendencies that have the goal of healing.

She calls the first of these actions or principles Helicy. Helicy is an explanation of the *intent* of healing behaviors. Rogers observed that for both humans and the rest of nature, the tendency and direction—or intent—of energy is toward harmony. We all strive toward balance, within ourselves and with the world around us. In Ani's case, this information was very important to her own healing process. She was aware of being at odds with herself before beginning therapy with me. This discomfort was her clue that she needed to come into better harmony with herself on all levels, a process that was now occurring. She also saw how contact with nature's beauty, order and harmony help her healing as well.

Rogers' second principle of healing—Resonancy—describes the *field motion* or movement toward harmony and health. She says that as we move toward increased health, our energies vibrate at higher and higher frequencies. This field motion allows us to have more experiences of spiritual transcendence that take us beyond time, space and matter. As Ani and I discussed this phenomenon, I reminded her of her meditation experiences. The more Ani meditated, the less she experienced stress and "dis-ease" in her body. The less stress, the more health, inner peace and harmony—or higher frequency of vibration, in Rogers' terms. As these qualities strengthened through meditation, Ani sometimes slipped past the constraints of her body and experienced the timeless transcendence of spirit: Rogers' field motion.

The last of Rogers' three healing actions is Integrality, which refers to the essential *connectedness* of all beings. This connectedness is promoted through Humor, Empathy, Altruism and Language, all of which lead to Transcendence and Harmony: H E A L T H. Ani saw herself moving toward Integrality. As she directed her attention and intention toward self-healing, she developed a better sense of humor, compassion and empathy for others, a desire to serve in some way, and an improved ability to communicate. All of these qualities moved her outside her narrower, self-absorbed limitations and she felt a deeper sense of connection with others. At the same time, she experienced more inner harmony and more harmony with her environment. She grew healthier.

In an earlier chapter, I remarked that harmony and beauty are the same word in the Navajo language: *hozhone*. In reflecting on Rogers' theories and hozhone, I told Ani that healing is a process much like that of the "primitive" artists who strip away all but the inner spirit of their piece of wood or stone. As we, too, strip away all that is not our own inner spirit's beauty, we heal. Our spirit emerges in its true form and goes on to touch the world with greater beauty, harmony and healing.

Rogers offers one more concept Ani found intriguing, the idea of "conceptual motion." What Rogers describes is a shift in the way we view dis-ease or "negative" symptoms. She cites anxiety, restlessness and disorientation as examples of what we usually judge to be negative. Roger's alternative view is to look at these symptoms as motions of our energy field, preludes to a new resolution or pattern.

I asked Ani what she liked so much about this conceptual motion perspective.

"I often judge myself harshly—my feelings, my physical problems, my actions—and then I go and judge others too," she began pensively. "It would be a big relief to see myself as an energy field that's always changing, and to see my 'problems' as signals that I need to move toward more harmony! I think I'd stop being so hard on myself and others, and begin having more faith in the healing forces of the universe if I shifted my viewpoint in this way."

I told Ani that I'd started looking at people, health and the healing process more in terms of energy when I learned my first energy-based healing art: polarity therapy. This system, developed by Dr. Randolph Stone, includes a hands-on approach in which the healer balances a person's energy field by placing her hands in various positions on—or just above—the body. This helps direct the healee's energies to arrive at increased harmony and vitality.

Shortly after I began practicing polarity therapy, I treated a client with a very heavy coffee habit. As soon as I placed my hands on his head and neck, I felt the caffeine in his system as an erratic and jangled pulse disturbing the overall harmony of his energy body. As I held my hands over his body, continuing to focus healing power, the pulse gradually smoothed out and the client gave a contented sigh. The restless, disruptive energy pattern induced by coffee shifted in the direction of healing, and internal harmony was restored.

We are remarkably adaptive people. When disruptive factors change with the support of a healer, as Rogers has noted, the energy body strives for harmony and reintegration at higher levels. If we are too stressed or depleted to mobilize ourselves toward harmony, the healer becomes an additional energy source. Like a conductor of an orchestra's energy patterns, she redirects them toward a higher order, harmony and unity of purpose.

Dr. Rogers' concepts create an attitude of openness that embraces healing as a journey for both healer and healee, and have had an increasing influence on nursing practitioners interested in holistic systems of healing. Two systems of healing that use the openness and shared journey qualities that Rogers promotes are Therapeutic Touch and Healing Touch.

Therapeutic Touch

As Ani's interest in spiritually and energy-based healing practices grew, I suggested she come to a workshop I was giving on the subject. The workshop introduced participants to cleansing programs, herbs, shamanistic healing, healing rituals and polarity therapy. At the end of the workshop, Sally, one of the other participants and a Registered Nurse, described a healing system she was studying. The system, Therapeutic Touch (TT) was developed in the early 1970s by Dora Kunz, a physical therapist, and Dr. Dolores Krieger, a nurse-physiologist. TT is based on their theory that the ability to heal is both innate in every person and can be developed in any person. Sally explained that TT—derived from the ancient practice of laying on of hands—incorporates elements from quantum physics theory and Eastern knowledge of human energy. It can be taught to most people, including children.

Sally described the basic practices of TT. The process involves five phases for the healer. First is *centering*, which includes coming to an inner quiet, setting aside any personal bias. Centering is key to accessing and transfering life energy while avoiding adverse reactions. *Assessment* follows, attained by passing the hands over the patient just outside her skin and "listening" through the hands for areas of imbalance. This is similar to one of the exercises in "Gathering Power," the process of "scanning" to feel someone else's energy field. The TT healer's hands are then used to *unruffle the field.* This generally involves long, slow sweeping motions of the hands down the length of the patient's energy field, with the goal of relieving areas of accumulated tension or static congestion. The healer is quite literally smoothing out the ruffled feathers of a cranky energy body. The fourth aspect of TT is the *direction and modulation of life energy*, accomplished through mental healing imagery focused on the patient. Last, and considered equally important to the other elements, is *knowing when to stop.* That moment comes when either the therapist no longer perceives any cues to energy disturbances or when there is a sense the patient has received enough energy for that particular session. According to Krieger, it is generally better to underdo than overdo. Too great an infusion of fresh energy can be difficult to integrate. And if the healer is insensitive or overzealous, the patient may end up irritable, restless or with a headache.

I was fascinated by Sally's description of TT and its resemblance to a shamanistic approach to healing I'd demonstrated in the workshop just hours earlier. In the mid-1970s, a Huichol Indian shaman first introduced me to the basic technique which I then further explored on my own. In this approach, I hold one or more feathers in my hand. After a period of centering and unfolding my will toward the patient, I use the feather as an additional tool to scan my patient's energy field in a way similar to the TT process. Again, using the feather instead of my hands, I proceed to "unruffle" the field. I use sweeping motions—as in TT—as well as several other techniques I developed. In one, I use the feather to draw disruptive energies out of the patient's field and then release them into the earth. I may also help seal up any energy leaks I find in the energy field by gathering the leaking energies together with the feather, coalescing them and then creating an energy "patch" which I place over the hole. In the final stages of the process, I send an intention of healing and harmony and use my will to sense when enough has been done for the time being.

Sally agreed that this shamanistic practice was similar to TT. She noted other similarities between what I'd taught the workshop participants about energy and what Krieger and Kuntz developed. They considered healing through TT a complex pattern of interactions among three unbounded fields of energy: the infinite source, the healer and the healee. They found that chi was abundant in the healthy and was depleted in the unwell. Ideally, TT healers are healthy, with a vital abundance of life force or chi. In that state they can most effectively direct the chi—primarily through their hands—and fill the deficit in the ill patient. Although TT healers are largely regarded as channels and catalysts for healing energies, they are also a source of some of the chi. If they are in a depleted state themselves, they risk the danger of becoming drained through their work. Sally commented on the value of some of the power-gathering techniques she'd learned in my workshop, saying this would be helpful for insuring high levels of energy in TT healers.

Sally also told us that Krieger and Kuntz not only developed the TT healing system, but set standards for TT practitioners that are in keeping with the goals of both the nursing profession and most other healing disciplines. An intent to help or heal was first on the list of standards. Since energy follows our attention and intention, this is a key attribute. Accepting the importance of intuitive skills and developing them through visualization and meditation were next. The therapist's physical wellness and emotional calm while administering TT were third on the list. The last elements considered the therapist's attitude. Empathy and concern for the client's needs must take precedence over the therapist's needs and ego involvement. Of final importance were the therapist's confidence in Therapeutic Touch's potentials and in her own ability to accomplish those potentials.

The main goals for the recipient of TT are similar to those of healees in general: having a sincere desire to get better and having an open mind that the method used will contribute to healing. However, Sally assured us TT is definitely not faith healing. The focus of mental healing imagery (directed toward a patient) can by itself have an impact—without the healer even being in the same room! Nor does the patient have to be aware that TT healing is being sent her way.

Sally told us about an example of this *in absentia* form of TT healing. In a fascinating research project, patients were separated from the TT healers by a wall, so neither could see the other. Half the nurses—the control group—simply read books during the sessions, while the TT group actively focused on healing imagery and sending life energy toward their patients. None of the patients knew what their specific nurse was doing on the other side of the wall. After repeated sessions, the findings showed an obvious acceleration in the healing process for the TT recipients. They recovered faster and in marked contrast to the control group's patients with similar injuries or illnesses.

"What else can clients expect from their Therapeutic Touch sessions?" Ani asked Sally with great interest. Sally told her that within the first five minutes of therapy most clients experience relaxation, and within about 20 minutes painful symptoms significantly lessen or disappear.

Although Therapeutic Touch is now incorporated as a recognized and valid form of therapy in some hospitals, the efforts of TT nurse practitioners to make this happen has met some resistance. Sally said that in recent years a group of nurses from a large city hospital decided to go to a weekend workshop to learn TT. The hospital's director of nursing was infuriated by this manifest interest in alternative healing techniques. When the nurses returned from their workshop, fresh and full of inspiration, they were met by a large sign the director had posted on the nursing department's bulletin board. It said: THERE WILL BE NO HEALING IN THIS HOSPITAL!

Besides being a training in nonjudgmental sensitization to energy and in the development of intuition, Sally told us TT is a spiritual journey of exploration for the practitioner. The centering experience is key in the journey, for it gives the practitioner access to the inner self/teacher/guide who is a reflection of her individual power.

I spoke in agreement at this point and added a few more observations. In TT as well as in other healing practices, the healer can be most effective when centered and in a meditative state. This leaves her own ego and personal concerns temporarily on the back burner and gives her access to inner guidance. Her awareness is then attuned to the healee and she can readily discern what is needed. Healers also are clearer conduits of spiritual "energy" sources—beyond "their" own—when their thoughts and emotions are at rest and their intention is focused on healing the other person. The following exercise offers a way to help anyone, including TT and other hands-on healers, become centered and clear conduits of spiritual healing energies.

OPENING AND CLOSING EXERCISE FOR HANDS-ON HEALERS

Do a few minutes of "Gathering Power from the Earth" or some other power-gathering exercise so you begin with extra reserves of chi or energy. Then spend time doing "Breathing Toward Inner Silence" until your mind is calm and empty of thoughts or expectations about the healing session. Next, invoke whatever higher spiritual powers you trust to assist you in the healing session, expressing your desire to serve by your own efforts and to be a conduit for other spiritual healing forces.

When your invocation is complete, begin focusing into your belly. Do the "Unfolding the Will" exercise from chapter 2, but rather than unfolding your will directly out from your belly, pull it up through the center of your body and direct it out through your hands. You now have mobilized your spiritual power and sensitivity in your hands, making them instruments of healing and awareness. You are ready to begin the healing session.

At the end of the session, consciously pull your will's energy away from the healee and back through your hands, arms and upper torso until your will is firmly regrounded in your belly. Thank both your inner guidance and the outer spiritual forces for their help. Clear any remaining energies you may have picked up from the healee by shaking your hands vigorously, rinsing them in cold water and shaking them again. You may also pass them through the smoke of burning sage, a cleansing herb.

The healee also can make her healing session more effective by centering herself—through methods like "Breathing Toward Inner Silence" or other meditations—and by focusing her attention on internal shifts of energy. This is powerful spiritual action and counteracts some of the Western medical model in which patients are encouraged to be more passive recipients of their doctors' ministrations. When both healer and healee are attentive, they engage in an intimate duet of dancing forces, of energy moving to and through them. Eventually a balancing of energy flows takes place in both the healer and healee.

What passes through us always effects us. When I first started giving polarity therapy healings, I found if I practiced the basics from the "Opening and Closing" exercise and stayed in a centered, meditative space throughout, even after eight sessions in one day I was more energized and balanced than when the day began. I've had similar experiences after conducting Womb Lodges and other healing ceremonies as well as after a variety of hands-on healing sessions.

As we listened to Sally speak about TT and other holistic approaches adopted by growing numbers of nurses, it became clear that nurses—primarily women—are a spiritual vanguard. They are creating a bridge between Western allopathic medicine and alternative healing practices. Nurses have long been concerned with healing in its more holistic sense. The addition of energy-based healing systems such as TT is a natural outgrowth of that concern. After hearing Sally's descriptions of the spiritual revolution, Ani decided to explore it further. She not only took a course in TT, but in the process discovered Healing Touch.

Healing Touch and the American Holistic Nurses' Association

Healing Touch (HT) is not one system, but a program for the exploration of many healing systems. It was developed by Registered Nurse Janet Mentgen, who has been practicing energy-based care since 1980 in Denver, Colorado. Like myself and other "pioneers" who pushed the early edge of holistic healing forward in the West, Janet also explored a variety of healing systems, and then incorporated a number of them into a training for others. HT became a certificate program of the American Holistic Nurses' Association in 1990.

Although I had already done some reading on HT myself, Ani did her own research in the program and came to her session one day brimming over with enthusiasm and knowledge that she *had* to share with me! She informed me that the HT program is an energy-based therapeutic approach to healing. She'd had one HT healing session and couldn't get over the similarities to the polarity therapy sessions she'd had with me. "I could really feel the energy moving!" she exclaimed. "I felt like all my cells were vibrating. And I was very relaxed afterwards, just like with polarity."

She went on to tell me HT uses touch to influence the human energy system and affect physical, emotional, mental and spiritual health and healing. The goal is to restore harmony and balance in the energy system and help a person to heal herself. Unlike TT, HT is not one method, but incorporates TT, headache techniques, Magnetic Unruffling, and other energy-based practices based on the knowledge of chakras—energy centers—and chi flows.

To complete HT certification, students must document at least 100 cases of their own hands-on healing efforts and then both present and prepare them for publication. The hope of the HT Program is that a written body of healing information will be compiled and passed on in much the same way women have always shared this kind of knowledge with one another, whether it be through recipes for chicken soup, herbal remedies or helpful childbirth knowledge.

As Ani continued her adventure through TT and on into HT, I pursued my own desire to understand more about the HT program. Sally referred me to Millie Freel, R.N., a certified HT practitioner and instructor who also has completed the four existing phases of AHNA's Holistic Nursing certification program. Millie taught nursing for 30 years at a Midwest university, and with her considerable personal determination, she managed to get some holistic nursing and practical holistic methods into the university's curriculum. This energetic woman then retired early to do full-time healing work. She noted wryly, but with compassion, that among her many clients are the occasional physicians who demand that their involvement in holistic healing be kept secret.

Probably the only person I know who's never taken any medication, not even aspirin or antibiotics, Millie has both a personal and professional interest in holistic healing. In 1963 she was diagnosed as having multiple sclerosis (MS). Her doctor told her to cut her work back to half-time, and declared that she would never bowl again—a favorite activity of hers. Millie told me she got "pissed off" and promptly went out to bowl her best game ever. She also continued working full-time and over the years managed the MS through diet, energy-balancing, exercise, some creative visualizations and rest.

In 1980 Millie decided that if she could manage the MS, she could also release it. She proceeded to do so by once again applying her in-depth program. "Ever since I was a child," she confided, "I've always felt I could do whatever I wanted if I just decided to do it, and then the Higher Power would always move in and help me and support my own efforts." Millie has been going stronger than ever since making her decision.

She also attended holistic healing conferences and workshops. Her conclusion after years of healing research and practice: "I see spirituality as the major, overriding force in all healing. I believe that true healing brings us into right relationship with ourselves, with others, with the greater environment and with God. What is unique about holistic healing practices is the state of consciousness of both practitioner and client: seeing wholeness rather than separated parts."

Millie appears to have an endless and voracious appetite for learning more about healing that has taken her to many countries. In her studies to date, she has seen no incompatibilities among the many world healing systems she's investigated. In October of 1993 she went to Moscow with three other women and two men for the purpose of teaching HT and Reiki to interested Russian healers. They made contact with the Russian Healers' Association, an organization that survived as an underground movement until the early 1990s. With the new and more open political environment, the association surfaced and continued to grow. The Russian healers Millie and her group met were enthusiastic about learning and adding HT and Reiki to their practices. Millie was stimulated by the exposure to yet more healing systems, including shamanism, the use of herbs, the laying on of hands and faith healing.

She embarked on another excursion—to China and Mongolia—with 35 other holistic nurses as part of a people-to-people ambassador program. During her visit to Mongolia, Millie was approached for help by the mother of a 14-month-old child. The little boy had been diagnosed with cerebral palsy and he didn't use his left arm, nor could he stand or walk. Millie gave him a slight spinal adjustment and a 45-minute HT session.

Afterwards, she demonstrated playing patty-cake, and the little boy proceeded to imitate her successfully, using *both* arms and hands. Then she offered her fingers, which the child grasped with each hand. He pulled himself to an upright position and walked, for the first time in his life, across the bed.

This healing event was dramatic in its alleviation of symptoms. But Millie feels healing practitioners must keep their expectations for specific results at bay. She noted that sometimes the healing is a spiritual preparation for and acceptance of death. "We don't necessarily know what is best for a person at any given point in her evolution," she commented, reflecting not only her personal views but those of the HT program. "Only the individual's deepest self knows, and will seek the kind of healing that aligns with that purpose." I agreed with her that the healer must have ultimate respect for this innate knowledge within every individual, and support personal freedom to the best of her ability.

In Shanghai, Millie visited the largest medical facility in the world. There, as in Mongolia, patients chose their preferred method of treatment from both Eastern and Western modalities. Millie's comment on the freedom to make such choices was: "I feel that ultimately we are each the best expert for ourselves, and that health care needs to increasingly go in the direction of letting individuals determine their own care, including what methods and practitioners they wish to utilize."

After my talk with Millie, I went one step further in my own exploration of the nurses' revolution. I called another woman whose name Sally had given me, one who was directly involved with the formation of the AHNA's holistic certification program.

Veda Andrus, Ed.D., R.N., joined the AHNA as Northeast Regional Director in 1985, and has since acted as Vice President, President and International Director of the program. At a board meeting early in her involvement with the AHNA, someone raised the idea for a holistic certification program. Veda told me that through an immediate and profound internal spiritual revelation, she felt certain that this project was going to be "her baby." I'm familiar with this kind of inner guidance. Some may call it intuition, but when there is a keen sense of foreknowledge about a dramatic change in one's future, it is enough to make most of us believe in other levels of reality.

Veda followed her vision and helped cocreate the AHNA's current four-phase Certificate Program in Holistic Nursing. This program teaches a philosophy of life and way of being in the universe. It both includes and extends beyond specific nursing applications to an awareness of the greater planetary environment. Veda says the training "shifts the way the soul listens."

The four-phase program includes theories from Martha Rogers, whom I've already mentioned, Jean Watson, who explores the energetics of love, heart and caring, and Margaret Newman, who expounds the philosophy that nurses are coparticipants in the healing process. The program emphasizes care and responsibility in the holistic nurse toward herself first, and then toward other people and the greater environment. Maintenance of physical health is explored on all levels, including exercise, nutrition and relaxation techniques. The role of spirit in healing is also respected. Nurses in the program gain a transcultural perspective on the power of attitudes, beliefs and values about spirit and healing as well as an exposure to many energy-based healing systems.

While describing her involvement in shaping the program, Veda told me "the heart of nursing has always been one of caring and love, and I continued weaving these two strands into the core approach of the Holistic Nursing Program." She also explained that the original nursing process was always holistically interactive with staff, patients and to some extent, the environment. She related a simple illustrative story. Upon the request of her hospitalized patient, a nurse relocated the patient's bed to a window—despite the minor inconveniences to the staff—because her patient felt oppressed by being constantly indoors. The view of the larger environment and the cooperation of the staff are all important factors in the patient's healing process.

Like other holistic nurses I've listened to, Veda feels it is the feminine energy that is involved with the healing process, be it in a man's or a woman's body. She also dropped the terms "healer" and "healee" from her personal vocabulary. "Both are coparticipants in the healing journey," Veda says, "and both are mutually affected by the healing energies moving between them."

Laying on of hands still exists in some of our Western churches. Sometimes it is a function of the priesthood with little healing power behind it. Other times, as in evangelical or snake-handling churches, it is wild and energetic but not systematized in such a way that anyone could learn it. Until the nurses' revolution, hands-on healing at least had a place in some churches, but it had none in our Western hospitals. Spirit or infusions of chi were displaced by drugs, surgery and other forms of medical technology.

The spiritual and holistic nursing revolution says there is room for both approaches, and that laying on of hands can be systematized *and* energetic *and* has a place in our hospitals. The revolution is more democratic than our churches in that women can learn hands-on healing as well as male priests. And the renewed awareness of spirit in healing brings an important balance to our Western medical system. Holistic nurses also say there is room for many approaches under the umbrella of holistic nursing. With TT, HT and the AHNA, nurses opt for inclusion rather than competition. These women confirm by word and action that there is room for many paths to the truth of healing.

6

Carrying the Weight of the World in Our Bodies

In her warm bed, Ani rolls over and sinks deeper into sleep, into the timeless magic of dreams. She is a young girl once again, running through a golden field of wheat, legs pumping with boundless strength, arms slicing the air, feet pounding the earth, blood surging its fierce song through her veins. She shouts with delight as she nears her Prince, takes a flying leap and lands perfectly on his back. Grabbing his silky mane, she shouts again as he rears up once and then takes off across the field, racing toward the startling crimson of the setting sun. Ani locks her thighs around his rippling torso, feeling her power to guide this massive beast wherever she wishes.

They gallop on into the wind until the sun sets and the once gold field is a sea of blood-red waves. Prince leaps over a fallen tree and suddenly Ani loses her grip and falls, tumbling through space and time until she lands in a foreign place. She is alone. Fog swirls about her, obstructing clear vision. Slowly she makes out the shapes of drooping, moss-hung trees and smells the unmistakable odor of swamp. Ani rises to her feet and navigates her way through this grey, confusing world. It seems like only moments before she felt strong and exuberant, filled with enough power to do almost anything. But now, with every cautious step, she grows mysteriously weaker.

As she stumbles through the swamp, she feels an oppressive weight on her shoulders, as if some invisible hand is trying to crush her. Finally, too weak to travel further through this foggy terrain, she sinks to the ground. She reaches behind her, trying to throw off the crushing force, and comes in contact with something solid. She grabs it and pulls it off her back, discovering it to be some sort of bag or pack. Curious, she loosens the strings at the top and dumps the contents on the ground.

Ani finds before her a strange collection of fashion magazines, advertisements for weight-loss programs and volumes of assorted papers with messages written in bold print. She picks them up one by one and begins reading. "You must dress for men," says the first. "Your body is not your own, which is just as well since it's not that great," says the next. "Keep your power secret, or better yet, give it away to others. It could be dangerous to keep any for yourself," instructs another. "Abandon your dreams—they'll only bring you heartache," says the fourth.

Ani might have read further, but she suddenly realizes she has collapsed, not on solid ground, but on quicksand. And she is being pulled steadily downward in its grip. She no longer feels most of her own body. Just before her head is drawn into the murky embrace, with her last breath she gasps, "Help, somebody save me! I don't want to die like this." And she wakes suddenly in her own bed, trembling and covered with sweat. "Oh," she groans to herself. "My therapist is going to have a field day with this nightmare."

Many women are trying to recover from a similar nightmare. Our adolescent insecurities are fostered and played upon by media images. We have lost touch with our childhood power and dreams. Once set in motion, the momentum of our anxieties and our need for acceptance often continue forward into adulthood. Our perceptions of ourselves become externalized as we try molding ourselves into a form attractive to others, especially men.

Women struggling to free themselves from the messages highlighted in Ani's nightmare face the challenge of reclaiming their bodies, of realizing they belong to themselves and not to some outside force. Since the human spirit resides primarily within the human body, the struggle can be seen as one against spiritual dissociation. It is for that reason that I include the problem of women and their body image in this section of the book. Learning to see and then mend the split between the external image and the internal experience is a process of healing.

Over the course of Ani's therapy, we discussed her dream and the cultural roots of her later anxieties about her body and self-image. From early in life, women are exposed to the covert and overt operations of the image makers. But their impact is more intense at the flowering of puberty—symbolized by the blood-red colors in Ani's dream. As a young woman's body begins to mature inside and out, she struggles daily to reorient herself to these massive changes. Her self-definition, based partly on the body-identity, is in flux. She frequently grasps outside herself for help in grounding a new identity. Clothing and cosmetics take on fresh meaning, a chance to hide or enhance physical features. The pages of fashion magazines often flutter in young women's bedrooms and lockers like new leaves in the spring winds. The models are scrutinized, as are other youthful female media stars. Girlfriends are important in new ways, enlisted for consultations on crucial issues of appearance. Mothers are invited for their opinions less often. They are old-fashioned, they don't know what's really going on, their perspectives are highly suspect and not to be taken too seriously.

At the same time their bodies and identities are in flux, most young women are surrounded almost daily at school by the ongoing attention of lusty young men, fixated on the progress, shape and size of girls' breasts. This interest has a natural foundation. So does the young women's attention to their own bodies and to the young men's. Hormones pump out the ancient song of life and procreation, and nature means for the song to be heard for the survival of the species. But however compelling sex may be, it is not the sole function nor source of enjoyment for young and healthy bodies.

In the West, young men are encouraged to keep building on their youthful vigor through sports and other physically demanding activities. They enjoy a domain in which body pleasure and physical mastery are separate from the mating dance. Meanwhile, at the natural peaking of their physical strength and endurance, young women receive much less support for athleticism than do their male counterparts. As a result, many girls shift their focus to flirtation and allure. While the guys are out on the football field, wearing knee and shoulder pads to protect their bodies from the physical dangers of athletic competition, the girls are padding their bras to protect their psyches from the bruises of social competition.

At the same time, young women are subtly pressured to be less intelligent, particularly if they don't want to intimidate potential boyfriends who may have shaky egos. Girls' grades often decline in math and science particularly, as if this is a male territory they dare not trespass. Of course these are generalizations, and some young women excel in both fields and are happy to be bright despite the "Keep Out" signs they may encounter.

"I've always been good in math," Ani chimed in at this point in one of our conversations. "But I had pretty large breasts by the time I was 14 and I figured if I wore my sweaters tight enough the guys would forget I was brainy and ask me out. It worked too well! They always wanted to make out with me, but if I displayed any desire for intelligent conversation on a date, forget it. I felt like I always had to be on the outside watching myself, watching what I said, using my body to get dates but not letting the guys get too far with it or I'd get a bad reputation. It was exhausting to always be wondering what everyone else thought of me, boys and girls both!"

I told Ani how I'd first been warned by a girlfriend against showing my own intelligence. Throughout elementary school, I'd been happy to be bright and excel in my classes. When I was 11, my father, a university professor, was granted a sabbatical leave and our whole family spent a year in France where I attended an all-girls' public school. The first few months were very difficult as I struggled to become fluent in French and to meet more demanding academic standards than those I'd experienced in the United States. Finally I gained mastery of French, and was soon competing for first place in my class. In addition to my studies in school, I accompanied my family on excursions to museums and to most of the countries in Western Europe, absorbing a great deal of European culture and history in the process.

Upon returning to the U.S., I entered junior high school. Socially, it was a bit of an adjustment to be around so many boys again. But Spanish classes were easy as the words often resembled French, and much of history class was already familiar to me from both French school and my travels. I frequently shared personal experiences from my year abroad. Naively, I thought I was helping make a slightly dry history course more lively for all of us. Then one day, my new "best friend" took me aside and told me I was getting the reputation of being a show-off. If I wanted to fit in and have the friendship of other girls and the interest of the boys, I'd better keep my mouth shut. I was devastated, but peer acceptance was a critical issue for me in my new school. I became as invisible as I could be in class for several years after that, although I did continue to do well on tests, rebelling silently against hiding my intelligence.

The pressures of male attention and the messages for young women to seduce rather than compete in the physical—and sometimes mental—domain continue to mount throughout adolescence. During that time, many a young woman's focus and body awareness begin to shift. Both go from being kinesthetically within her body and enjoying its sense of life, motion and sensory experience, to being outside herself and telepathically transported into the minds of the males viewing her. Or at least she hopes she is telepathic in her efforts to divine what makes her attractive to men. This shift of attention from the internal sense of self to the externalized male viewpoint is the beginning of a pattern. The pattern is for women to give their power away to men through an effort to read men's minds and accommodate what might please them. This was part of the message in Ani's dream, and her growing weakness in that dream reflected how she'd given her power away from adolescence on.

Since most men are equally programmed by media images, the entire culture shares standards in much the same way members of a religion share certain beliefs. Not participating in the agreement puts one outside, on the dubious or unacceptable fringe. Like the seasons of nature, however, these standards change from time to time as the economy, the effects of wars and the capricious inspirations of fashion designers consort to keep us hopping. One of the problems for women trying to conform to any current fashion or fashionable body image, is that we all have highly individual body shapes and physical characteristics. But do we celebrate the sweet and spicy diversity? No, we bemoan our individuality, negate the uniqueness that is each one of us and repeatedly try to hammer our rounded selves into square holes. Even those who fit the current image rarely believe they do. They seek the ever-elusive manifestation of perfection as intensely as the "misfits" do.

Being skinny with generous breasts has been the standard for several decades, but most women's bodies don't match this difficult and rare combination. Some women internalize this pressure to conform to a near-impossible image. They frequently starve themselves or get breast implants for image "success." Self-starvation becomes as uncontrollable an addiction as the fixation on "image." The anorexic woman is blind to the reality portrayed in the mirror: a geometric abstraction of bone-defined jutting angles and screaming concave shadows that might well be titled "Portrait of a Dis-embodied Spirit." She sees only a vision of "Fat, Fat and More Fat."

As young women struggle between taking joy in their bodies and trying to match socially imposed "acceptable" images, many feel out of control in the crossfire. Some overeat, claiming their right to enjoy food and rebelling against image pressures. Becoming overweight may also be a defense against the intense sexual interest and advances they are not yet prepared to contend with. Others confront the same pressures and sexual tensions by starving themselves and becoming asexual in appearance. Often sexual development and even menstruation are temporarily arrested in the process. Anorexia nervosa and bulimic behaviors are experienced as ways of controlling the body. Ironically, this sense of control—in both the overweight and the painfully thin—is an illusion. Instead, it is a capitulation to the very pressures young women are trying to escape: the battle for ownership of their bodies. And both extremes in body weight are threats to health and life.

Even those who have no serious eating disorders are for the

most part still struggling with the hypnotic efforts of the image makers. They bear the weight of this massive and constant burden of propaganda *in* their bodies, like the heavy sack in Ani's nightmare. Though they may be as svelte as a gazelle, most women still worry that they might become fat if they slip in their daily vigilance. And these concerns about weight are in addition to myriad other preoccupations: about the shape of their eyes, lips and breasts, the color and texture of their hair, the length of their legs. . . . The social hypnosis is successful and many women are in an ongoing state of partial trance. We are simultaneously possessed and dispossessed of our own bodies. Is it a wonder so many women suffer depression? Their spirits hover anxiously outside their occupied bodies, waiting for an exorcism of the demons of self-rejection and self-hatred that have invaded them, waiting for a chance to come home.

Full-figured Ani struggled daily with her fear she was too heavy and with her resultant love-hate relationship with food. She had never gone to the extreme of anorexia or bulimia, but "to eat or not to eat" was a daily mantra with no spiritual resolution. "What can we women do to heal our relationship with food?" Ani asked me. "It feels like we're trapped. We have to eat to live, but trying to live with food can be hell!"

I suggested that she first start thinking of her body as an expression of spirit. Then she should try to think of nature in the same way, including the earth, sunlight and plants. Every time she ate a plant or plant-eating animal, she could see herself incorporating a variety of spiritual energies. "In this way," I told Ani, "we really are what we eat! Take time to pay attention to this spiritual interaction we call eating, and you just may find a new appreciation for food and your body." For women who tend to overeat, this process allows them to slow down and take in less food with more pleasure. For those who undereat, it can be a key to experiencing food in a more positive way. And for women with a love-hate relationship with food, this process may help them heal that relationship.

SPIRITUAL HEALING FOR EATING CONFLICTS

Take a few minutes to try this simple exercise. Go to your kitchen and get a piece of fresh fruit or vegetable. Now sit someplace pleasant and comfortable, perhaps even outdoors on the earth if it is warm enough to do so. Hold your piece of food cupped in your hands as if it were something sacred and filled with spirit. It is. Visualize the seed it originally grew from, a seed packed with energy and containing the entire map for its eventual growth. See that seed nestled in the warm body of the earth, soaking in the life-catalyzing moisture of repeated rains, beginning to sprout both upward-reaching leaves and downward-searching roots. Watch it pull energy from the earth and the sun, doing each process perfectly and instinctively. See it swell and elongate in both directions. Visualize its entire growth, up to the point where it produces the very food you now hold in your hands. Try feeling the fruit or vegetable's energy humming in your palms, humming with life and spirit, singing "eat me, enjoy me, merge your spirit with mine." Before you do so, bless the food with additional energy. Take a few deep breaths and on each exhale send some energy through your hands and into the food. Now go ahead and respond to its invitation by eating it. Chew slowly, savoring its taste and texture. As its physical and spiritual essence enters your mouth and then your stomach, try feeling the duet of energies your own body plays in response. Let the knowledge sink in that food, especially organic food, is a special gift of creation. Every snack and meal in your future can be a spiritual experience.

Using this exercise, with time and practice Ani slowly developed a more positive relationship to food. I also gave her an excerpt of a poem from the late author Don Marquis' delightful book, *archy and mehitabel*, to support her growing spiritual relationship with food and her own body.

"*. . . how beautiful is the universe*
when something digestible meets
with an eager digestion
how sweet the embrace
when atom rushes to the arms
of waiting atom
and they dance together
skimming with fairy feet
along a tide of gastric juices . . .
. . . i have a yearning to hear
from my stomach
further music in accord with
the mystic chanting
of the spheres of the stars that
sang together in the dawn of
creation prophesying food . . ."

Part of our healing revolution involves setting aside imposed messages about ideal body weight and shape and finding a weight that is appropriate for us because there we are the healthiest, most comfortable and most free. On the level of health alone, being extremely underweight or overweight are both dangerous. For women who are too heavy, a variety of approaches remedy the situation. You can eat more slowly and savor the food's spiritual ingredients as suggested in the healing exercise. You can also practice kinesthetic awareness and be more conscious of the burden extra weight imposes on your body. From that place of *internal* awareness, instead of from the image in the mirror, a decision to slim down and feel better may emerge more *naturally* from within.

Because so many Americans are overweight, extensive research examines which methods really reduce weight and which are likely to fail and/or even cause worse problems. Restricting calories at too low a level may be counterproductive: in an efficient metabolic carryover from our distant ancestors—who sometimes had to go days without food—our bodies simply go into starvation mode and adapt by cutting back on what they use. When we return to a normal diet, the body—still in starvation mode—tends to store what it ordinarily burns up. This accounts for the frequent phenomena of rapid weight gain after dieting. Then the dieter becomes trapped between having to eat sparsely or having to gain weight. This is a terrible predicament. It is better to eat a modest, well-balanced diet and increase one's physical activity to burn up more calories without forcing the body into this survival routine.

Ani pressed me further to describe other ways women can escape the traps that lead them to become dis-embodied spirits. "How can we break the hypnosis you talk about," she demanded, "this trance that causes our physical bodies to become sources of constant anxiety instead of something we enjoy?"

"The key is in reclaiming our bodies," I responded, "as well as our minds, hearts and spirits. We have to own them and know they are for ourselves first and foremost. This shift in attitude is a revolution, and we'd better be prepared both to struggle and to strategize. We must become aware of the forces of oppression and how they operate. And we need a fierce grasp of our goal and the benefits of that goal. This revolution is essentially spiritual in nature. We have to exorcize the destructive forces we've allowed into our beings. Then our spirits can fully occupy their homes: our bodies!"

How do we reoccupy the body we abandoned in spirit to others? One way is to pay more attention to feeling the body from within rather than wondering how it appears to other people—particularly men. This is an important shift in focus. Concentrating on our internal experience of Self is empowering and re-energizes the body. Often relaxation exercises promote this awareness, guiding our attention throughout the body, first to locate tension, and then to release it. I told Ani about a variety of other therapeutic techniques, including the Alexander and Feldenkrais methods, that help develop awareness of inner tensions and energy blocks in order to improve posture and health. All internal awareness techniques are forms of spiritual healing. They restore us to a sense of wholeness and ownership of our own bodies.

I studied one such method—the Skinner Releasing Technique (SRT)—for a number of years. The process was developed by an inspired and creative former dancer and choreographer, Joan Skinner, and has four related aspects:

- attending to the uninterrupted flow of breath;
- using imagery to both release tension and return the body to its proper alignment;
- developing a deep and multifaceted awareness of one's body parts at any given moment in time;
- utilizing internal and external sources of energy for both everyday activities and dance.

In the initial stages of their SRT training, students spend most of their time on the floor, flat on their backs and eyes closed in deep inner concentration. The teacher periodically gives verbal instructions—usually in the form of evocative imagery—and allows the students time to work with each image before proceeding.

The images promote the four primary aspects of the Skinner training. For example, to increase awareness and uninterrupted breathing, the instructor might have students visualize air as light, and then see the light streaming in an unending circle in and out of their lungs. As their concentration increases, the students will then practice holding this image—and other images from training—while standing and then moving about.

For example, a typical Skinner image for the release of muscle tension and for proper skeletal alignment is the suspended string. Students imagine a string attached to the crown of the head, the shoulders, elbows, wrists, fingertips or knees. Each string is held by an invisible force. The various body parts are lightly suspended from each string. While still prone, a student may "allow" the knee-strings to pull her knees until they're bent and her feet are flat on the floor, and then to draw her knees out to the side and back again. Having these magical strings do the work allows all but the essential deep muscles to stay relaxed during movement and promotes better skeletal alignment. Later, these strings help the students rise to their feet and begin experimenting with walking, running and leaping.

As the students progress in their work, they integrate this kinesthetic awareness and other results of the training into their daily lives. A student might find herself attaching a head string while driving—allowing her head to float more freely and in a more centered manner on her neck—thus preventing tight neck and shoulder muscles. Another student might notice during an intense business meeting that she is barely breathing. She can use the "light cycling" image to restore relaxed breathing patterns. In both cases, the student is still able to simultaneously focus on the other task at hand—driving or business negotiations. The Skinner Releasing Technique helps practitioners hold many focuses at one time.

Learning Skinner's system of kinesthetic awareness was profoundly revelatory and integrative for me. I found it was possible to actually feel my entire being from within, sometimes right down to the cellular level. These repeated experiences gave birth to a sense of awe and appreciation at my own existence. Over several years I reprogrammed my body, stripping away a lifetime of external conditioning, internalized messages and emotional charges still held in my muscles: my body memories of pain. As these messages, energy blocks and pain were recognized and released, relaxation, power and revitalizing fresh energy moved to fill the emptied spaces. Each time this happened I experienced the exhilaration of remaking myself in my own image.

"And that," I told Ani, "is what it takes—each and every day—to be free. The external messages and pressures are always with us, so to continue to be our own embodied spirits we must be like snakes and slough off the skin of what-is-not-me on a regular basis.

"Some regular form of exercise is also invaluable in succeeding with the revolution," I continued. "As you've learned, rhythmic exercise allows the mind to calm and be absorbed in a flow of motion. Once our minds are quiet, the internal perceptions of our bodies can be brought to heightened awareness, every gesture a profound celebration of life. Regular stretching exercises are also important. While allowing our bodies to remain supple and less prone to injury, flexibility of body also brings flexibility of mind, heart and spirit. The same is true with building strength and endurance through exercise. Not only are there health benefits, but we gain a certain confidence about ourselves that spills over into areas other than the physical.

"That's why I often encourage women to learn self-defense. It's been found that women who project a victim energy through poor posture and lack of confidence are more likely to be victimized. Self-defense and other forms of exercise increase our self-confidence. We then project this confidence and aren't so attractive to bullies."

Ani practiced some Skinner awareness techniques I gave her while continuing her yoga and aerobic classes. Her appetite for personal growth, as I'd seen in others who began a path of healing, was voracious! She began changing her physical posture, walking taller, shoulders back instead of hunched, head balanced evenly on her neck instead of tucked down like an anxious turtle. These changes were motivated from within as she found herself more comfortable holding her body in these new ways. But a secondary result was that Ani projected a more confident image, and others responded to the change by treating her with more respect. Both business and personal relationships improved. Her increased physical flexibility also was mirrored in other areas. She gradually became more flexible in her attitudes about herself and others, a change from her previously rigid and sometimes dogmatic way. Her physical flexibility gave her more faith in her ability to adapt to the ever-changing nature of life.

In this revolutionary process of reclaiming our bodies, there are many spiritual actions we can take. Any practice that helps us experience the chi or energy flows in the body is a spiritual action, including yoga, Taoist meditations, chi kung, tai chi or other energy-based healing systems. Ecstatic and spiritual dance forms such as eurythmy, belly dancing, Sufi dancing and other sacred dances from various cultures help women experience their bodies in motion as a holy event.

Eurythmy is a dance form that was developed in the early 1900s by the brilliant and spiritually committed visionary, Rudolph Steiner, whose approach to education is still utilized in contemporary Waldorf schools. The goal of eurythmy is to communicate spiritual energy through the body of the dancer to the audience by certain formalized gestures. The dancers' emotions and personalities are held in abeyance while they perform, their faces kept in a neutral mask and their bodies draped with loose-fitting clothes to likewise mask their gender. Through eurythmy, the human body is the sacred vessel of spirit in motion.

Belly dancing was not originally performed for men as a dance of seduction, contrary to popular opinion. Some rumors assert that belly dancing began as a dance women performed for women giving birth, and that the movements were meant to imitate and harmonize with the rippling movements of the pregnant woman's belly. Whether this is true or not, belly dancing was once intended to be done by and for women as their own spiritual celebration of female power, beauty and grace. And Sufi dancing is a means of approaching ecstatic union with the Divine—a prayer of motion—through repetitive movements and chanting that put the dancers into a trance state. In that state, normal consciousness of the world is replaced by heightened awareness of the sacred.

Dance experiences of a spiritual nature are fairly rare for Westerners. Most of our dancing is either social, replete with concerns about how we look to others and with frequent sexual innuendos, or it's performance dance in which we're sitting and watching others—or occasionally on stage ourselves. Dancing as an approach to spiritual union or as an expression of our spiritual essence, for our own experience of joy, vitality and a touch of divine madness, is something no one should miss! Especially women.

Caring for ourselves in ways that maintain health, pleasure

and awareness is part of a wave of change taking place in Western attitudes. Spiritual awareness is part of this wave. Other, more "primitive" cultures weren't and aren't so shy about making the connection between body/spirit and health. In fact, in those cultures spiritual forces and imbalances are often identified as the cause of many physical health problems. Healers and shamans alike draw on spiritual sources both within and outside the patient to facilitate healing. Typically, shamans begin their calling after surviving a major "initiatory" illness or injury. A person's battle with death or life-threatening forces is won not only with the result of health, but with the onset of unusual spiritual powers. The new shaman then uses her powers for healing and other spiritual activities, invoking beneficial forces and encouraging harmful ones to leave. Body and spirit are seen as inseparable expressions of one another.

We all need to know our physiospiritual natures, the indescribable miracle and gift of our bodies, and to enjoy them as our own. To accomplish this, we may need to fight, first recognizing and then separating ourselves from the haunting voices that entice us toward spiritual and/or physical death. We must overcome the evil spirits that burden us with the message that our bodies belong to others, with the command that we must conform to an externally imposed mold. When we succeed, we discover that like the shamans, we too have come through our journey with new powers. With these powers we can cast the weight of the world from our bodies and dance more freely as embodiments of spirit.

7

Cutting Free
of the Past

Jenny and Paul sat up, stunned by the immediate and perceivable results of their cord-cutting ceremony. Jenny's body visibly vibrated from the combined effects of release and a new infusion of energy. Paul wept quietly. "I never realized how much my ongoing connection to my ex-wife was draining me," he said, "and I also didn't see how much I'd been pulling on my brother's energy and draining him. If I hadn't done this ceremony, the patterns would have probably continued for the rest of my life. I'm so relieved I cut those cords! And I'm determined to cut the cords to the rest of my family and to every past girlfriend so we can all get on with our lives with more freedom and energy!"

We all engage in a lifetime process of movement between dependence and independence in our attachments to other people. This activity first develops in our relationship with our mother. After birth, it continues with an expanding network of other people. The surging spirit of growth within us constantly seeks balance between need and freedom, stretching us inexorably between autonomy and community. One of our greatest challenges is to forge meaningful alliances with other people without sacrificing our souls. Another is to gain choice about the spiritual and energetic nature of our connections to others.

The Cord That Bonds

There are several natural elements common to all people that create the deepest bonds between those sharing them. These are pregnancy and birth, sex and love. Birth and sex, with their ties to the life process, create a unique spiritual/energetic bond.

"What is this bond exactly," asked Ani the day we first talked about it, "and where did you learn about it?"

"I first encountered the concept of the bond in the writings of Carlos Castaneda and his associates," I said, "and later a shaman/seer further expanded my understanding of it. Not only that, but he and I created a ceremonial process for those ready to sever such bonds to people in their past. The shaman and I sat on a power spot in Wales. We were at the top of a sacred mountain that looked like a pregnant woman's belly. And we were right next to the inverted 'navel' when inspiration struck. I think the idea for the ceremony must have popped right out of Mother's bulging belly and into our minds."

"What kind of ceremony?" Ani demanded. "And why would people want to get rid of a bond that's spiritual?"

"If you'll have a little patience," I laughed, "I'll tell you all about this bond: how it is formed, its properties, and about the ceremony to disconnect it. Whether we experience this bond as real and perceivable—as I and many others have—or whether we regard it as a metaphor, we can all still profit from learning about it. Once you go through the ceremony, you'll have a better idea of its nature, Ani."

Every time sex takes place, the spiritual will of the two individuals gathers itself within them, and then flows outward from the belly to connect with each partner's energy. This creates an energetic cord between the couple, similar to an umbilical cord. Its purpose is twofold. Firstly, whether or not the partners intend to make a baby, the spiritual will automatically acts as if that is exactly what is going to happen. The cord bonds the couple and channels some of their joint energies to the potential embryo. Secondly, the energetic cord ties the partners together spiritually in an enduring connection as permanent mates and prospective parents. Again, this occurs on the energetic level whether or not the two people intend to become pregnant or even have more than a one-night stand.

If conception takes place, the energetic bond between the parents expands. It embraces the fetus and nourishes it throughout the pregnancy. By birth, it is strongly established. Although the physical umbilical cord is severed just after delivery, the "energy bond" is not. The child remains firmly connected to each parent. This is true even if either one or both biological parents are absent in the child's life. The cord also stays intact if the parents remain with the child, whether their relationship is positive or difficult. Just as in the womb, after birth the child continues to be "fed" energetically—both through the cords to its parents and, by virtue of its shared bonds with the parents, to any blood siblings.

This energetic link to the parents is as it should be. The child needs it to grow and thrive *until he or she reaches adolescence.* At that point, as the young person arrives at sexual maturity and an increasing need for independence on all levels, the cord should ideally be "cut" through some kind of puberty ceremony. In fact, in many cultures a variety of such ceremonies existed, although they may not have consciously addressed the energy cords. Many Native American tribes sent their young people on vision quests at puberty. These adolescents were completely cut off from the human community for several days, fasting and praying alone out in nature, searching for a vision or revelation to guide them through the next stage of their life: adulthood. When the young person returned to the tribe, frequently one or more relatives who were not the parents were increasingly responsible for taking care of the girl or boy until he or she were full adults. Often this meant no longer living with one's parents. Both the dramatic vision quest ceremony and the new relationship to the parents served to energetically separate the young people and their parents somewhat, while leaving intact shared love and affection. Other cultures had different puberty ceremonies, but the results were similar.

As Ani continued in therapy, struggling to pare away that which was not her real self, I shared with her more information about the energy bond.

"Why is disconnecting the cord between parents and their kids so important?" she asked. "I thought I was supposed to be learning connectedness, but this whole idea of cutting cords makes me wonder."

I laughed and reminded her how in her own adolescence, she needed to increasingly perceive herself as an independent person. Teenagers are distinct and unique people in their own right—despite inheriting some of their parents' physical characteristics, intelligence or talents—and they need to know this. However, as long as the cords remain intact, their energies and identities are still too intermixed with those of their parents. And in Western cultures, we either don't offer our young people puberty ceremonies, or the ones they experience through the Judeo-Christian religions don't have the same effect of disengaging them as do the initiation ceremonies of other traditions.

"Look how many Westerners like you, Ani, are already in their

30s, 40s or even older and are still trying to sort themselves out from their parents. 'Who am I?' we're all murmuring to ourselves, our counselors, our friends. Those uncut cords help sustain identity confusion for all of us."

Not only is it important for adolescent or older children to disconnect the energy cords to their parents, but, as I explained to Ani, it is also beneficial for the parents. The cord is like a two-way street: energy flows in both directions. As long as the cord is still connected, it is partly draining for the parents, since its original purpose was to nourish the young. And this bond also keeps the parents' identities too interwoven with their children's. That can result in possessiveness and emotional entanglements between parents and their children.

"I can relate to that!" Ani exclaimed. "Sometimes I feel like my mother and father are inside me, influencing my thoughts and emotions. They even show up in my dreams."

Ani could also see how she might inadvertently still "pull" on her parents. Although she wanted to be an independent adult most of the time, she was sometimes overwhelmed with a desire for her parents to take care of her as they had when she was young. When she got in these moods, her mother frequently called her more often on the telephone, as if she sensed Ani's needs. Her mother's tendency to give advice and be overly controlling then intensified. Ani gradually shifted from welcoming her mother's input to finally having her fill. She then became rude or cool, pushing her mother's energies back to a more comfortable distance. Her mother would get insulted, and both would be alienated for a while until the cycle began again.

In the case of adoption or sometimes divorce, when one or both biological parents are absent, parent-child dynamics are both similar and dissimilar to those of the nuclear family. The energy cords are still there—for they remain intact unless consciously disconnected—but the absent parents are not as psychologically intertwined with the child as they would be if they'd raised him or her. Nevertheless, the ongoing existence of the cord keeps all parties bound up in each other's lives in a subliminal fashion. Two or three people, unknown to each other in the usual sense, may still push and tug on each other without conscious awareness.

If we have arrived at or passed puberty, we might seriously consider the spiritual action of cutting the bonds between ourselves and our parents. "I think I'm convinced," said Ani. "How do we do it?"

In response, I first told Ani about my retreat participants and their vision quests. I explained that the vision quest attaches us more firmly to the universal flow of spiritual power in nature, and is potentially a more fulfilling, less hazardous attachment than those to our parents. Doing such a ceremony can be helpful in partly cutting the cords. A second and more total disengagement comes from *consciously* disconnecting the energy bond. The ceremony that my shaman friend and I created in Wales serves this purpose well. The result, for both child and parents, is more autonomy and freedom of choice in future actions and interactions. Even if our parents are dead, the ceremony can be helpful, for we often remain spiritually attached to people who are no longer here on Earth. The ceremony is also useful in cutting cords to blood siblings. And because the energy bond is usually established during sex, cutting cords to past sexual partners is especially useful.

You may wish to record the instructions for this ceremony on tape first, so you won't have to interrupt your process to read them.

CUTTING THE CORDS

Before beginning the process, choose your method for cutting the energy cord. You can use the side of your hand like a knife edge or sword, or you can grasp the cord along its length with both hands, one hand higher than the other, and yank it in two. You may need to cut or yank the cord more than once until you are certain it is severed. And with each cutting or yanking gesture, you will need to exhale forcefully and make a loud sound of some kind. This is just as important as the physical action, because the power of breath and sound—as with the martial arts ki'ai—helps push the other person's energy away from you.

Once you've decided on your cutting method, sit or lie down and make yourself comfortable. Now close your eyes and focus on your breathing. With each exhalation, release all thoughts, emotions and physical tensions until body and mind are calm. Then, on the blank screen of your inner vision, bring up an image of your mother from a moment in time when you enjoyed her company. If you never knew your biological mother, ask Spirit or your imagination to provide an image that you can focus on during this process.

As you gaze at your mother, sift through your memory for anything and everything positive that you gained from this woman. This includes her part in your having life, any skills or talents she nurtured in you or passed on to you and any gestures of kindness, generosity, affection or love she gave you. Envision anything else you appreciate and remember. At each new memory, look at her and thank her for this gift.

Next, explain to your mother that although the umbilical cord was cut at birth, there is another cord that still exists between you that was never cut. Describe your understanding of the dynamics of this cord. Then tell her that neither of you need it any more and that cutting it will free both of you to be more yourselves and to have clearer choices about your future relationship with one another. Assure her that cutting the cord in no way severs whatever bonds of affection exist between you.

While keeping her image in focus, breathe deeply into your belly. Place your hands over your navel. Visualize a luminous energy cord extending out of your navel, growing clearer with each breath, a cord that is connected at the other end to your mother's navel. When you see its entire length, remove your hands from your belly and place them several inches away from your navel and from each other, palms facing one another. With your eyes still closed, try feeling the energy cord with your hands. Slowly move your hands as far up its length as you can reach and back down to your navel. Do this several times until you feel confident you know where the cord is.

Since severing the cord may take a number of gestures—either cutting or yanking apart—and since you want to act with as much power as possible, gather some energy for the process. While still keeping your hands around the cord and your mother's image in sight, take some more deep belly breaths, summoning energy and power to your spiritual center. Again, calm your mind and emotions as much as possible. Cutting the cord is not an act of hostility or of any other emotion. It is an act of pure and neutral power. Continue slow, deep breathing until you arrive at this neutral and powerful state of readiness.

As soon as you are ready, inhale deeply, focus on the cord and ACT! Cut or yank and exhale loudly! Take a few breaths and do it again. Make your action big and powerful. Breathe and do it again. Now place your hands in the air above your navel. See if you can feel if and where the cord was cut. Has it been completely disconnected? If not, go through your actions as many times as you need until you are satisfied the cord is cut. You will know when you are done. Trust yourself.

When you are done, allow your mother's image to recede and fade away. Then place your hands around what is left of the cord, which is now made only of your energies. Inhale deeply and with each inhalation pull the cord toward your body, in through your navel and into your belly. When you have all your own energy back inside, take the palm of one hand and slap it firmly several times over your navel to seal yourself up. Now relax and rest for a while. Notice your overall energy and state of being. If some emotions are surfacing, allow them their place in your healing, for they are part of the energy release. Take whatever time you need.

When you are calm and relaxed, do another self-inventory to decide if you have enough energy to go through this process again with your father. If so, the format is identical except for calling up your father's image instead of your mother's. Remember to call up his image from a pleasant time you shared, to thank him for every positive result of your relationship, to explain the process, feel the cord, gather your power and focus, do the action with a vocalized loud exhale as many times as needed, release your father's image, return your part of the cord to your belly, seal yourself back up and rest.

Now take some more slow, deep breaths and with each inhalation, fill your entire body with light. Choose any color light you desire. Begin at your feet and progress toward your head until you are completely filled with light. Then take a few more breaths and let the light spill out your pores until you are totally surrounded in a cocoon of glowing light. Feel your revitalized and more autonomous energy body. Thank yourself for your efforts, for benefiting not only yourself but each individual on the other end of the cord. You are all more free to live your lives as yourselves. Exhale several times with a sound, wiggle your fingers and toes, rub the back of your neck and gently stroke your face. Whenever you are ready, open your eyes and return to the room in which you began this process.

When I personally take a person through this process, as a shaman/therapist I sometimes add some of my own energy in support of the cord-cutting, if needed. I may offer verbal encouragement or use a drum, among other things. The aftereffects of these cord-cutting ceremonies vary and are highly individual. The results may be subtle or very dramatic, and some may be truly surprising.

I guided a client named Marcy through this process of cutting cords to her parents several years ago. Marcy had struggled unsuccessfully for years to end a strong and ongoing addiction to smoking pot. A few months after the cord-cutting ceremony, she told me that not only had she effortlessly stopped smoking pot, but that she'd understood the part the cord-cutting played in her ability to do so. She realized that she began smoking pot in her early teens as a form of rebellion against her parents. It was an effort to assert herself as a separate and distinct individual, particularly because she knew her parents did not approve of this activity. Once the cords were cut, she truly was separate and distinct from them. There was no need to smoke pot any more as a means of establishing her autonomy. The entire addictive pattern was halted with the release of her parents' energies.

I found this a very exciting result, consistent with the goals and dynamics of the cord-cutting process. Many of us develop behaviors at adolescence for similar reasons. These patterns may not be particularly supportive of our overall well-being, either then or later in life. The cord-cutting allows the source of these behaviors to be illuminated and released more easily than through other therapies or personal efforts. As a result of the cord-cutting, people frequently also notice improved relationships with their family, a refreshing sense of freedom from their past and an increase in energy and emotional stability.

During the months following Ani's cord-cutting ceremony between herself and her parents, she tried to be aware of any energetic shifts in their mutual relationship. What she noticed primarily was a diminishment of the push-pull cycle between her and her mother. Ani's own collapses into neediness and her mother's subsequent "smotherings" decreased, and both women were pleased with the improvement. Meanwhile, Ani also spent time exercising her will out in nature. Although she hadn't yet done a vision quest, these new spiritual attachments to nature were partly fulfilling the same role. She was gaining more energetic nourishment directly from "Mother" and needing less from her human mother.

Sex and the Energy Bond

The invisible cord that grows during sex supports the spiritual bonding between a couple, even when the two people have no conscious knowledge of the cord itself. With awareness of this bond, they can capitalize on the spiritual potentials of their relationship via Taoist energy exercises, by praying together or through any other spiritual activities. However, they also need to know that a variety of energies pass through the cord, back and forth between them, for better and for worse, including reverberations of their emotional, mental and physical states.

Here is a commonplace example of this kind of exchange. One day, Mr. Jones suffers a severe injury at work. Mrs. Jones isn't notified for several hours, but during that time she feels unaccountably anxious and uneasy. When she is finally contacted about her husband's condition, she says to herself, "I knew there was something wrong today, I just knew it!" What she didn't know about was the invisible "telephone" cord through which she first received the information. That cord might explain numerous other examples of telepathy between couples, as well as between parents and their children.

Many couples have experiences similar to the Jones'. Even more common is the day-to-day effect of one partner's moods on the other, the ways in which an unexpressed thought, positive or negative, can have an impact. Conscious knowledge of the energy bond between couples can further deepen their understanding and awareness of these energy exchanges and encourage them to live in a more conscious manner in relationship to one another.

Understanding the impact of the cord also provides a different perspective on the issue of extramarital sex. According to the marriage contract, it's not supposed to take place. But it frequently does, and with a variety of destructive results to the primary bond. Setting aside moral and emotional perspectives for a moment, let's look at how it can be destructive on a pure level of energy. Try to picture a spiritual cord between two people, extending from belly to belly, which tends to get stronger and more substantial over time and repeated sex. Then picture a third person with whom one of the couple has become sexual. Now there is a new strand going from one of the original couple to the new person. Since energy flows back and forth between each cord, all three are immediately interconnected. Not only that, but since the amount of energy held by any individual is limited, the initial cord between the original couple will grow weaker and thinner as part of its energy is siphoned off to the third party in the triangle.

This simple illustration of the sexual energy dynamics shows two things. First, it helps us understand why the extramarital activity of one person is felt by the other and why, on some level, that person "knows" that his or her spouse is being unfaithful without being told verbally. Secondly, it shows how these activities subtly weaken the primary relationship, even if there is no intention to leave it on the part of the wandering member. Both elements can be crazy-making for the "faithful" spouse who doesn't have the conscious understanding of what he or she may sense. If the "wanderer" is confronted directly with the spouse's suspicions of an affair and denies having one, the situation is even more troublesome.

As a therapist, I often deal with these complicated and disruptive dynamics. I also see that teaching energy cord-cutting brings clarity to relationship issues and gives couples a deeper understanding from which to make choices about their relationship. Ani's marriage finally dissolved because of her husband's affair with another woman. Although they were already divorced when I first met her and there was no marriage for me to help her with, my descriptions of the "triangle" dynamics helped her sort through some of her own experiences during her husband's affair and see them in a new light.

"I'm going to cut those cords next!" Ani exclaimed. "I don't need any more of my ex's energy hanging around, or any vibes coming through him from his girlfriends either!"

Ani's comments reminded me of other aspects of the energy cord. In our society, very few adults have been sexually involved with only one person. Many have had at least one sexual relationship before marrying their current mate. Some have had extramarital sex. Some have never married and have had a variety of sexual encounters. Of those who have married, many have divorced and gone on to other relationships that involve sex. This means that many adults, beyond the cords to their parents, siblings and offspring, also have at least several and sometimes numerous cords attached to people they have been sexual with. Those cords include "one-night-stand" folks from their past as well as individuals from more long-term involvements.

Ani was slightly uneasy at this point as she recalled her recent history of one-night stands. I saw her trying to calculate just how many cords she needed to cut. Then she changed the subject slightly and asked about the energetic effects of close but non-sexual friendships. "I've felt more intimately connected to some of my friends than I ever did to my husband. Are there cords, energy bonds between me and these friends?"

"Not exactly," I said.

There are definitely a variety of deep mental, emotional, physical and spiritual connections that can be established between people who are not parents, children, siblings or sexual partners to one another. And energies can pass back and forth between them. The cord of the energy bond is only one type of energetic connection among myriad possibilities, but tends to be the most permanent unless consciously disconnected.

Sometimes it is helpful to have "visual aids" in order to better grasp the extent and impact of our will bonds to others and to inspire us to action. I gave Ani the following exercise for that purpose.

THE WEB OF CONNECTIONS

Find a big sheet of blank paper and a pencil. Put a dot indicating yourself in the center of the page and then draw a large circle around it. Next, place the names of your parents—unless you already did the cord-cutting ceremony with them—and any siblings or children around the edge of the circle. Then draw a line from yourself out to each one of their names. Your picture will resemble a bicycle wheel with radiating spokes and yourself at the hub. Now add to the circle any person you ever had sex with, including unwanted sex of any kind. It is important to be accurate and honest with yourself, and no one need ever see your picture besides you. Draw a line from yourself to each one of them.

Now reflect on the amount of time you've spent with any of these people, including your blood relatives. Then retrace the cord lines to each one so that the people you've spent the least time with have the thinnest cords, and the most long-term relationships have the thickest ones. You now have a diagram of one facet of your energetic and spiritual reality.

Look at your diagram, remembering that the thickest cords indicate the strongest fusion of identities and greatest opportunity for a variety of energy exchanges between you and the person on the other end. The overall picture gives you a sense of how you have spread yourself out energetically and in how many lives you are spiritually enmeshed. Do not despair if your circle is densely populated! You can use the cord-cutting ceremony to disconnect from all of them. Simply do the same process used for cutting the cords to parents, substituting siblings, children older than 13 and past sexual partners. Limit yourself to three or four cord-cuttings per session to prevent fatigue.

I then told Ani some of the other effects of a highly populated circle. If people have had numerous sexual contacts through personal lifestyle choice or by profession (as in the case of prostitutes), their energies, identities and spirits are going to be in a rather confused state. Bits and pieces of their selves are scattered all over the map, while fragments of others' selves are circulating through their own.

Numerous energy bonds confuse and possibly drain our energies. They weaken the only thing that is truly ours—and the foundation of our spiritual life—our sense of Self. Both of these factors make true intimacy with another increasingly difficult: we continue both knowing ourselves less, and having less of ourselves to give. Long-term prostitutes and sexually promiscuous individuals all have trouble with intimacy over time. This is particularly poignant when they finally meet someone they would like to "settle down" with.

There is an additional dilemma with which our spirits must grapple. If we have had numerous sexual partners, the chances

are that we may not have known them very well before we got
involved. Once we did, we probably found we didn't like them
all that much. If we had, we would have stayed with them. This
means that we are carrying around energies from people that are
quite possibly not harmonious with our own. The result is internal conflict, a broken spiritual home in which our indwelling
spirit cannot find peace.

Of all the kinds of sexual contact we can have, rape or other
forms of sexually "transmitted" abuse are the most shattering to
our spiritual harmony. In these situations, someone else's energy
is forced upon us against our will, creating trauma for body, mind,
heart and especially Spirit. The spirit that automatically creates
a bond to the attacker through the sexual act—because our
spirit's nature is to form a will bond *whenever* sex occurs—is then
held prisoner with a hostile cellmate. It is locked in an ongoing
struggle from which it seeks release. It is no wonder this kind of
trauma puts the survivor in a type of dissociative state; on some
level the spirit is trying to leave the body to escape its intolerable
dilemma, placing the survivor in a partial and sustained out-of-
body experience. And because of the intensity and negativity of
the assault, the survivor's attention returns again and again to
the memory. This strengthens the bond to the very person and
event from which she is trying to heal.

If a woman is a survivor of rape or other sexual abuse, cutting
the cord to her past attacker is an act of power and healing, and
one that may allow her to finally feel free of the trauma's impact.
If she is going to take this particular action, I recommend she
familiarize herself with this process by cutting cords to parents the
first time, and perhaps one or two siblings or past sexual contacts
of choice. When she is ready to do a session to cut the cord to the
person or people who abused her, she might want to devote the
entire session only to that purpose. The session will be most

effective if she has already done as much healing prior to the cer-emony as possible so the bulk of the emotional and physical trauma has already been worked through. When she comes to the part in the process where she would ordinarily thank that person for any benefits from their mutual association, she has a choice to make. She may not wish to thank him for anything. She may want to simply tell him what he did was wrong and that she is now going to disconnect herself from him permanently. However, she might also wish to reflect for a few minutes, to see if there is anything positive she has managed to extract from the event. This may sound strange. But sometimes a person can walk away from a horrible situation with new skills. She may be able to share compassion and understanding with others who experienced something similar, or she may have learned to tap some hidden wellspring of inner strength she hadn't realized was there. If the survivor finds anything like this as a result of her experience with the abusive person, she can either thank him for being the cata-lyst, or, if that doesn't feel right, she can look at him and thank herself for not only surviving but for having an indomitable spirit that created something positive from a negative situation.

Among the many people who have done the cord-cutting cer-emony to free their energies from past lovers, there have been a variety of effects, including one type that is sometimes amusing, sometimes exasperating. Fran cut the ties to her ex-boyfriend Matt. She had once hoped to marry him, but his initially keen interest in her dissipated over time as his interest in other women increased. He finally broke off their relationship a year ago and had not spoken to her since. It took Fran months to heal her emotional wounds. She finally got to a point where she could completely let go of Matt and cut the cord as her "grand finale." Within days, Matt called her on the phone, asking her to go out with him and try again. Fran was no longer interested and told him so, but she was intrigued by the timing of his actions in relation to her cord-cutting.

Several other people have related similar stories to me. What we concluded is that the person on the other end obviously feels the energetic results of the cord-cutting ceremony. People like Matt thrive on pursuing rather than being pursued. Once they feel they have something or someone, they lose interest. When Matt felt Fran literally remove herself from him, suddenly he no longer "had" her and his desire to pursue her resurfaced. You may need to be aware of this potential aftermath of disconnecting from old flames, so you can decide in advance the wisest way to deal with such repercussions should they occur.

Many people have asked me if they should cut the cord to someone they're currently involved with sexually if it is a positive and ongoing relationship. Generally, there is no reason to do so as the cord spiritually enhances a good partnership. However, there may be times when one or both people decide to cut the cord for a specific, short-term purpose, knowing it will be reestablished the next time they are sexual.

Let's look at a fictitious couple named Kerry and Bill. Kerry has a deadline to complete several paintings for a gallery exhibit. Although the marriage is generally good, Bill is currently in a rotten mood due to stresses between him and his boss. Knowing the energy cord between them is a factor in causing Kerry to be adversely affected by his mood, they decide to cut the cord between them until Kerry finishes her paintings. Some of the disruption coming from Bill is alleviated, Kerry finishes her project, and after a week of celibacy they return to sexual relations and reconnect the cord.

Sue and Andy, another fictitious but representative couple, have been in a nonmarried relationship for over a year. Although it went well for the first year, Andy has felt increasingly uneasy with Sue over the past few months. After finally expressing his discomfort, the ensuing conversation reveals that Sue has been seeing another man—Phil—with whom she has been sexual during the period of Andy's mysterious unease. Andy and Sue agree to give their relationship a few more months to see if they can improve it, and to see if Sue can drop Phil and become monogamous again or if she and Andy should terminate their relationship. In the meantime, Andy is unwilling to be sexual with her and to be caught up in the energy bond between Sue and Phil. Andy and Sue decide to cut the cord between them until Sue either stops her sexual connection with the other man or until Andy and Sue decide to end their relationship. Both know cutting the cord alone will not solve all their problems, but it will free Andy from an undesired energy entanglement and perhaps allow each of them to see themselves and the other more clearly. Then they can make their decisions from a more solid perspective. Knowledge of the energy cord is spiritual knowledge. A decision to cut a cord is a spiritual action. Neither the knowledge nor the action contain moral judgments or blueprints for sexual behavior. We must each come to our own decisions and ethics, hopefully with clarity and thoughtfulness. What the knowledge of the will bond and sexual dynamics *does* provide is a new basis for and understanding of the spiritual and energetic results of our choices. And cutting the cords that confuse, drain or imprison us is a vehicle for healing and energetic freedom from the past.

Ani cut all her cords over a period of several months. She felt increasingly whole, energized and free and began suggesting the ceremony to many of her friends. In the "wounded healer" tradition of shamans and modern healers alike, Ani initially embarked on a necessary journey of self-healing, only to find some of her focus and power shifting over time to the healing of others. Through counseling,

*healing rituals and exercises, courses in reflexology and other holis-
tic systems, she gained tools, knowledge and power along the path.
In her final counseling session with me, she announced that in the
future, she wished others to call her Anima rather than Ani. This
was her statement of wholeness, symbolic of an embrace of her total
self: the sign and goal of all healing.*

PART THREE

Spirit Turns to Face the World

8

Spiritual Ritual: Theater of the Human and the Divine

Ritual provides a sense of order and grounding amidst the often unpredictable and tumultuous forces that challenge every human. Secular rituals are set on the stage of the known world. They provide small pauses between the dramas of everyday life through actions of comforting regularity. Spiritual rituals take place against the star-strewn curtains of the unknown, invoking invisible forces to play out their drama within a partly structured scenario. And Western women make their contributions to the spiritual revolution by creating rituals to meet their own needs and those of the global community.

Our secular rituals—coffee breaks, the habitual evening walk or warm bath, birthday celebrations or the weekly bridge game—link separate moments in time into a sense of continuity. These repeated patterns ground us and give the feeling that something in life is known and controllable. We need this sense of security up to a certain point, but too much of the known and the comfort of habit can put our spirit to sleep.

Our innate understanding of this danger leads us to find ways to reach out to the unknown to awaken and illuminate our beings, to give the human drama more depth and to avoid terminal narcolepsy! Spiritual rituals link us to each other. But they also connect us to that which is not human and is less familiar: to cycles and elements of nature and to the Divine. Spiritual rituals ground us in our relationship to both the known and the mysterious and are a unique milieu for spiritual action.

In most cultures, people created rituals that celebrate the turn of seasons, planting, harvesting, the successful hunt and sometimes the phases of the moon. Birth, the onset of puberty, marriage and death are almost universally observed with rituals, as are the birth and death of prophets, saints and messiahs. Prayer services give participants time away from mundane concerns to meditate on or communicate with Creator and lesser divinities. Some individuals and families turn their attention ritually to the divine several times daily, often at meals or upon waking or preparing for sleep. For these people, the theatre of daily living is suffused with the awareness and sometimes the experience of numinous forces weaving through their secular activities to create a rich and durable backdrop.

Through creation myths and cosmologies, the religions of the world anchor people to their origins and orient them toward the forces that shape their lives and environments. Meaning and identity are thereby shared. Many rituals enact myths. Through participation in such rituals, community members reconfirm their shared identity and meaning. Pilgrimages to holy places are another way for people to revitalize their ties to a collective identity and creation myth. Their efforts and rituals throughout the journey may also bring them spiritual blessings of unusual dreams, visions or healings.

Spiritual ritual can and should inspire the creative, joyful potential of a community to renewed vitality and celebration. As we have seen throughout history, should a people's religion and accompanying rituals be disrupted or destroyed, the meaning of life itself is shaken, the continuity of the drama broken. And the people can literally lose the will to live. This situation was exemplified here in North America in the recent past through the suppression and disruption of Native American religious practices, with devastating results to the minds, hearts and spirits of much of our indigenous population. And what happens to the joyful potential of a ritual when only half of the community can fully identify with it? What happens when the ceremonial leaders are only men, when the symbols or deities are described as primarily male, when the holy objects or altars are only accessible to males? What happens to the spiritual will of the women attending these rituals? I believe everyone is deprived when only half the cast is allowed to stand in the ceremonial spotlight. The wills of both women and men are cheated of their full spiritual expression when the feminine element is deleted from the ceremonial script.

This has been the predominant situation in the West for several millennia. In the Judeo-Christian traditions, usually the ritual officiator has been male, although that has been slowly changing in recent years. Nonetheless, women have rarely been encouraged to become spiritually active and powerful, and as a result, have too often become relatively passive spectators in their churches and temples. This is often true of the male half of the congregation as well. However, they at least have had male spiritual role models or figureheads leading them to believe they too might strive for spiritual power and an active relationship to Creator.

This general state of spiritual gender imbalance is now true in most places in the world, although it has not always been so. In the past there were more priestesses and woman shamans in various religious traditions. All across Asia, for example, women once played extremely important and powerful roles in the rituals, primarily as shamans and trance mediums. Women's intuitive nature was appreciated and utilized in these spiritual endeavors. In a powerful yearly Indonesian ritual, the local shaman used the dreaming or visionary abilities of the community's young women to help decipher the needs and appropriate actions for the next year's cycle. Here again, the feminine was valued.

However, in many cultures where women once held strong ceremonial roles, today those roles are increasingly rare. This is partly due to a larger issue, the fact that increasing numbers of indigenous traditions are being disrupted and lost through the massive influx of Western influences. And because Western culture at this time is still predominantly patriarchal, it leaves a certain patriarchal impression on the people it touches. In its wake, whether here in the United States or abroad, women's intuitive spirit and spiritual roles are often left neglected in the dust.

There are some exceptions to women's diminished role in spiritual ritual. One example is found in current Afro-American spiritual movements. In the Brazilian Candomble and Voudouin ceremonies, women have respected spiritual roles and leadership. As high priestesses, they initiate and train fledging novitiates. These women officiate at the rituals in which the saints and gods and goddesses of their religions are called upon to choose group members for temporary "possession": the embodiment of the holy powers and personalities. Interestingly, in these religious communities women are regarded as more sober and balanced vessels of the gods and goddesses than men. Some Australian aboriginal vestiges of female ceremonial leadership and power have also survived; women still group together to perform their own rituals, handing down aspects of the rich Dreamtime cosmology to the younger generations. In the Western world, women of the past quarter century are finally reinstating their spiritual roles in childbirth. Many have taken back the ritual roles from the over-riding control of male doctors and insisted on playing their parts more the way nature intended them to.

Again, everybody benefits when women and men have equal opportunities to perform in the global amphitheater, whether it be in secular or spiritual activities. Within each of us there exist both feminine and masculine qualities. And both need to be exercised, acknowledged and respected in order to arrive at the experience of internal wholeness and holiness. When one gender is disdained or excluded from our inner spiritual life or from external activities such as spiritual rituals, we *all* lose part of the balance of our own beings.

Acting to Empower Spiritual Rituals

Aspects of the unknown and of divine powers come into play through strong rituals, but only after we take the initiative to invest our own time and energies. When we do, those powers often respond to our efforts. What are the factors that make spiritual rituals both potent and spiritually effective, and what can we, the actors and playwrights, do to make them more so?

Over years of both participating in other people's ceremonies and creating many myself, I have witnessed several empowering factors that address these questions. They are:

- the level of personal power of the individual or individuals involved;
- the degree of preparation by the participants before the ritual begins;
- the amount and quality of individual participation once the ritual starts;

- the appropriateness of the ritual form to the circumstance and/or environment in which it's being practiced.

These issues of spiritual action will be explored one by one so we may understand the importance of our individual roles in ritual, how we might further empower rituals, and what the overall dynamics are that make rituals effective.

Spiritual ritual is a gesture of and toward power. Divine power resides within us and within all creation. Performing a ritual is an attempt to reconnect with that power. Power follows power. Since spiritual power is attracted to itself, the more of it that is already held by those performing the ritual, the more will be drawn by the event. Each participant is therefore important, as necessary as every ingredient in a loaf of bread. Because many rituals designate a ceremonial leader, we tend to forget this fact and depend on the personal power of the leader, hoping for the best. But even in the rare cases where the leader is a spiritual powerhouse, the entire group benefits still more when each person adds her own energy to the ritual.

Whatever we can do in our lives to gather and sustain our ongoing connection to power will positively affect the spiritual balance and quality of the rituals in which we participate. There are hundreds, perhaps thousands of spiritual practices that raise our energy level. These include sedentary and inner-focused meditations, postures and prayers, moving meditations such as tai chi, energy-focused martial arts, spiritual dance forms such as eurythmy, and gathering power from nature. Gathering power is not only beneficial for our day-to-day experience of life, but can be regarded as our individual responsibility and contribution to any ritual in which we participate.

This brings us to the second point concerning effective ritual: the element of prior preparation. Our ongoing spiritual practices increase the amount of power we can add to a ceremony. But what are we doing the five minutes or hour or day just before a ritual begins? Where is our focus? All too often, we arrive at a prayer service or other kinds of rituals with our energies, thoughts and attention scattered in every direction. Frequently we chatter away with friends as we arrive, up to the very moment when the ritual is about to begin. Unless we have a very strong meditative practice that allows us to silence our internal dialogue on command, once the ritual begins we'll have trouble being fully present with our power and attention. Most of us just barely arrive at this state by the time the ritual ends. Then we wonder why we didn't experience much—and blame it on the ritual, the leader or even on Creator.

Some rituals may engage our full attention faster than others. However, taking responsibility to prepare ourselves in advance will make the most compelling rituals even more effective. And we'll be more present to enjoy them! There are many ways we can prepare ourselves ahead of time. Meditation, fasting and other forms of purification often decrease the distractions of body, heart and mind so we can better focus on spirit. Even making a decision not to talk to anyone for a period of time right up to the beginning of a ritual can be extremely helpful for gathering our focus. Everyone can contribute to the overall energy of a ritual and all can personally benefit.

Now we come to the third question: how does the degree of group participation effect the overall strength of a spiritual ritual? As with most group events, quite a bit. Gathering our focus and personal power are two ways everyone can participate. However, our attention tends to wander if we don't have a more active role to play than listening to someone give a sermon—unless it's highly inspirational and engaging. Spiritual ritual works best as a performance in which everyone present has a part to play and when each of us is an actor in the drama rather than a passive audience. What activities exist that can increase our involvement?

Group singing and dancing are two of the most powerful ways to enliven a ritual through group participation. Both tend to engage our entire being and add a great deal of energy to the collective process. Most religious communities have a body of commonly known songs and singing together always changes the emotional climate in a positive way. Some rituals also include special dances to invoke, embody or celebrate spiritual entities. Such dances allow us to shift from passive or sedentary roles into full physical expressions of the sacred. Circles automatically encourage democratic involvement of ritual participants while allowing everyone to see and be seen by each other. The circle also subtly promotes a sense that everyone in it has equal access to the Divine. A third way to make a ritual inclusive is to give each person an individual blessing. Communion, being anointed with blessed water, oil or incense, or being prayed for specifically by the leader or entire congregation are some good examples. Another powerful engaging factor is for each person to contribute something physical—such as food or flowers—for the altar. In some New Age rituals, a blanket is spread in the center of the circle. Everyone both leaves a small gift and takes a gift someone else has left: a variation of the potlatch ceremony.

The fourth element that affects the power of ritual is the appropriateness of the ritual form to its purpose and environment. Our lives, cultures and environments are in a constant state of flux, from the subtle to the dramatic. What may have been intensely relevant a century ago, or even ten years ago, may now seem outdated. Religious purists often hold the view that a ritual originating one, two or even three thousand years ago was good enough for our ancestors and should be good enough for us. And there may be aspects of this perspective that are true. Ceremonial ties to our ancestors can be very grounding for human identity. However, most rituals change at least subtly over time. Whether a Catholic priest or a Sioux medicine man says, "This is the way we've always done it and this is the way it's always going to be," the statement is still incorrect. The quiet or dramatic influences of great visionaries, of individual interpretations or of changes within the cultures themselves have always shifted the form of rituals over the years. Inspirations for positive change should be a welcome element for revitalizing all religious ceremonies. They keep the rituals from becoming stagnant and assist in making them more relevant and appropriate to the people involved.

For a ritual to be in harmony with the flow of life itself and thus with the participants, elements of the familiar and of the creative or spontaneous are both needed. This is especially true if the ritual occurs regularly within the community. When certain aspects of the ritual are known and performed the same way every time, the participants feel a sense of comfort and security. And when a place is made for at least some aspects to be *different* each time, the changeable nature of life is reflected to all. These ritual variations also link our awareness to the new and unknown—both powerful aspects of spiritual reality itself.

A ritual that adapts to individual, societal or environmental events and concerns will maintain a dynamic and relevant quality for the community it serves. And new rituals can be created for specific occasions and needs. I especially encourage women to do so for two reasons: first, creating a new ceremony can be an extremely empowering spiritual action; and second, doing so provides a positive counterbalance to the predominance of male spiritual leadership.

I recently created two simple rituals for my women's writing group. At one of our weekly meetings, a member of the group told us she'd just received the results of her latest pelvic exam, and some questionable cell activity required an exploratory biopsy. I suggested a brief healing ritual and after getting her consent, the rest of us formed a circle around her. I quickly taught the women in the circle how to pull energy up from the earth as they inhaled. Then, on the exhalation, we all directed this energy to our friend at the center. As we did, I had her inhale and concentrate on absorbing the healing energy, particularly into her womb. We performed this simple process for about five minutes. Afterwards, everyone felt refreshed, energized and inspired about ritual potentials.

The second ritual I created was for Tanya and Dee, whose birthdays fell close to one of our meetings. This time I was asked in advance to prepare a ritual as a surprise for them. The day before our gathering, I selected four of my ceremonial fans to use for a four-direction blessing. I also put together a bowl of sage for purification, cedar for new beginnings and sweetgrass for bringing in positive energy. I took the fans and bowl of herbs to our gathering the next day. Once again, everyone formed a circle, this time with the two birthday women in the center. First I burned the herbs and bathed everyone in their pungent smoke. Then I called upon Creator's power, the energies above us—stars, sun and moon—and the energies of Mother Earth to strengthen and balance each of us. Next I picked up the fan I'd chosen to represent the south and called in the powers of the south wind. As I felt its energy I gathered some of it with the fan and touched it to the head, hands, heart, belly and feet of Tanya and Dee. I then used the respective fans to do the same with the west, north and east winds. As we all faced east everyone drew on that direction's renewing energies, and I told the women they could do likewise in the future whenever they felt the need. I then asked Tanya, Dee and any of the others who wanted to, to meditate on any moments of joy, beauty and power they recalled from their lives. I showed them how to gather the energy from those experiences into a ball of light between their hands and to take its power into their bellies for strength and empowerment. Finally I gathered all four of my ceremonial fans into one hand and touched them to each of the nonbirthday women so they too could be part of the four-direction blessing. Every one of them ended up feeling included and deeply moved by this simple ceremony. They all gained a new appreciation for the power of ritual and were heartened to learn they could create their own rituals in the future.

Here are some suggestions for creating rituals of your own.

PLANNING A RITUAL

Spend some time thinking about the people you know well, including close friends and family members. Is there anyone among them who has gone through a very difficult experience recently or is searching for a new direction in her life? Is someone getting ready to die? Or is someone due for a significant event like a birthday, marriage or birth? Is someone getting a job promotion or beginning college? From these various possibilities, choose the person to whom you are most drawn and create an empowering spiritual ritual for her.

Take some time to think about that person. Consider her temperament, the colors, foods, music, incense, flowers or other plants, people and activities she most enjoys. Write down whatever you know. Try to find out what information you need that you don't have. This is all excellent material for assisting you with ideas for setting the stage and creating a physical environment for the ritual.

As with any stage, don't forget the element of lighting. Will your ritual be most appropriate and/or most enjoyed by this person in sunlight, moonlight, candlelight, the light of a bonfire? Do you feel she would prefer it indoors or outdoors, weather permitting? Lighting has a big effect on setting the mood of the ritual, so give it adequate consideration.

Next, focus on the purpose of the ritual. Is it to heal from recent difficulties, to bring clarity for a new direction, to honor and bless someone preparing for death, to celebrate an upcoming positive event or for some other purpose? Take some time to think about the various physical, mental, emotional or spiritual implications and details of the person's situation. What could the ritual give her that would be healing, clarifying, honoring or celebratory, given her situation and the purpose of the ritual? What does she most need or what would she most enjoy? Again, write down whatever comes to you as you look at these issues. Gaining clarity about the purpose and goals of the ritual will help you set up its deeper content and structure, and you gain a sense of the words and actions that might help move the ritual toward these goals. Let your subconscious and creativity have free rein. At first you may get a wide variety of fleeting and seemingly unconnected images. Write them all down. Eventually you will get the sense of a pattern, or you'll find a thread that weaves all or many of those images together and allow you to discover others that fit. Trust your process.

Now you need to consider the person's religious/spiritual beliefs. These are critical to take into account and to utilize in the ritual. Whether or not you share the same beliefs and practices, if you want the ritual to be effective for this person, it must harmonize with hers. Her beliefs will dictate what spiritual powers you call upon in the ritual, as well as influence what kind of altar you might create and what, if any sacred objects and images you use.

Her spiritual preferences might also dictate the music you choose, although the music could be her favorite secular choices as well. Music has a great influence on the tone of the ritual, with its powerful effect on human emotions. Consider carefully the moods you wish to create and their purposes. Does the recipient of this

ritual need a chance to shed tears, laugh, to become calm, energized, uplifted or reminded of her past with some golden oldies?
The music you choose will be evocative and will effect not only the
main person it is for, but everyone involved. That brings us to the
next element in creating the ritual: who else will be involved?

Think about the people she knows, including family, friends,
business associates, members of her church or spiritual community. Who among them would support and enhance the ritual's
purpose? The person it's for may have the best sense of this, and
you might want to consult her if you are unsure. Of the people
you end up including, are there some who you would like to give
specific roles in the event? Do you see yourself as the sole "mis-
tress of ceremony," leading the flow of events alone, or is there
someone you'd want to share that role with? Are there ways to
include everyone in group activities like singing, praying or dancing together, lighting candles or placing a flower on the altar?
Remember that the higher the level of group participation, the
more powerful the ritual will be for everyone. Can you place
everyone in a circle for that purpose?

As you continue creating the ritual, don't forget the importance
of each individual's efforts to gather power and focus ahead of
time. You might want to suggest this in your invitation by request-
ing that each person set aside time the day of the ritual for some
kind of energy-raising spiritual practice. Let them know this will
help increase the power of the ritual. Meditating and fasting or
eating lightly that day might be on your suggestion list. If you
don't feel confident that the people invited will respond to these
kinds of requests, there is a second option for ensuring advance
spiritual preparation. That is to make the opening of the ritual
itself a time for silent prayer, for sustained group chanting or for
sedentary or moving meditation of some sort. Building this kind
of energy-raising and focusing activity into the ritual is quite practical, given the fact that people often can't or won't set aside time
for such preparations.

Finally, look at the rhythm or pacing of the event. You are the
choreographer of this drama. Do you want a slowly building
rhythm escalating to a powerful crescendo? Would the purpose of

the ritual be better served through a series of more subtle ups and downs of intensity? Is there some element you particularly want to highlight, and if so, do you want to lead the group gradually toward it or surprise them suddenly? Give special consideration to the ending. Its tone and energy is what people will most consciously take away. Do you want to end on a high note or would it serve the purpose better to end with calm? Also consider the possibility of a postritual shared meal of some kind. Not only is this an enjoyable social activity, but it allows everyone some time to integrate the effects of the ceremony and perhaps share some of their experiences. Leaving the setting abruptly at the conclusion of a ritual can be rather disconcerting to our spirits. It's a bit like spending an hour in a warm hot tub with your friends and then jumping into a cold shower alone! A shared meal, especially one that includes a communal blessing of the food, provides a nice bridge between the spiritual event and the more secular activities that participants will engage in once they leave.

There may be other kinds of details that come to you as you plan. Be open, continue focusing on the person you're trying to serve and the goals of the ritual, and pray for the highest guidance possible in your efforts. Most of all, enjoy the process. Creating a ritual can be just as much fun as our childhood efforts at making up skits with our friends, deciding on our costumes and props and audience. The process and the ritual need not be somber, no matter what its purpose, in order to be effective.

And a sense of play has another advantage. Ritual is a theater of the human and the divine, and both have their unexpected qualities. Once the ritual begins, the unknown and the spontaneous may contribute their own roles. Be prepared and make room for them in your own mind in advance. Stay focused on your overall purpose, be flexible and most of all, delight in the opportunity for spiritual action and experience that you've helped create!

Looking at the elements that go into ritual and the factors that empower ritual has several benefits. We gain a new perspective from which to observe any ritual we attend, a deeper understanding of why it either does or doesn't work well. We build an effective foundation for creating our own rituals. Finally and most importantly, we gain faith in the fact that we can play an essential part in any ritual. It doesn't matter if we are one of eight or eight hundred present. Our presence, level of power and attention, and our link to Spirit are all elements of a unique role only we can play. If we enter it fully and with gusto, the characters of the Divine will rush to meet us at center stage.

Women's Search for Meaning in Western Spiritual Traditions

Women have long participated in the rituals of the world's religions and have taken meaning and identity from the shared beliefs of their spiritual communities. Today, we look closer at the nature of the meanings that shaped our identities and find serious problems of both meaning *and* identity woven into the beliefs and resultant rituals.

Many of us are angry or disillusioned with Judeo-Christian religions. We sometimes mistakenly transfer our anger to Creator and cut ourselves off from all spiritual life. Others of us have switched allegiance to what has become known as the Goddess movement or are trying paths from other cultures, such as Buddhist or Native American practices. Or, in an explosion of spiritual creativity, we are making up our own personal or group rituals.

All of these alternatives may present certain challenges to those of us who left the mainstream religions. Often, we end up missing the embrace of those larger religious communities. Some of us may return to them and try to find our own balance within them, despite the problems. Others may try exploring and utilizing the extant feminine cores in the Judeo-Christian religions, resurrecting those elements that provide more balanced imagery and focus for our rituals.

For example, within Judaism, women around the country are holding their own *Rosh Hodesh*—full moon—ceremonies, building on an existing tradition but adding their own creativity to the form. Some delve into an exploration of the *Shekhinah*, the feminine aspect of Creator, described as both indwelling and outside in the human community and nature. The Shekhinah aspect brings the vast and mysterious power of Creator closer to all in an intimate, more tangible manner. This is a powerful image and presence for Jewish feminists to incorporate into mainstream Judaism. Nonetheless, it is still a challenge to overcome several millennia's inertia of relating to the Almighty as a solely male force. Even the aspect of Jewish mysticism that always acknowledged the Shekhinah predominantly viewed her as the bride: a spiritual counterpart but of lesser stature and status than her groom. Despite various obstacles, efforts are being made to establish her unique value. Some Jewish women, including women rabbis, are also trying to change the more male-biased wording in the traditional rituals and are looking carefully at the words they use in their own alternative rituals.

Similar issues and efforts exist in the Christian religions. Some feminist Christians who don't wish to entirely abandon their churches are trying to bring forward the aspect of Sofia. The Sofia is a presence of feminine wisdom similar to the Shekhinah, and is sometimes interpreted as one and the same as the Holy Spirit. If these feminists can convince their congregations that God is androgynous, and that the union of Christ to the Holy Spirit is to a female bride, then the Holy Trinity becomes a balanced force for both men and women to relate to equally.

In addition to a stronger focus on the feminine aspect of the sacred, there is an encouraging increase in the number of female ministers. Some of them are even creating their own churches and services. Other nonclergy women are trying to change the church from within. They attend the regular, often male-led rituals. But by sharing their own perspectives, they attempt to raise the level of awareness of sexist and patriarchal biases amongst their fellow worshippers.

Whether from within the mainstream Judeo-Christian communities struggling against massive currents from ages past, or from the new feminist offshoots, rituals are powerful vehicles for creating change. Through evocative imagery, spiritual action and prayer, rituals enable us to integrate spiritual meaning, connectedness and community. The predominantly male-oriented Judeo-Christian forms must shift to accommodate the growing need of the people for spiritual balance. There may be growing pains, but Spirit can prevail and heal.

Grounding the Goddess

The present Goddess movement is in a fluid state that makes defining it a challenge. What is most obvious is that it includes a deification of the feminine and a distancing from the patriarchal religions. Simultaneously, the movement celebrates past matriarchal religions and elevates the status of various ancient goddess figures. Some women of Jewish and Christian faiths also participate in Goddess rituals without conflict or animosity toward either style of worship. Many of them transpose the focus on Sofia and Shekhinah imagery into the Goddess rituals. Other women gravitate to the Goddess movement out of pain. They are distressed by the prevalence of male power and symbols in the Western churches, and wonder if and where there was a place to be unabashedly spiritual while being empowered as women.

The origins of the Goddess rituals vary, drawing from the

creativity of the women's circles performing them as well as from neo-pagan and earth-based paths. Women are encouraged to explore the mythologies of other cultures, seeking feminine spiritual imagery to add to the growing Goddess movement. Many have benefited from their experiences of nonpatriarchal ceremonialism and of forging a new spiritual identity and identification.

One of the most positive aspects of Judeo-Christian feminism and the Goddess movement is the spiritual quality of "immanence": being near or immediate. As with the Shekhinah, one of the Goddess's primary attributes is accessibility. The Goddess is a spiritual presence manifest here among us, within the human community, and touching us through the body of Mother Earth and all of nature. This more tangible immanence of spirit is contrasted with other religious traditions such as Christianity and Buddhism, where the goal is transcendence—transcendence of the lures and limitations of the earthly, physical domain. Instead, the Goddess is within reach, present in what we touch in daily living. She is a positive counterbalance to a predominant focus on transcendence and escaping the traps of the material world. Both pathways have their merit in the spiritual scheme of things. The fact that involvement in the Goddess rituals doesn't preclude pursuing other spiritual pathways is a powerful statement about its inherent strengths and flexibility.

The Goddess movement contains much that is positive and healing. The movement also has some rough edges that hopefully will smooth out as it moves through its growing process. The following brief overview is offered in the spirit of supporting future balance in the Goddess rituals and philosophy.

Most of us were raised with the impression that God is male. This is a biased and sometimes harmful concept. Many of us are now understandably angry about the issue, and as a result, some who gravitated to the Goddess movement encourage one another to consider Creator as solely female. Creator is most likely male, female and unfathomably beyond either. Giving that Power a solely female identity, the Goddess instead of God, once more creates a biased image. As women, should we really push the pendulum to the opposite extreme to feel our spiritual connection to the divine? A healthier approach might be to represent Goddess rituals as celebrations of the feminine aspects of Creator and creation, so that we don't repeat the mistakes of spiritual vanity men made in the past.

As the Goddess movement matures, we also need to be careful about romanticizing past Goddess worship. Doing so is part of our nostalgic tendency to believe that long ago things were better than what we have now. There undoubtedly were positive aspects of prior Goddess religions. But one of the more destructive idealizations I've heard is the elevation of the ancient sexual role of temple priestesses. In recent years, those figures have been repeatedly portrayed in various women's publications and gatherings as some kind of consummate spiritual prototype. In reality, all too often the priestesses were slaves captured as young girls and sold to the temples to perform as prostitutes for the pleasure of the local males. Ritualized sex gave the mask of a divine union, when quite probably the divine or ecstatic rarely entered into it, especially for the women. I don't believe the sexual priestess image served women well in the past, and I doubt that it adds much to empower women in the present. In our longing for a more utopian society and our search for positive and healthy models, we need to guard against romanticizing images and practices from the past whose reality wasn't as rosy as we now fantasize.

Another Goddess-movement aspect that may be counterproductive is the fixation on goddess figures from ancient Greek and Roman pantheons. As Western women, we may seek powerful female spiritual role models as sources of inspiration and emulation. Unfortunately, many of the Western goddesses were, according to the myths, raped by gods, by human males or even monsters, or were born from the loins or foreheads of male gods. Although their lives may have also contained appealing elements such as courage, love and spiritual talents, their origins or fates may not be positive models for modern women. In addition, none of these goddesses were ever human beings. It seems more fitting for human women to have human role models. Also, some women may psychologically identify with their goddess(es) of choice without having a real spiritual experience of them. Dressing like Diana or Demeter for a ritual is quite different from years of training and preparation to embody a spiritual entity in a Candomble possession dance, for example. When Western women act out their goddess roles in rituals, emotional excitement is often mistaken for divine power. Fantasy can be fun, but it is not Spirit.

The Goddess movement contains many positive elements. It also presents challenges of balance and discernment. As in all arenas, knowledge, sobriety and awareness each have their place in the creation of Goddess rituals. Bringing forth women's active, more egalitarian participation and creativity in ritual has been one of the movement's strongest positive qualities. Looking toward a feminine, imminent facet of Spirit has been another. We can best support what is real, grounded and healing in the Goddess movement by making an effort to avoid the twin pitfalls of fantasy and vanity.

Ritual's Darkest Face

One of the most serious issues facing millions of women—sado-rituals—has been thoroughly addressed by Mary Daly in her book *Gyn/ecology*. There have been and still are some ongoing rituals in various cultures that involve mild to major mutilation of the body. The traditional foot-binding of Chinese women and the ritual immolation of Hindu widows are but a few examples of these sado-rituals. Fortunately, the first practice has been dropped and the second has substantially diminished. Ritual genital mutilation of girls and young women—particularly clitorectomy—is one of the worst sado-rituals still being widely practiced. The origins of these rituals—practiced predominantly in the Middle East and Africa but rumored to still exist in other parts of the world—are unknown. Some speculate that their Middle Eastern origins were with the ancient royalty of Egypt, and then emulated increasingly throughout the rest of the population. Apparently nothing in the written religion of Islam supports this practice, and yet many young Muslim women are subjected to it, as are many non-Muslim black African girls, sometimes as young as three or four years old.

The results of these rituals vary in degree of severity and damage from traumatic to deadly. It is common for many girls in a row to be mutilated with the same unsterilized rusty knife or jagged piece of glass. Beyond suffering the pain and terror of the moment, they often become ill from infections and all too frequently die. The inadvertent spreading of AIDS is another unfortunate by-product of these practices. Of those who survive, many live out the rest of their lives in physical pain or discomfort. Most are unable to experience any pleasure in sex, and often suffer limited mobility. Walking itself may be a daily source of misery.

In addition to these physical issues, deep psychological effects need to be taken into account. Try imagining what would happen to your trust in your mother, if one night she, and perhaps some of your other adult female relatives, woke you and told you this was to be an important night for you. You were going to be initiated and celebrated as a woman, with a special ceremony after which you would have adult status. Perhaps you are ten or twelve years old. You are led through the dark to the hut of the tribal female "doctor," where you enter a room crowded with many of your friends and some of their younger sisters. Anticipation is high, and you and the others alternately giggle or stare wide-eyed as you wait for the ritual to begin. Then the first of your friends is led through a door into the other room. You wait with the others for your turn. Suddenly the air is pierced with screams of pain and terror, which go on unabated seemingly forever. Then, almost worse, silence falls as your friend—lively and high-spirited when you saw her only a brief time ago—staggers through the door, pale with shock, legs almost folding under her as the "doctor" or an assistant supports her back into the room. She lays down off to one side of the room moaning as the next of your friends is called. Soon it will be your turn.

The images of this entire scenario were both sensitively and vividly portrayed in a 1994 television program on the subject and in a documentary film by author Alice Walker called "Warrior Marks." The theme of the program and the film was an extension of Walker's novel, *Possessing the Secret of Joy*. While viewing both, I imagined what I could only surmise must be a sense of ultimate betrayal in these young girls, led to this excruciating fate by their own mothers, aunts and the local female doctor after being told this was going to be a wonderful initiation into womanhood. Why are these rituals perpetuated when the older women know full well exactly what their beloved daughters and nieces will experience and the considerable health and life-threatening risks involved?

A large factor, besides the inertia of tradition itself, is the issue of marriageability. Most mothers in these societies wish to see their daughters married. Somewhere along the way, prospective husbands decided their wives should be virgins. To ensure this, part of the sado-ritual sometimes includes stitching the outer labia together, leaving only a tiny opening for urine and menstrual blood to escape. Sexual penetration is thus impossible, and the stitches remain in place as proof of virginity until the marriage ceremony. And those men who worry about their wife's passions straying from home believe their marriage will be more secure if the woman feels no pleasure in sex. To try to assure this, the women's clitoris is removed as part of the ritual. In many African tribes, the price of a bride has traditionally been so high that often a man cannot afford to marry until he's in his 30s or older. Then he takes a wife often one or more decades his junior. This state of affairs probably exacerbates the men's sexual anxieties. For all of the above reasons, the sado-ritual is supported to the degree that historically, many men of Islam or parts of black Africa only marry a woman who has gone through it. And at a primal level, the ritual itself programs the young women to be overwhelmed and controlled, a deep imprinting which makes them more susceptible to later domination from their husbands or other social forces.

Since the mothers want to see their daughters married, the oppressed become the oppressors, perpetuating the cycle of pain and betrayal century after century. Even in the United States, there are still women of African or Arab descent or of Islam who make sure their daughters go through this ritual mutilation, although perhaps sometimes in more sterile medical environments.

One would question why the United Nations and World Health Organization have not more effectively intervened in this obviously life- and health-threatening situation. Is it because the victims are female? Or because they are black and Arab *and* female? In one television documentary on the subject, United Nations' officials were pathetically closed-mouthed or incoherent when challenged. The main point that emerged was their ostensible reluctance to interfere with the religious traditions of other cultures.

This pitiful excuse is unacceptable, but if such is the case, women need to take the situation into their own hands. Such a movement is growing in black Africa and in the Middle East, often at considerable danger to the women trying to raise the consciousness of others and put a stop to the sado-rituals. Yet the numbers of these courageous women are increasing, from female doctors and intellectuals with some influence on the government, to artists, students and concerned mothers and daughters alike. Just as in the West, it seems women all over the world are daring to act in ways that their grandmothers and even mothers only dreamed about.

Rite of passage ceremonies for young men and women can be extremely positive and need not be eliminated from these cultures. However, there are no positive spiritual or physical benefits from genital mutilation of girls. In the men's spirituality movement, similar concerns are raised about circumcision of baby boys. As an alternative to sado-rituals, new life and body-celebrating rituals could be created to fill the vacancy left by abandoning the dangerous practices. This would also turn around the destructive cycle which leads too many women into harming and endangering their daughters, making the mother-daughter bond a trap filled with deceit and betrayal. Positive alternative rituals could only benefit all concerned, and take away nothing but pain and confusion.

Given the multiple problems in the world's religions and their rituals as women have known them, some feminists and other women activists advise abandoning any and all spirituality in favor of sociopolitical action. Without denying a great need for the latter, taking such a stance is like saying the world would be a better place without fire, because fire is sometimes dangerous. The warmth of nonsexist spiritual community and communion can serve both men and women well; without it, part of human nature is left in the cold. This spiritual amputation proposed by some feminists severs women from potentially profound sources of inner strength and power, and from enjoying the pervasive presence of the divine within and around us. Cutting ourselves off from a life of spirit allows patriarchal forces to be ultimately victorious. Since this is the very issue all feminists struggle against, there is a more constructive solution to the problems of religions. This solution is for women to challenge one another to find spiritual knowledge and rituals—or create new ones when needed—which empower them with fresh meaning, identity and a more balanced perspective of themselves in relation to the vast Mystery.

Applications of Ritual in Healing

There is one final issue that I touched on in the "Spirit in Healing" section that I want to bring up again here. This is the role of ritual in healing, one I've explored extensively and encouraged others to do likewise. Because spirit is part of our multi-faceted nature, Western healers might consider incorporating more spiritual ritual in therapeutic processes. In most cultures that utilized shamans, such practices were common, but a good many of these practices are now lost or dying out, replaced increasingly by Western medical methods and technologies. Ritual is deeply integrative, and its potential role in holistic approaches to health is near-infinite. It would be a great loss if ritual's therapeutic potentials were completely abandoned in the future.

Western medicine has many strengths, but it also has its limits and drawbacks. The ways it has been practiced have too often reflected patriarchal tendencies of disempowering women, especially in childbirth practices or in the number of unnecessary surgeries performed on women's bodies. Male doctors frequently elevated themselves to the status of high priest and discouraged their patients from asking questions or challenging their authority. Health is one more area where women must and are reclaiming growing control over their own bodies. In addition to becoming more knowledgeable about our bodies and the effects of herbs, nutrition, exercise and energy-based therapies, exploring and utilizing the potentials of ritual in healing is another exciting option. I have used rituals extensively in physical, psychological and spiritual healing, and have found them extremely effective. If healing—whether mental, emotional, or physical—has wholeness and wellness as its goals, the individual spiritual will and the cosmic divine must both be engaged as allies in the process for it to be complete. And healing rituals are one place where wholeness and holiness can dance hand in hand.

Contemporary Western culture has been poignantly bereft of powerful rituals, despite the existence of Judeo-Christian puberty ceremonies such as confirmation or bar and bat mitzvahs. Even within the past few decades, the once-popular ritual of May Day, with its colorful baskets and May poles, has almost completely disappeared. Native Americans are struggling to hold on to some of their rituals like the Sun Dance, Maiden puberty ceremonies for young women and sweat lodge ceremonies. But the rest of us need a strong, fresh infusion of meaningful spiritual rituals that empower men and women alike.

We don't need to wait. We can create such ceremonies. Spirit is an endless spring waiting to bestow its sustaining and healing properties on all who care to drink from it. We are all inherently thirsty, and the innovative use of spiritual ritual is a practical and uplifting chalice in which we can serve ourselves and each other while quenching our thirst for the Divine.

9

Our Spirituality Teachers: Danger or Delight?

"We're off to see the wizard, the wonderful wizard of Oz . . .
if ever a wiz there was. . . ."

As we begin our tour through the geography of spiritual figure-heads and power dynamics, let's first give the map an overview to familiarize ourselves with the general lay of the land. There at the center of the map you'll notice a large river. It is called the Mainstream and is where secular issues of power are thrashed out between men and women. Some of its tributaries flow through the spiritual realms.

Right next to The Mainstream runs the jagged Mea Culpa Mountain Range where some Christian priests and ministers have given wise counsel to their congregations while others have sexually or monetarily misused power. Among the darker peaks you can see Mt. Bakker, Mt. Swaggert and Mt. Koresh.

Below these mountains is a long canyon that stretches from the present far back into the past. Although it looks innocent at first glance, Cult Canyon is actually full of quicksand. Jim Jones Gulch and Manson Bend are perhaps familiar.

A large area slightly off to one side contains dense and varied foliage. It is the New Age Jungle and numerous spirituality teachers dwell there. Although partly hidden from the general public eye, we know some of these teachers are guiding followers in the direction of spirit. Others use their roles as camouflage to better stalk the bodies and bank accounts of their followers. It's as yet unclear if they've been taking lessons from their Mea Culpan counterparts or have come to similar strategies on their own.

What looks like a yin/yang symbol near the Jungle is actually the East/West Frontier. In front of it is a large sign saying "Kindly Leave All Your Possessions Here." Nearby are two famous landmarks: the First International Bank of Enlightenment and the gold-plated Guru Throne.

The convenient supply shop marked at the trailhead is called "What Women Students Are Looking For." And slightly down the trail but surrounded by camouflage is another shop: "Hunting Supplies and Emergency Rations for the Male Spirituality Teacher."

There is valuable buried treasure in this territory—not at the end of the trail but in many places along the way. Sometimes the treasure is easy to get to and sometimes it is surrounded by traps.

My journey as a seeker of spirituality was filled with both adventures and misadventures. In following my teachers' spiritual treasure-hunting maps, I encountered fascinating fellow human travellers, other-worldly vistas and mysterious beings and forces. I also ran up against dead ends, staggered at the edge of dangerous cliffs and wandered lost in circles for periods of time because either a map was inaccurate or my own naivete misled me.

Spirituality teachers are mortals like everyone else. I've now created my own map to help demythify them, to encourage greater self-awareness and integrity among teachers and students alike and to decrease hazardous waste of time on both their parts.

The interface between spirituality teachers and students can create great delight. The contact can also result in complex dangers when the potent issues of power, sex and money enter the scene. The following explorations are aimed at maximizing the delights and minimizing the dangers between students and teachers along the path where increasing numbers of Westerners seek out spiritual teachings. The map is the best I can give you at this time. Gather your energy and attention and prepare for an unusual tour of spiritual awareness. Remember: we can't change what we aren't aware of.

The Glow of Power

"Sam" is a spirituality teacher and part-time ethnic jeweler who travels and teaches around the United States. He is legally married, but keeps this bit of information conveniently to himself. Wherever he goes to teach, Sam becomes sexually involved with at least one—and usually several—women students. While enjoying sex and often small to large financial gifts from them, he eventually and privately proclaims his love for each woman and they become "engaged." Sam has numerous "fiancees," unknown to each other and his wife, all over the country and isn't above using drugs and alcohol to increase the vulnerability of the women. In one community, this man (who is also an alcoholic) took one of his new young female students to a bar. After plying her with enough drinks to impair her judgment, he "candidly" revealed to her he felt she really needed a special healing ceremony to deal with some deep problems he'd sensed in her. Upon arriving at her home, the flimsy excuse of a healing rapidly progressed—without ceremony—to the bedroom. Although

*the student wasn't physically forced into drinking or sex,
her trust in Sam as a teacher was taken advantage of, and
for the next few months she had various difficulties recovering from the "healing." Eventually word of Sam's many
inappropriate behaviors circulated from city to city, and in
response to his abuse of power, some of his female sponsors
refused to invite him back to their communities for subsequent workshops.*

The story of Sam was confided to me by some of his former
women students when I was giving workshops in a community
he'd recently visited himself. Although bizarre, only slightly less
obnoxious examples are endemic in the New Age and mainstream
spiritual teaching circuits. In nearly every place I've gone to teach
for years, I've heard more and more stories reflecting the misuse of
power—primarily by male teachers with female students.

Power is a bright flame that either lights our path or entices us
toward destruction. When power is embodied in spirituality
teachers or leaders, those people are often challenged to choose
how they wield their fire. Will they use it to become masters in
the art of service or adepts in the art of seduction?

Whether or not you are ever confronted with inappropriate
behavior on the part of a religious leader or spirituality teacher—
or become a teacher yourself—issues of power dynamics are relevant to your life. We all face issues of balanced and unbalanced
uses of power in our secular relationships and in the global
community at large. And if you begin using the knowledge and
practices contained within this book, your personal power and its
effect on others will grow. Awareness and responsibility must
expand as that increasing power is channeled into spiritual and
secular actions.

We are drawn like moths to the glow of power, whether it be

spiritual or worldly. Some people work, fight and even kill to attain it, while others are more passive and content to simply bask in the secondhand aura of someone else's power. Among those who have spiritual or worldly power, what they do with it varies. The story of Sam described a teacher who benefited some students but who also misused his power through a variety of mental, emotional, sexual and material manipulations. Nonetheless, it became clear from several firsthand accounts that Sam's status and position of power as a spirituality teacher were at least temporarily attractive to a number of women.

Why are we drawn to both spiritual and secular power? Both kinds can give us more options, and most people appreciate having a variety of options. The power of money allows many choices for pleasure, control, selfishness and generosity. Often the power of wealth and status go hand in hand. Top executives of successful corporations have both. Their status and power give them numerous options, including the ability to make decisions that may affect the lives of many people. Teachers also have power, the power of knowledge and authority that can also affect many lives. The energy-gathering practices of chapter 1 provide other kinds of power and options: power that can be used to improve the quality of both spiritual and secular life. Most of us are attracted to at least some of power's many options.

Individuals who glow with more than average spiritual or worldly power are often charismatic. But they may also be intimidating to those who have—or feel they have—less power. Those who use power to harm others are clearly intimidating because of their actions. Those who use power for positive goals may sometimes be perceived as both attractive and intimidating to others who envy their seemingly unattainable position.

As children, many of us felt a mixture of admiration and relative weakness in relation to our parents' power. The road to maturity involves a struggle for increasing power and independence. Even if the power our parents wielded was mostly beneficial, we have to find our own strengths to finally realize our parents—and later other authority figures—are not awesome gods but simply humans like ourselves.

Imbalances of power between individuals exist in most families and societies. They also exist between groups such as nations, and perhaps always have to some extent. And they often exist between men in spiritual/religious roles of power and their women students or followers. We will see some ways women may contribute to these imbalances as we peek in the windows of the trailhead shop. . . .

What Women Students Are Looking For

I will tell you some of what I was looking for.

I was in my mid-teens when I realized my own rather fierce, determined predilection for spiritual experiences. By the time I was divorced in my late 20s, I also felt I wanted a male partner who shared my somewhat esoteric thirst for spiritual knowledge. But as I looked about, it seemed such men were a rare species.

This surprised me. I imagined among the tens of thousands of men who'd begun ingesting mind-altering substances only a decade earlier and reading *Autobiography of a Yogi* or Carlos Castaneda's tales of power and separate realities, that many would have continued on a serious spiritual quest. But when I attended spirituality trainings, most participants with equal interest in such a quest were either women or married men. Or they were the male leaders of the trainings.

This situation created a baffling predicament for me. As a healthy, single, spiritually dedicated young woman, I often was flooded with passion around these male teachers. But I was confused about whether the passion was for the knowledge they possessed, the power I imagined they could bestow on me, their care for my spiritual progress, or sex. In other words, did I hunger for their bodies, minds, hearts, souls or all of the above?

I was both extremely naive and idealistic in my expectations as I imagined potential relationships with some of my teachers. I fantasized the qualities of Jesus, Buddha and Castaneda's Yaqui teacher Don Juan all rolled into one man, and would unconsciously project this impossible image over a teacher's much more modest attributes. I'd think about how wonderful it would be to have a relationship with that person: the ultimate teacher-student-yet-somehow-simultaneously-egalitarian-soulmate connection. With exquisitely cosmic and spiritual sex, of course. And there were several teachers interested in auditioning for the role, but for the most part they were simply method actors.

I learned a great deal from my experiences, both from the valuable spiritual directions some teachers pointed me in and from the mistakes I made. The main conclusion from my mistakes is that the spirituality teacher-student relationship is very much like others in which one person has a role of authority and the other is coming to them for some kind of help. As between doctors or counselors and their clients, there is an inherent imbalance of power in their positions. Even if in reality the student or client may have equal or even greater personal power, this usually doesn't match her perceptions of the balance between them, nor does it usually match those of the authority figure. The one seeking help or guidance tends to look up to the person in authority. A perceptive and ethical teacher/healer knows this tendency and encourages the seeker to develop her own strengths. But if he is less ethical and crosses the line into a personal relationship to feed his own ego desires, there is bound to be trouble.

The trouble in such relationships is inertia. When a teacher-student relationship moves into a personal one, both parties tend to stay locked into the teacher-student pattern, which then permeates the entire relationship. In male-dominated societies such as ours, the imbalance is even more pronounced if the teacher is male. As the relationship progresses, both people keep seeing the man as more powerful and the woman as less so. If the woman eventually tires of her lesser role and desires a truly egalitarian relationship, one of two things usually happens. Either the man resists stepping off the pedestal and bails out of the relationship, or in rarer cases where he too wants greater equality, the relationship is in for a bumpy ride as the balance of power shifts. Many such relationships either remain imbalanced or break apart. Few survive the turbulence and shift to a healthy equality.

The difficulties posed by personal relationships which begin as teacher and student should come as no surprise, nor should it be a shock that problems arise when the former student begins demanding a more egalitarian balance of power. Here in the United States we've all been witness to the turmoil as African-Americans demanded equality. Or when women did. It is difficult and uncomfortable for those who have been dominant, in control and authority, to relinquish some of their power, even if intellectually they may believe it's better to do so. Usually the oppressed or less dominant have to struggle hard for their rights. Expecting a free ride to equality is an idealistic fantasy, and highly unrealistic if we understand human psychology and power dynamics.

So what do spiritually interested women really want? The following conclusions come from my own experiences and from conversations with many women friends and students.

First, women seekers want practical, applicable methods that will deepen the spiritual quality of their lives. Being for the most part gregarious, they also want spiritual company along the path.

Many would also prefer a male partner who shares at least some spiritual interest, for the bond between a couple that sets out on spiritual explorations together can be quite fulfilling. In the absence of such a bond—and many women complain that the men in their lives are either baffled or put off by their spiritual interests—women may content themselves with platonic spiritual company. Others will focus their unfulfilled desires on their male spirituality teachers and become personally involved with them. Such relationships are often problematic, as we will see shortly. There are also considerably more interested women students than there are male teachers. This ratio may then cause an additional problem: competition between the women for their teacher's attention.

There is one more key ingredient women spirituality seekers want, whether consciously or not. They want power. On some level, all are seeking the power of increased spiritual awareness, experience, knowledge and personal energy, and all are seeking to enjoy the spiritual power inherent but hidden within themselves. The attraction to power is a natural one. But both male and female spirituality students are often deluded in thinking they can get that power simply by having a close relationship with their teachers. Although this may come as a big disappointment, it doesn't work that way. Even though a few teachers have gathered enough personal power to temporarily elevate the energy level of their students, eventually that energy dissipates until the students learn to gather and maintain personal power for themselves.

Because of our cultural conditioning, many women still don't believe in their right to empowerment in many arenas. So to experience the power they are naturally seeking, they attach themselves to those they perceive as having it—usually men. The same is true in the spiritual world, where women still tend to look for their own power in their male teachers. Not only that, but sometimes they also give away much of the power they *do* have to their teachers, projecting it onto them through fantasies or going out of their way to indulge their teachers' personal whims in order to be close to them.

Although the need for spiritual companionship is what usually catalyzes women's sexual involvements with their male teachers, some feel it is the way they can get closest to their teacher's power. In other spheres this is called "star fucking." The practice is symptomatic of a feeling of powerlessness and lack of self-esteem, although it may appear as an act of great confidence on the surface. When a woman feels unable to arrive at social recognition or power in her own right, she may seek out a man who has already attained those attributes. Perhaps he holds a political office, is a successful businessman, teacher of spirituality, or is in fact a star in the sports or entertainment industry.

Recently, a magazine article came out about "Buckle Bunnies: Women Who Love Cowboys and the Men Who Hate Them for It." Although these women prefer offering their sexual favors to the top rodeo contest cowboys, most will settle for whomever is available after the show. The women follow the contests everywhere, and beyond sex, frequently pay for the bed and board of their personal cowboy of the night. Since only the top few cowboys are able to make a living on the circuit, the buckle bunnies' financial aid may actually support much of the rodeo business. Are they appreciated for their efforts? Only marginally. For the most part they are considered a convenience and a joke, despised by the very men they wine, dine and bed. And yet the women persevere undaunted, apparently content with the glamor of contact with America's macho stars.

Whether with cowboys or spirituality teachers, a woman's sexual addiction to any of these figures is a conscious or unconscious attempt to imbue herself with some of their prestige through her association with them. She is trying to fill the power vacuum in her own life by drawing on the "star's" apparent power. This maneuver doesn't accomplish its goals, but the illusion of its success can be quite compelling as long as she's around the prestigious man. The fact that it doesn't work is illuminated when the star moves on across the horizon and the woman is left once again with herself. Often she promptly begins looking for a new star to whom she can attach her dreams. The cycle is perpetuated unless she becomes aware of the underlying dynamic and turns her energies to acknowledging and developing her own self-worth.

This pattern of sexual addiction to prestigious men has all of the qualities of many other forms of addictions: an experience of internal emptiness and even despair propels the individual to seek relief. Although the problem may have social causes, its core is an internal and spiritual one; and yet, the addict will inevitably search for external and worldly solutions. Drugs, alcohol, food, work, sex and a myriad of other possibilities can each become the domain in which an individual tries to find solace for the soul, forgetting or unaware that the kingdom of heaven is within. Caught in a trap in which the object of addiction provides temporary relief but never truly fills the empty space, the addict turns to the external hoped-for salvation and inevitably comes up empty only to try once again.

For a woman to recognize her own spiritual curiosity and thirst—and then to become sidetracked into pursuing power through the teacher instead of internalizing the teachings and gathering power to her own center—is a trap. That she is trapped so near the real object of her search—spiritual knowledge—is tragic. The teacher who supports this pattern does a great disservice to his role, to the woman student, and finally, to the return of spirit in her life. One could correctly say both teacher and student are responsible for their own actions. But when there is an imbalance of power, the one holding the greater power or authority carries the greater burden for right action. The star should hold to its role and purpose: shining light from within as a guide and example for others to do likewise.

Speaking of stars, let's move down the trail to see if we can penetrate the camouflage around the next shop and catch a few glimpses into . . .

Hunting Supplies and Emergency Rations for the Male Spirituality Teacher

Like their students, male spirituality teachers are also hunting power. And like their students, the ways they do so may be appropriate or inappropriate, constructive or destructive.

One of the places they are most likely to find power as teachers is right where they often stand: in the limelight.

It's relatively easy to look good when standing before an interested and receptive audience. In fact, being center stage often brings out the best in a performer of any kind. However, the glow and special effects may not necessarily emanate from within the individual before us. Both spirituality students and teachers can become confused about the issue of where the power is really coming from when the teacher is center stage.

Here is a "secret" about being in the limelight that I've learned myself as both a performing artist and a spirituality teacher: It's a two-way exchange. Whatever most performers or teachers admit to themselves or others, a great deal of power is generated when a group of people come together. And if those people all focus their attention in one place—their spirituality teacher for example—much of that group power is intensified and projected into the object of their attention.

At first glance it seems our teachers are the ones doing all the giving when they're standing before us speaking or demonstrating spiritual practices. Hopefully the teacher *is* giving something. But the students also are literally empowering that person with massive doses of their own energy. Male and female teachers can get quite addicted to such a source of readily available power. The best prevention or antidote for this potential addiction is for teachers to regularly—and independently of their students!—gather power for themselves. Then when they stand before their students, teachers can brim over with power. Rather than absorbing their students' energies, they'll reflect and return those energies back for the students' own use.

When spirituality teachers start their careers, many maintain a modicum of daily spiritual practices, personal power and vision. But over time they may slowly become addicted to their students' energies and abandon their own spiritual lives. It is so easy to ride on the power and adulation of students that a teacher may feel fine about skipping a day of meditation or taking care of his spirit in some other way. Then a day turns into a week or a month; and the years can fly by as the teacher abandons his own path and practices and becomes a student junkie. Or the minister loses his faith but won't abandon his pulpit. His personal power then disappears and he is increasingly dependent on an audience to feel good. He becomes a master of illusion.

Sometimes this predicament of losing personal power is used as a justification for enticing students into sex—more frequently by male teachers with female students than the reverse. Sex is yet another way to draw on the students' energies, to garner emergency rations.

Here are some frequently used tactics of male teachers who hunt power through sex with female students.

One favorite opener is flattery: "I can see you are a very spiritually powerful/unusual/talented woman."

Next comes one of three typical variations on emotional manipulation:

1. "I really need some of your energy. If you'd have sex with me it would be a spiritual act of service. I'd then be better able to carry on my exhausting professional responsibilities." This version is at least vaguely honest, as may be aspects of the second variation.
2. "I'm so lonely here on the path and you're so special . . ."
3. "Our spiritual/sexual union will be the cosmic yin/yang event of the New Age, and will turn the tides for the future with the blessings of all the higher beings of the universe. And when we've finished, we will go our separate ways with detachment and no future expectations of one another." This one is more in the nature of an impersonal energetic contract, and is most common among teachers of tantric styles of sexuality or some "medicine men."

If the teacher neglects his own practices—in favor of leeching off his students—and is now a burnt-out shell of his former self, he may use a slightly different tactic that is the most dishonest of all. He tells the woman that he is going to bestow mystic knowledge, spiritual enlightenment and power upon her through the act of sex, and that she should view this as her lucky day. Or night, as the case may be. Indeed, her heat-seeking missile of a teacher is now a good candidate for being nominated Energy Vampire of the Year! Ironically, in such situations the woman often has considerably more personal power than the man. She may actually practice some of the spiritual exercises her teacher recommends but has abandoned himself in favor of mooching off student energies. And she may have reaped the benefits of some power—glowing far more brightly than her teacher—but be completely unaware of that reality. And her teacher certainly isn't going to enlighten her on the subject.

Where else might a teacher become off-balance in his search for spiritual power?

Most who have developed a following have done so because they either have charisma, some level of real spiritual knowledge or a combination of both. Whether community-based or travelling around to interested audiences, teachers are constantly interfacing with people who look up to them. In the privacy of their own thoughts, these teachers know they are human beings like their followers, with good and bad habits, strengths and weaknesses alike. But in public life they are placed on a pedestal, whether they like it or not.

This is a difficult image to live up to and still remain impeccable. After a while the temptation to feed on and to take advantage of the lofty image's potentials presents itself to all spiritual teachers, even the most altruistic. A few fight the good fight with their own egos and never act on those temptations. They are the ones who encourage personal development and independence in their followers and maintain a degree of personal humility. But most spiritual teachers falter and weaken to various degrees.

When teachers buy the power of the pedestal image, the purchase includes the belief they are better than their students, even if they didn't feel that way in the beginning of their career. Such teachers often devote more energy to maintaining their own superior image than to furthering student progress. They may verbally exaggerate their level of training and knowledge and their spiritual experiences. Finally, at the extreme, they paint themselves as an indispensable element in their students' lives. Increasingly they demand personal homage be paid: emotionally, materially, spiritually or sometimes sexually. Although at this point such a teacher may see himself as being in control, actually it is a situation of mutual dependency. The teacher is dependent on his followers' adoration and support. In turn, his students are dependent on him and on the false power of being associated with someone they've all agreed is important. This end of the teacher-student continuum is called a cult. And so we continue on our tour to the quicksand regions of . . .

Cult Canyon

Although this is rather strange terrain, when a seeker sets off into the world for spiritual teachings, there is always the chance she may encounter and even become involved with cults and cult leaders. Despite the fact that not all cults are life-threatening, the seeker should still be aware of their potential hazards. Cults and cult leaders have not disappeared from the spiritual landscape in modern times—they just keep changing forms. Seekers are advised to consult the map and to use strong binoculars during the tour to discern possible wolves in sheep's clothing.

Historically, numerous religious cults have developed around mildly to extremely power-abusive individuals. Typically a cult leader gathers followers to foster student dependency and loyalty while demeaning the rest of humanity. This tactic encourages followers to feel special in contrast to everyone else in the ignorant/sinful/unenlightened world. Between many cult leaders and followers there is a core trade-off: "You feed my ego and I'll feed yours." Eventually, whatever real spiritual knowledge might have originally been imparted by the leader increasingly takes a backseat to the ego-stroking contract and all its ramifications. The true light of spirit gradually fades as the false light brightens. Some cult leaders are relatively harmless beyond supporting this mildly obnoxious mutual dependency. Others have gone off the deep end and taken their followers' wealth, freedom and sometimes, their lives. Then the intense lust for the power to control others becomes as dangerous a weapon as it has been in the hands of the notorious political tyrants of human history.

What other details does a seeker need to look for to help her identify cultism?

Most cult leaders strive to control their followers materially and/or sexually through some quasi-religious dogma or belief system. They may also try to increase cult members' malleability by encouraging drug and alcohol abuse. Like Timothy Leary and other drug gurus, they beckon substance-intoxicated followers toward exotic but often spiritually ungrounded terrains, claiming Shangri-la is just around the corner for the chosen ones. Many cult leaders demand that all personal funds and/or possessions be turned over to them, although some insist their followers simply take a vow of poverty without asking for their material resources. Either situation creates a certain dependency on the cult and cult leader.

I was once involved in a relatively harmless cult—one without sexual or substance abuse—although I didn't identify it as a cult at the time. It was lead by an Eastern teacher who never directly asked for money but whose close assistants did—frequently—on his behalf. Ostensibly the money was to take care of the teacher's material needs and travel expenses for him and his large entourage. However, the teacher's lifestyle was quite affluent, something his followers were encouraged to think he more than deserved because of the gifts of enlightenment he bestowed on them and the world. Meanwhile, most of his followers' resources were depleted and they often lived on minimal food in crowded, communal houses to get by.

Within this group there was a taboo against complaining about material circumstances. Devotees were encouraged to believe they were serving a higher being and were privileged to learn his teachings and be part of his following. Both the membership in this "special" group and the quite real benefits of the teacher's meditation practices combined as a potent force. The material hardships intensified followers' mutual dependency as the practicality of pooling resources grew. Nonetheless, in the spiritual domain meditation enabled each of them to be partly independent and powerful. Because of the positive spiritual benefits and the absence of real mistreatment of devotees, the group was a fairly benign cult.

Most Americans are familiar, at least by name, with the phenomena of tent shows, televangelism, faith healing, snake handling and the "holy roller" sects. Each rely on the power of the group, and the leaders manipulate that power. In itself, such manipulation is not negative, for respectable shamans and other spiritual leaders manipulate group power for the spiritual benefit of the members. And sometimes spiritually thirsty members of the cult-like groups have real and beneficial experiences. But often a large percentage are led into unrealistic expectations based on the group high so they will keep padding the pockets and/or egos of the leaders.

In many cults, the leaders control followers' sexual behavior but with some variation in style and degree. Occasionally and most rarely, celibacy is required by all. When the cult leader is male, which is usually the case, sometimes the male followers are required to be celibate and the women, often including their young daughters, become the sole sexual "property" of the cult leader. David Koresh and his followers were a most recent and infamous example of a situation that eventually escalated to such a point. However, even though the women and daughters were more obvious victims of sexual abuse, in truth the men of the community were also abused and dominated by being forced to put up with Koresh's increasing sexual manipulation of their wives and daughters.

Charles Manson and Jim Jones were two well-known cult leaders who also practiced sexual domination in a slightly different way. Although Manson controlled his followers with the help of LSD and Jones did not, both he and Jones insisted that all the women in the cult be sexual with them. In addition, they both orchestrated sexual scenarios among the rest of the cult members, male and female, in various combinations aimed at breaking their followers' psyches and destroying their morals. This practice made their followers increasingly vulnerable to other forms of control. Like many cult leaders, Manson, Jones and Koresh all cited a special connection to God as justification for manipulation, used sex as a tool for humiliation and demanded total devotion from their followers. In different ways, all three groups ultimately became death cults, with Koresh's followers allegedly prepared for suicide but killed by outsiders, Jones's group entering a true suicide pact and Manson's gang spurred into murdering others.

A little further back in this century, Adolph Hitler and his henchmen stunned the world with perhaps the worst "expanded cult" ever. They combined religious fanaticism, sexual mayhem and sadism with abuse of power unto death. Members of the upper political-military echelons frequently indulged in sexual orgies and had access not only to prostitutes but to many other females they desired. Their sadism and perversions were at their worst in the death camps. Hitler demanded total devotion from his followers and was not above using occult methods to back him in his goals. He even imported Tibetan sorcerers to Germany, adding their spiritual energies and efforts to his cause.

This strand to Tibet is intriguing in its connection to other aspects of cultism. Long ago, in the formative years of Tibetan Buddhism, one of its male leaders created and sustained a particular sect through a form of sexual domination. Using an aspect of tantra—a spiritual/sexual discipline—this man reputedly had sexual intercourse with 5,000 female monks as the primary spiritual initiation into his sect. The initiation was supposedly a form of *darshan*—transference of energy from the master to the disciple. Many Eastern gurus traditionally use a peacock feather as the instrument of energy transference, simply touching it to the top of their devotees' heads. But this Tibetan leader apparently did away with the feather and used sexual prowess in his personal darshan campaign. The echo of a few men having access to many women in Hitler's Germany—with Tibetan occultists hidden behind the scenes—is an eerie one indeed.

Tantric Buddhism, developed and practiced most heavily in Tibet, is based on the knowledge of sexual energy flows through the body, and has as its purported goal the channeling and directing of these energies for the purpose of spiritual enlightenment. While some of the tantric practices can be done alone—including by celibate monks and nuns—others are specifically designed for male/female sexual union and aim at the cosmic merging of yin and yang principles. Unfortunately, from the royal Mongolian court of the 1300s, through secret circles of European thrill seekers in the late 1800s to early 1900s, to modern day "experimental" sexuality courses and cults, tantra is frequently misused as an excuse for sexual orgies rather than as a serious personal discipline.

Recently I learned how tantric practices have been harmful to many women in Southeast Asia. Several months ago I participated in a women's studies conference. One of the seminars I attended was led by a petite and articulate woman from Thailand who spoke about the growing epidemic of prostitution in her country and throughout Southeast Asia. Although the situation is a complex net of economic, sexist and social issues—created to a large extent by the earlier presence of the United

States military and currently backed by the tourist trade—the speaker mentioned at one point that it had a certain historical precedent rooted in the tantric Buddhist practices of the priesthood. For centuries, young Thai village girls have traditionally been delivered on request to aging monks for the purpose of infusing them with youthful vigor. The modus operandi: sex. This apparently was an accepted practice and was probably proclaimed an honorable and holy duty for the young women. As tantric Buddhism is reputedly an extremely powerful discipline, one might wonder why these venerable monks with decades of spiritual discipline behind them need the sexual energy of young girls—particularly at what should be the culmination of an enlightened lifetime of meditations. There are also tales that other Tibetan tantric practices—shrouded in secrecy—exist where not-so-old monks also use young women or skillful prostitutes in sexual rituals.

The Thai seminar leader drew a parallel between parents allowing their daughters to be whisked away by monks for sexual purposes and city men coming to poor country families with promises of great wealth in exchange for their daughters' "brief" prostitution career in the city. In truth, some money does filter back to these impoverished families. But the "brief" stay is usually extended as the daughters are entrapped in a world of drug addiction, disease and abusive men. Sometimes they are also caught in a flow of traffic that streams out of their country—shipped to foreign ports as exotics in the international prostitution market.

I asked the speaker why, since Buddhism was so strong in Thailand, the monks weren't more actively protesting the situation. She commented wryly that many of the prostitutes, trapped in their profession but believing it was their personal bad karma, sent portions of their earnings to the monasteries as a counterbalance of good karma. Apparently many improvements in old monasteries, together with the building of new monasteries, have prostitution monies as their foundation. And so monastic silence on the issue is golden.

As with cults, once again we see the far-reaching effects—including economic ones—of the quasi-religious sexual manipulation of women. The "woman-as-holy-sexual-vessel" routine is neither holy nor healthy. And it has damaging effects on women's spiritual will and internal sense of value. If you encounter a "spirituality teacher" who suggests that the sexual "priestess" role is your highest calling, you should stare long and hard at him from a safe distance. Are there wolfish fangs glinting beneath his fluffy snow white exterior?

Now say a mantra and look down the road. We are fast approaching . . .

The East/West Frontier

Many of us benefit from contact with Eastern spiritual practices. Hindu and Buddhist meditations, yoga and martial arts classes, tai chi, ayurvedic medicine, Taoist practices and Reiki healing have all entered the Western health and spirituality marketplace. Great saints from the East such as Ramakrishna, Krishnamurti and Sai Baba have had a positive spiritual impact on the West in this century, as have a host of other gurus and spiritual leaders.

Many women include one or more Eastern practices as a foundation of their spiritual lives. Some shave their heads and become serious initiates of various Buddhist sects, some join Hindu ashrams, and a few have taken up martial arts or spent time with teachers in India.

Although the majority of Eastern teachers who settled in the

West have been men, women have found their typically gentle, nurturing manner a refreshing contrast to the more macho personas of many Western authority figures.

However, there have been certain elements of cultism in some of the gurus on the East/West Frontier. A few of the more famous and infamous have encouraged their followers to take vows of poverty to enhance spiritual progress. Without directly asking themselves—as in the personal example I gave earlier in the tour—the word often goes out through a guru's disciples that the burden of devotees' money and possessions are best placed at the master's feet. Then devotees never again have to be distracted from their spiritual quest. Of course, these enlightened teachers have no spiritual difficulties in handling the millions of dollars that come their way.

As for cultish, abusive sexual practices among gurus from the East, I have not heard of anything like the methods of Koresh, Manson, et al. Some gurus enjoin their devotees to chastity as a faster path to the light. Others say that both chaste and married people have equal opportunities for enlightenment if they are consistent in their disciplines and prayers.

Women are probably safer sexually with most Eastern spiritual leaders than with many of their Western counterparts. But men and women followers alike might want to be circumspect with their checkbooks. Although the spiritual/cultural exchange is largely a positive one, it seems that when East meets West, the lure of fame and fortune sometimes shakes the gurus' moral girders.

As we cross the Frontier, those peaks you see ahead are not the Himalayas, patient seekers. If you'll consult your map, you'll note they are the famous . . .

Mea Culpa Mountains

Cults and foreign spiritual emissaries aside, we have our own share of challenges with abuse of power coming from mainstream religious leaders. Christian evangelists Jimmy Swaggert and Jimmy Bakker were both disgraced through their practices of relieving the vulnerable elderly of their money, in addition to Swaggert's sexual peccadillos with prostitutes and Bakker's with a church secretary.

The Catholic Church spends hundreds of millions of dollars dealing with priestly misconduct that includes illicit sexual activities and child molestation. This is ironic indeed, since the Church always claimed that celibate male priests are more superior vessels for the holy work of God than are nuns or married men and women. The Church appears long overdue in revising its position. A happy, moral person dedicated to humanity and spiritual celebration—whatever his/her gender or marital status—would surely better serve the Church and God than those whose sexual frustrations interfere with their personal well-being and ethics and lead them into various abuses.

And there are many fine Christian clergymen and women exhorting their congregations toward strong spiritual and social actions alike. But while some staunch Christians warn of the spiritual dangers of other paths outside their domain, their leaders and followers are no more exempt from potential misuse of power than people of other religions.

As the media has given the entire mountain range fairly extensive coverage, tour participants are adequately informed and we can now move quickly on to the steamy regions of . . .

The New Age Jungle

The mid-1960s marked the beginning of a new era in the West, one that for many included radical changes in dress and hairstyle, taste in music, sexual behavior, a return to more "natural" life-styles and an awakening interest in various forms of healing and spirituality. Thirty years later, the interest in alternative healing and spiritual paths continues to grow. New Age book sections, bookstores and workshops proliferate decade by decade. A great deal of positive change and useful information was generated and made available to the public as a result of this New Age renaissance. But, as in all new movements, there are challenges as well. Even though the overall "spirit" of the New Age is toward personal empowerment, development and decreased authoritarianism, the existence of New Age teachers and leaders still presents a potential danger to students: giving their power away to teachers and letting teachers take advantage of that power.

More and more people are seeking spiritual answers and experiences outside the Judeo-Christian traditions. Such seekers interface with New Age teachers, shamans and gurus from many races and cultures. Often students are dazzled by the exotic plumage of these teachers and tend to make excuses for—and even encourage or support—behaviors they wouldn't tolerate in more "normal" circumstances. Women may be pressured or seduced into sex with teachers they barely know, enticed by the glamor or prestige of the situation. New Age spirituality contains great potential. But while drinking in its exciting possibilities, teachers and students alike can become intoxicated and lose their grip on balanced uses of power.

New Age teachers may or may not assume their particular roles with the goal of increased sexual liaisons with women. But day in and day out they are often surrounded by a variety of women looking up to them, hanging on to every word, seeking guidance and feeling flattered by any kind of special attention. Often, it's both too tempting and too easy for the teacher to turn this "special attention" into sex.

Many New Age teachers travel widely. Their professional and social behaviors are therefore outside the sometimes more restraining eye of a knowing community. Such travellers can either serve or take advantage of a larger population. Those who are truly dedicated to teaching and serving merit respect. But being on the road a great deal of the time is a difficult, challenging life.

Ironically, loneliness is one of the difficulties of such a lifestyle. New Age teachers may regularly be surrounded with students as they travel from place to place, but unless they return frequently to the same communities, they are always with strangers. Weeks or months without social intimacy can take a toll on a teacher's emotions. His need and search for intimacy may end up in bed, among the tangled sheets of imbalanced power, with the naive or needy women students who seem to be so plentiful.

When teachers abuse their position for sexual seduction, it is with at least some degree of consciousness. However, the women who end up entangled in a teacher's web are often less conscious of the effect of supporting his manipulations. These women are either naive or allowing their personal needs to supersede caution and wisdom. As a result, they contribute to the increasingly out-of-balance New Age teacher ego epidemic, and sometimes to personal problems of their own.

One of the odd exceptions in this teacher-student pattern is found in "Dana," a female teacher. Dana draws students with her promises to reveal allegedly ancient and secret knowledge which she is the sole carrier of in these modern times. At one point in her career she seduced a male student several decades her junior and they became lovers for several years. He finally ended the relationship. For some months after doing so he was a nervous wreck. He claimed Dana was jealous and using witchcraft on him to make his life miserable and trying to bind him to her in hopes he would return. According to his story, he then became wildly promiscuous for some time and eventually felt he'd broken free of her. This unusual example illustrates that women spirituality teachers are not exempt from temptations to misuse their positions.

Preparing for the Journey

Being of a practical bent, I generally put together a checklist of things I might need before I go travelling. In addition to the map I've just given the reader, I also offer a two-part "Checklist of Awareness" to consult for a spiritual journey. The first part suggests what to observe in teachers. Although I use the masculine gender to refer to them, a great deal of that list applies to either gender. The second part encourages self-awareness and self-empowerment in the student seeker. Although some elements are specifically for women, much will also be useful for male students who navigate the spirituality landscape.

Checklist of Awareness

Your Teacher

Power

- Does he encourage students to think for themselves, to challenge the information he presents? Or does he demand unqualified acceptance of everything he says?
- Does he promote spiritual explorations beyond his own teachings? Or does he elevate himself as an ultimate spiritual authority and claim he has the only valid teachings and spiritual answers?
- Does he give students knowledge that will help them empower themselves and take independent, responsible spiritual actions? Or does he encourage student dependency on him as a source of their power?

- Are his actions basically in harmony with his teachings? Or is he only talking the good talk and encouraging students to do as he says, not as he does?
- Does he state his goals and do they encourage positive, empowering and egalitarian actions for humans? Or are they elitist, authoritarian, racist or sexist?
- If he is of a different culture or race than most of his students, does he use this to enhance awareness and understanding between peoples? Or does he elevate his culture or race and subtly bully or put down those students who are not of his culture or race?
- Does he encourage students to take charge of their own lives? Or does he encourage them to drink alcohol and take drugs so he can more easily manipulate or control them?

Money

- Does he charge reasonable teaching fees by which he can support himself? Or does he directly or indirectly request that all—or a large share—of his students' financial/material resources be turned over to him in the name of spiritual service?
- If he is not comfortable setting a fee for teaching, does he tell students in a straightforward manner that he is nonetheless dependent on their financial donations? Or does he tell them he's too "pure" to charge teaching fees while he moves into their homes and lets them know he needs new clothes, a car, a teaching center, a "loan," etc.?

Sex

- Does he pressure his students to "push their boundaries" and engage in sexual activities—with or without his direct participation—under the guise that sexual "freedom" equals spiritual freedom or enlightenment?

- Does he claim that sex with him will heal or empower students?
- Does he sexually seduce students with flattery?
- Does he manipulate students into sex with promises of revealing special teachings?
- Does he claim he has a very high level of sexual energy and that students would be doing him and themselves a favor if they'd have sex with him?
- Is he married—but assuring students his wife understands the loneliness of teaching and travelling?
- Does he have a reputation as a womanizer or is he obviously trying to start his own "harem"?
- Does he manipulate students into sex with a "poor me" routine?

Yourself as Student

- Do you feel you are your teacher's equal as a human being— even though he may have some knowledge you don't—or do you place him on a pedestal?
- Do you turn a blind eye to behaviors in your teacher that you are generally uncomfortable with? Or do you apply the same psychological and moral standards to him as you would to anyone?
- Do you generally trust your instincts about people but ignore them when it comes to your spirituality teachers?
- Are you interested in applying the spirituality teachings you're learning from your teacher so you can further empower yourself? Or are you looking for secondhand "power-by-association"?
- Are you secure in your own social world? Or are you hoping

a "special" relationship to your teacher will elevate your status in the eyes of your peers?

- Are you comfortable being responsible for your own life and actions? Or are you looking for an authority figure to tell you what to do?
- Are you comfortable having money to use for your pleasure, needs and the needs of others? Or do you feel money is really the root of evil and are vulnerable to requests for all of it from your "enlightened" teacher?
- Are you secretly envious of your teacher's wife/significant other? Are you looking to "one up" her through an intimate relationship with her mate, your teacher?
- Do you tend to idealize and give your power away to people with secular status roles—media stars, doctors, politicians—and to carry this pattern over to those with exotic spiritual roles such as shamans, medicine men and psychics?
- Do you think teachers of Native American, Australian, African or Eastern cultures are more spiritually pure or elevated than Western teachers?

Clarity about a teacher's attitudes, beliefs, motives, goals and behaviors as well as your own is the goal of this checklist exercise. It is part of the journey of awareness and a foundation for more conscious spiritual actions between you and your teacher.

Teachers of spirituality and religious leaders best serve themselves and their followers through continuing to take care of their own spiritual growth and development. Meditation, yoga, power-gathering and vision questing all reduce tendencies toward exhaustion, depletion and reliance on students as a source of energy. And teachers who practice what they preach set a good example for their students by glowing with power from within.

The same application of effort holds true for students. Rather than relying on the charisma and spiritual power of the teacher as a substitute for personal effort, practicing the spiritual methodologies offered is a much more enduring fulfillment. For the woman student, doing so helps create a balance of power that makes her less susceptible to teacher manipulations and less drawn to "star-fucking" as a mode of feeling spiritually valuable. Finally, the more spiritually developed a woman becomes, the more astute she will be discerning the real lack or level of power in any teachers she encounters on the path. She will probably find that not everyone who wears mystical robes and waves a wand around is a true magician or wizard!

Despite the problems and challenges to women students, what is most positive in the current panoply of spirituality workshops and teachers is that real spiritual knowledge and technologies are more available. Women can use them without being burned at the stake as witches. Whether or not teachers' ethics are shaky, students can still use the learning opportunity to hunt power and knowledge and apply both in positive spiritual actions. Women are quite capable of rejecting their male teachers' poor habits while still extracting some good out of their teachings. If students continue firmly supporting that which is good in their teachers and not supporting the misuse of power, they will encourage more impeccability in their teachers and draw out the best they have to offer. And perhaps fakes and flakes will disappear from the spirituality landscape.

Not only is there great learning potential for women students now and on the expanding horizon, but women are also venturing more into roles of spiritual leadership. As we move toward a more egalitarian society, women will face the same joys, temptations and responsibilities that men have experienced. And women will most likely make their share of mistakes in the process. Every woman who chooses to act as a spiritual teacher or leader will have the opportunity to face both the light of spirit and its twin shadows—the seduction of power and the power of seduction—as she too dances with power's bright flame.

10

The Invasion of the Body Snatchers and Will It Be Good for Us Too?

The village idiot stands on the land, eyes turned beseechingly toward the sky. "Save me!" he whimpers pathetically, hoping angelic beings will descend in response to his pleas. "I'm starving!" Off to one side his oxen bellow, stamping their hooves impatiently and looking at the nearby plough rusting useless on the ground. The village idiot's fallow field stretches all around him, barren despite the warm summer sun and earlier spring rains. At his feet lay full sacks of wheat, rye and barley grain, corn and squash seed: the unopened, unplanted manna from heaven that could feed him for years. Ignoring it, he starves, he begs, he complains.

One of this book's main purposes is to counteract our human tendency to wait for outside forces to bring salvation. As an alternative to that passive approach, I've offered empowering options for spiritual actions, actions individuals can take on their own behalf and then on behalf of the global community. I've described nonhuman sources of power and methods for interacting with them, but I've also encouraged awareness of our own inherent spiritual power and equipment.

As we approach the prophecy-laden millennium, let us consider meeting it from a place of power. If we don't, the future may continue to feel like an overwhelming monster that some supernatural force must save us from. We have embraced a disempowering perspective for too long. It is time we put to rest the viewpoint that externalizes all real power; time to acknowledge our own spiritual essence and apply our resourcefulness to help ourselves; time to give birth to a cycle of faith in action.

But in order to give birth to a new cycle, we must acknowledge our proclivity to externalize power, to abdicate spiritual development and salvation to powers outside ourselves. Waiting for supernatural forces to save us is both an ancient and a contemporary cherished theme. Our myths and beliefs are generously strewn with references to coming interventions of God or avatars, messiahs and other powerful and benevolent beings who have the potential to save us from ourselves—or lift us out of our more mundane pursuits. As the millennium approaches, Muslims await the Reformer, Jews await some other messiah than Jesus, Christians hope Christ will return despite the fact he was treated rather badly last time around, Buddhists anticipate Maitreya the returning Buddha, and Hopi look for the True White Brother.

Major improvements like world peace are expected as the result of messianic and supernatural interventions. Some Christians believe the dead will rise from the earth and the spirits of the living will be snatched out of their bodies to meet with the spirits of the airborn dead in the Rapture. Many of those who await God's direct intervention entertain the strange fantasy that Creator will come as a mass murderer to destroy anyone whose race or religion the fantasizers personally dislike. Or they believe that God will descend like a cosmic atom bomb to destroy this whole beautiful planet and then recreate and repopulate it again immediately—but only with people, plants and animals who all get along perfectly with one another.

What about the possibility that Creator already made a perfect planet for us to enjoy and live in peacefully? And those awaiting a messiah might look to the past to see what really happened when enlightened beings such as the Buddha and Christ *did* bless this earth. Life for their devotees was a spiritual blessing. It was also a difficult challenge that demanded hard work and sacrifices and confronted self-importance and ego. The two great leaders weren't body snatchers who invaded, took over, possessed everyone and solved all their problems. No; Buddha and Christ offered the spiritual tools for us to save ourselves, and they demonstrated how to use them. Despite our persistent tendency to hope such beings would do our work for us, they instead left our salvation to us.

Our messiahs have been quite human. They had bodies, ate, were faced with the vast range of human problems, worked hard for spiritual knowledge and illumination, and died. They may have urged us to join them in their divine vision of human spiritual potentials, but they also encouraged us to work on our own worldly problems. Despite their humanness, after their deaths we dressed them up by giving them strange births and powers they never had. We placed them on impossible pedestals, dehumanizing them and disempowering ourselves in the process. We made salvation their business, not our own. And within the religions that followed our great visionaries, the religious officials encouraged this mythification of the few and the disempowerment of the many. Why? Because such strategies increased their own self-importance as holy intermediaries, gave them control over others and maintained structures of bureaucracy—jobs—that would make any true messiah weep to hear what was being done in his or her name.

Despite both the value of messiahs and the confusion created in their absence, the choice to save ourselves is still available to us every moment and day of our lives. In fact, the ability to make choices is a sacred gift and one to be utilized in all spheres, spiritual and secular. We *can* choose to be good to ourselves and others.

To care for ourselves, to seek knowledge and to take responsibility for the choices we make are signs of maturity. While we do not expect an infant to feed and dress herself, a ten-year old who cannot do so has a serious problem. And though we don't expect a normal ten-year old to drive a car, we do expect an adult to do so, when she has received the necessary training and license. Developmentally, the human race hasn't quite reached worldly and spiritual maturity. In many ways we still long for a divine Mother or Father to "do it for us" and to clean up the messes we make.

When I counsel clients, I let them know early on that despite their wishes to the contrary, I can't cure their problems. I can offer psychological tools and an environment in which they can better heal themselves, and I can accompany them on the healing journey. I also tell them that if they really wish to make progress, most of their work will take place between sessions, not just when they're in the office with me. And when I teach spirituality workshops, I'm fairly blunt about the fact that I offer information and techniques conducive to spiritual growth and enlightenment, but I can't do the work for the participants. The collective group energy and intense spiritual focus I encourage effects a temporary high while we're together. But simply being present in such a climate does not evoke a magic that permanently transforms everyone. To maintain and then increase spiritual awareness, personal power and development, the participants need to apply the tools and knowledge they've been given.

Sometimes this comes as a rude shock. We still have a strong belief in the quick fix, the instant high we can easily shop for and buy. We don't think we should have to work for spiritual enlightenment. If our fantasy savior is not available to raise our consciousness for us, then we think enlightenment should be available—preferably for free but we'll spend a few dollars if we must—at the spiritual supermarket of our choice. The result of this attitude is that many people with an interest in nonordinary experiences take "consciousness expanding" substances and/or go to spirituality workshops. If they exercise no sustaining spiritual practices between these events, their experiences eventually wane. And when this happens, they simply go for the next fix.

Why don't we fathom that spiritual development takes time and effort? We don't emerge from our mothers' wombs fully grown on any level—mentally, emotionally, physically or spiritually. We are born with the basic equipment: a brain, feelings, a body and spiritual will. When each of these areas receives proper nourishment, each aspect of our being develops and flourishes. Our spiritual nature is the same as our other aspects—it needs nourishment, exercise and stimulation. If we take care of our spirit and give it these things, our spirit too will thrive.

Some of our attitudinal problems stem from the approach of our churches. We often receive the message that if we just show up at church every week, we have a free ticket to salvation. If we're Catholic, we must also regularly go to confession. Catholics may very well feel relieved after going to confession and receiving the priest's absolution. And Christians generally may feel safe and virtuous through weekly church attendance. But if they revert to actions that weaken or oppress themselves or others in between times, their actions obliterate any spiritual upliftment church attendance provides. The clergy, despite whatever status and authority we have given them—and they have taken—cannot imbue our lives with moment-to-moment high spiritual quality. Jesus's message—to live a life of love toward oneself and others, to seek the inner kingdom of heaven and to do even greater works than he—was a pretty obvious one for attaining spiritual maturity. But this message has been largely ignored and replaced with going to church and waiting for him to physically come back again and take over. It's like a spectator sport. We expect Jesus to return one day—not only to play but to be the whole game himself! We watch from a great distance, as if we were before a television with our remote control, flipping from channel to channel so we won't miss any action elsewhere while waiting for the big game. Meanwhile, precious moments tick by in which we could all try to nourish, enjoy and share the spiritual light within us.

Jesus's suggestion to do great works ourselves was excellent advice. Rather than hoping he or some other messiah will come clean up our messes, why not use our God-given abilities to do so ourselves? We are capable of arriving at world peace through our own actions, of combatting the darkness of endless wars by first seeing clearly who or what is really preventing peace and abundance for all. We are also quite capable of cleaning up the environment, protecting future resources, stopping erosion and desertification, and of fighting racism, sexism and other forms of oppression and violence. Some people hold cherished but unrealistic fantasies of immortality or of living only on air in a world with no mosquitos or other annoying elements. Why not replace those fantasies with actions to replenish the earth's depleted resources, so we may enjoy her beauty and live here in peace with our fellow humans? Why not take the spiritual action to grapple with our own morality, our own potentials for good and evil, instead of hoping God or a messiah will fight and permanently defeat the Devil? If we all held the vision that we are each a real part—a cell or hand or heart—of the second coming of Christ, then pooling our collective light and abilities would allow us to actually manifest the prophecies of heaven on earth.

In fact there are efforts being made in this direction. Despite various levels of individual, industrial or political attempts to sabotage global progress, we have a growing "green" movement of ecological awareness and action, a demolished Berlin Wall and Cold War, Middle East peace negotiations, a black president of South Africa and increasing numbers of women taking positions of secular and spiritual authority. Jesus might deem these actions great—if not greater—works than his.

It is uniquely satisfying to achieve something through our own efforts. Deep down, we all know this, even if at times we wish for a divine housecleaner to clean up after us, a cosmic therapist to make us automatically love ourselves or a messiah to drive all evil from the world and suffuse us with instant spiritual enlightenment. The sense of accomplishment derived from applying skills we've developed makes us feel solid, whole, resourceful and even ecstatic. We feel good about ourselves, and no one can give us that feeling nor take it away from us.

SELF-EMPOWERMENT EXERCISE—STAR CHART

Try this exercise of self-empowerment. Its purpose is to help you consolidate the power of your past accomplishments by listing and appreciating them, and to encourage you in future efforts.

To make this exercise even more fun, buy yourself a supply of shiny stick-on stars, the kind grade school teachers place on grade "A" tests or papers. Reserve a large, separate sheet of paper for these stars. Place one on the sheet for every accomplishment you recall. You can even make a design out of your stars. Every time you look at those stars, take a few deep breaths and fill your belly with the light and power they reflect, the power of your efforts and accomplishments.

Get a notebook and pen. At the top of the first page, write "Mental Accomplishments." Then make a list of your intellectual achievements to date. These may include mastering your native language, your education, original ideas you've had, on-the-job skills you have learned—in or out of the home, productive decisions you've made, your ability to teach your children necessary skills and anything else that is appropriate. This list does not need to be completed in one sitting. In fact, in this category as well as the following ones, you may find yourself recalling other accomplishments for days or weeks after you begin the process. Simply add them to your list as you do. Each time you recall a mental achievement for your list, spend a little time remembering the sense of satisfaction it gave you. If you did not allow yourself this sense at the time, give it to yourself as a gift in the present.

Next, review the emotional category. Write "Emotional Accomplishments" at the top of a new page. Reflect on your past efforts to mature emotionally or to enlist your heart and feelings in the service of someone else. Recall the times you've offered love and compassion to yourself or another person, when you've confronted an inner fear and acted wisely despite it, when you finally saw a destructive addiction or emotional pattern within yourself and stopped it, when you realized you could choose if, how and when to express a feeling, when you took responsibility for your own emotional well-being and stopped blaming your parents for all your problems. This list will probably also be an ongoing one.

At the top of the next blank page write "Physical Accomplishments." This list includes utilitarian objects you have made, technical skills for making or repairing things, outdoor accomplishments such as chopping wood, building fires, tracking, farming or gardening and camping know-how. Finally there is the area of physical body accomplishments. Included are crawling, walking, running, learning dance, sports and body-building skills, hiking, and doing health-related activities such as cleansing fasts, conquering physical addictions and learning and applying hands-on healing skills.

Write "Spiritual Accomplishments" as the heading for the fourth area. List any spiritual disciplines you have learned and practiced, any helpful spiritual inspiration, teaching or counseling you have given to others, spiritual rituals you have helped create and spiritual knowledge you have grasped either from others' teachings or on your own. Because of the link between creativity and spirit, you can also include any artistic skills you have learned and artistic creations of any sort with which you have been involved. The latter can include performance arts as well as physical creations such as paintings, sculptures, fashion or architectural designs and creative literary works.

Each time you look over your list and your resultant "Star Chart," try remembering the good feelings you had as a result of your accomplishments. Despite any struggles along the way, allow yourself to recall—or create now if you didn't allow it in the past—the sense of satisfaction you had from learning and doing something to the best of your ability. Bring those good feelings back to awareness when you need the reminder for encouragement in new endeavors or when fantasies of having others do everything for you dominates your daydreams! Holding your power in this way buoys your confidence in future spiritual actions and helps you build on your spiritual strengths. Since our society—including our churches—doesn't provide much support in either of these directions, we'd better give it to ourselves.

Our efforts and accomplishments can reward us with at least as much satisfaction in the spiritual domain as in other areas of life. This is not to say that working at something precludes delighting in gifts or help from others. Those elements that come to us without effort on our part can be a welcome balance to hard work. However, while fantasies of total salvation have their appeal, an exclusive diet of gifts and outside help does not encourage us to grow strong and healthy. Instead, it eventually weakens and disempowers us.

I certainly welcome and enjoy gifts of Spirit—what some call grace—when they come to me. But my own experience is that I generally receive more of those gifts when I avail myself of them through my spiritual efforts and practices. My part is to create the proper climate in which those blessings may then surprise me. I've raised plants from the stage of seeds to full fruition. I can't make them produce flowers. What I can do is tend them and give them what they need. If conditions are right, my efforts are rewarded with the gift of a rose or gardenia.

My various art projects are the same. I don't expect a song or poem or book to spring full grown onto paper without first sitting down with pen or computer, writing out ideas, thinking about them and reworking them. However, once I put myself into the process and evoke a creative climate, I often receive gifts of inspiration as precious to me as the many other blessings in my life. And when it comes to Spirit, I use the tools and knowledge I've shared in this book to create a spiritual greenhouse. Within its nourishing climate, not only does my spirit thrive but I also receive an abundance of gifts.

Mostly I enjoy this balance of effort and grace. If I'm fatigued, if I feel temporarily weak and overwhelmed by life's secular and spiritual challenges, then I tend to indulge more in salvation fantasies and my prayers resemble desperate bleats for a Supermom/dad to take care of everything. But if I rest, gather power, recover—and maybe find some new resources for support and encouragement—then I arrive at a very different space. I'm back on life's dance floor stretching, flexing my muscles, leaping, tumbling, breathing hard, breaking a sweat and immensely enjoying my efforts and increasing sense of mastery. Although I may seek out enjoyable dance partners, I'm certainly not looking for a body snatcher to occupy and take over my being. By then I'm having too great a time possessing my own body.

Myths, Images and Realities of Possession

In the immense anthology of human experiences, there are many tales of possession by both human and supernatural forces. Control and loss of control, domination and surrender, strength and weakness are all recurrent themes within the individual psyche and the human race as a whole. Before addressing the near-endless speculations about possession by supernatural forces, let us first consider those of a more secular nature: the undeniable realities of human-to-human domination.

I cannot imagine the possibility of any person in history going through life without dealing on some level with this issue of domination. We've all had parents or parent substitutes. Even if their dictatorship was benevolent, inevitably at various points in raising us their power and authority overrode our own desires—either for our own good or because of a parental bias or mood of the moment. I clearly recall many of my youthful struggles for independence from my parents' control, struggles that escalated throughout adolescence and into early adulthood. As I gained confidence in my own abilities—including being able to take responsibility for and learn from my mistakes—the balance of power slowly shifted. Finally I dropped most of my fears and resentments of my parents' prior authority—right along with the early hopes they could make my life perfect. By then I'd both made a fair share of mistakes and had a number of accomplishments on various fronts. My appreciation and love for my parents grew fuller, as did a much more egalitarian relationship between us.

As a therapist I do my best to help others resolve similar issues with their parents and move along to increased autonomy and maturity. I try to help heal the results of the abnormal: the wounds from domination gone over the edge in the forms of parental abuse, rape and street violence. And as a citizen of the world, I'm familiar with our shared history, one that includes nasty characters who have exerted and abused their power over others. Some of them are well known, and include the infamous Roman Caligula, King Henry VIII, Hitler, Stalin and, more recently, Sadam Hussein. What each of these men had in common was substantial secular power and authority and the ability to enlist the support of others. And there have been many others whose names are less known but whose titles describe their style of control: political dictators, slave owners, soldiers of the Inquisition, sacrificial priests, pimps, murderers, thieves, rapists, child molesters, violent gang members and other characters in the drama of human-over-human domination.

In order that the negativity of history not endlessly repeat itself, we need to learn from it and plan our future actions on the basis of the knowledge and understanding of power dynamics. I believe that fostering real but balanced power is, perhaps ironically, one of the greatest deterrents to the development of violent and tyrannical people. In an effort to understand the dynamics of power abuse, I've searched through my own personal history for the times I've felt the angriest and most capable of violence or desirous of imposing my will on someone else. Inevitably I found that I experienced those intense emotions when I was in situations where I felt helpless, weak or at a disadvantage. In contrast, I've noticed when I'm filled with self-confidence and self-respect, I enjoy supporting those same feelings in others, have less desire to control people and am much more flexible and compassionate in my interactions. Again, nurturing this kind of balanced power within ourselves and others seems to be a key to inner and outer peace and ending our history of power abuses.

DE-ESCALATING DOMINATION

An exercise I once did myself may prove useful for the reader as well. Spend some time reviewing your personal history for experiences of great anger, for the desire to inflict violence on another—whether you acted on it or not—and for the desire to dominate another. Make a list of these moments.

Then look at each one and try recalling other subjective states that may have been below the surface of the anger and the desire to control. Are there any themes in common? Did you feel weak, helpless, at a disadvantage or out of control yourself at those times?

After you've made your list and looked for underlying themes, use the power of knowledge you've amassed from the process. Use it to understand yourself and others. Use this knowledge to sensitize yourself to future situations in which you or others may feel powerless to some degree, so that you can explore means for empowerment *before* the situation escalates to the point of unnecessary anger, violence or domination.

When individuals or groups feel oppressed and abused by others, they in turn perpetuate the cycle of oppression and abuse. This is true whether it is women oppressed by men, one race or religion by another or children by parents. If we can't fight off our oppressors, we either turn our anger and violence toward ourselves or toward vulnerable others. Suicide, child abuse and riots are frequently expressions of anger which originate in feelings of helplessness. Understanding this does not excuse the violence. However, our understanding does clarify the dynamics so we have tools to prevent future violence. Violence and oppression are forms of possession. They exemplify the imposition of one force over another. The free will of the oppressed is imprisoned, its choices restricted by the will of the oppressor.

If we are healthy when we are young, we are voracious megalomaniacs, desirous of bending the entire universe to our will. If we grow up healthy, we learn to respect the "will to power" of others and take our place in a shared universe. In order for the human race to mature into a new phase which is more cooperative and less tyrannized, every person must have access to knowledge and skills that foster self-empowerment, self-respect and personal responsibility.

And what about the myths and realities of spiritual possession in our human anthology or the longing to be taken over by divine forces? They go hand in hand with the tales of human domination.

Earlier in this book I mentioned various cultural traditions in which spiritual forces are called upon to temporarily inhabit or "possess" human beings. I briefly described the dynamics of certain African-based ceremonies in which saints, gods and goddesses are invited into the dance circle to choose appropriate human vessels through which they can express themselves. Usually these people have gone through years of spiritual effort, initiations and training in order to be strong and clear enough to be vessels of spirit. Finally, when both spirits and humans are willing and able, possession takes place in a given ceremony. But only temporarily! Clear spiritual parameters are agreed upon in advance by the priestesses and the spirits, and when the dance is done, the inhabiting spirits know they must "vacate the premises" until the next ceremony. The human participants reclaim their own bodies and rightly so.

Possession is not meant to be a permanent state. It may be enjoyable and productive on a short-term basis, if the occupying forces are benevolent. But our minds, emotions, bodies and spirits are already divine gifts. It makes no sense to permanently abandon them to some other force. What does make sense is to bring ourselves closer to the Divine within our own beings.

Whether productive or not, beliefs, fascination and imagery around possession persist, including possession by negative forces. Many cultures developed elaborate systems of protection against vampires, werewolves, evil spirits and the effects of witchcraft. Images of demons and their dark master Satan are scattered liberally throughout Christian theology, right up to contemporary sermons. They are often counterbalanced with beliefs in and prayers for large-scale Divine interventions by God, the Holy Spirit and the second coming of Christ. Movies like *The Exorcist* contain images that play on fears of dark possession and anxieties about whether evil is stronger than good. Even a 1994 episode in the television soap, "Days of Our Lives," portrayed a modern woman in Salem—attacked by evil forces that caused her to float in the air and that moved her furniture dangerously about—and a hospitalized priest who was trying to save her. And although hard-core Christians may deride some New Age beliefs and vice versa, both are preoccupied with possession issues.

There are several predominant strands of possession images, myths and realities in New Age circles. Channeling is an increasingly popular one. The human channeler is a person who temporarily either consciously moves or is moved aside by an outside force wishing to communicate through the channeler. That force then speaks through the channeler's mouth in a different voice, or transmits its message via a process called automatic writing. Some channelers only channel a single entity, while others play host to many. The identity of the entities range from the disincarnate spirits of former humans to beings from other dimensions, all of whom allegedly wish to serve the living with helpful advice and guidance.

Over the past decade, channelers have become numerous and in vogue. Some even have regular columns in some of the more offbeat New Age magazines, written under science fiction-like pseudonyms and in the "voice" of their entities. Few New Age channelers seem to go through any training—unlike the spirit possession priestesses mentioned earlier. A few seem accurate and authentic in what they channel, as was the late and famous Edgar Cayce. Training for channeling may not always be a prerequisite for channelers, but trained spiritual awareness might help them answer their own and others' questions about whether they are channeling real spirit beings. For those who are channeling real beings, a lack of spiritual training may leave them ignorant about the true nature and intentions of the channeled entities. Those who are *not* channeling outside entities are simply speaking from different parts of their own psyches. When that is the case—which seems likely given the large numbers of untrained channelers—are they fooling themselves or possessed by their own subconscious? Or are they purposely fooling the many seekers looking for answers in some of the wrong places? Channelers' audiences would do well to check a channeler's references and track record, listen hard to what he or she is saying, go with their own gut feelings, and keep a firm grip on their checkbooks.

Such an audience might also reflect on the power of group possession. Many group leaders, including channelers, Christian preachers, encounter group leaders, shamans and rock stars, are skillful in whipping up group energies. They facilitate group bonding and openness—sometimes among total strangers, sometimes with drugs or alcohol added to the stew—and the audience is temporarily possessed by a group spirit. Depending on the goals of the leaders and the group members, this possession can be positive, negative or anywhere in between. Group energy is very powerful, especially when focused. Healing, ecstatic spiritual states and pure recreational enjoyment can be positive group intentions. When group leaders focus the power of the group on themselves and have a "story" or image the members really want to believe in, the leaders can take advantage of the group possession state to heighten their personal credibility. People tend to drop their critical faculties in such states. If the leader is a charlatan, this dynamic makes it easy for him to keep fooling many of the people much of the time. If our own friends have already praised the leader in advance, we are then even more predisposed toward abandoning discernment. We dive into the group whirlpool, believing in its shaman, preacher or New Age channeler.

Channeling is not new, despite its current New Age renaissance. In ancient days, the Greeks and Romans would have called the human vessel an oracle. Most of us have heard of the oracles of Delphi. Oracles of the past—from Greece to Egypt to China—were often respected consultants of monarchs, military leaders and sometimes priests seeking guidance in their individual domains. Another type of channeler—the trance medium—also existed in the past as well as today. Trance mediums channel the spirits of the human departed to family and friends seeking contact with them. As with the first type of channeler, the period of "possession" is temporary. Such mediums are more rare in New Age circles, but are still consulted throughout Latin America, Southeast Asia and Africa where contact with one's ancestors is considered important. Styles vary, and the medium may either be in direct contact with an ancestor spirit, or may rely on a spirit intermediary who is in contact with the ancestors.

Here in the United States, there is another group of New Age channelers who carry the strange title of "walk-ins" and are said to be no longer themselves at all—or in other words, are permanently possessed. A walk-in is a human whose identity has been displaced and whose body is occupied by an extraterrestrial being who typically communicates through them in strange and stilted accents. Undoubtedly many of these alleged walk-ins are New Age entrepreneurs seeking fame and fortune. But however extreme or unbelievable walk-ins may seem to most people, the preoccupation with UFOs and aliens grows. Counterculture and mainstream publications give time to the issue, including numerous articles in *Omni* and *Penthouse* magazines. Movies like *E.T.*, *Cocoon*, *Close Encounters of the Third Kind*, *Roswell* and others abound, as do growing numbers of related documentaries and books like Whitley Strieber's *Communion*, Timothy Good's *Above Top Secret* and *Alien Contact*, and Kevin D. Randle's *UFO Crash at Roswell*.

We are alternately intrigued by the possibilities of benevolent and enlightened aliens of superior intelligence coming to solve our problems, and apprehensive that such beings might be hostile invaders or body snatchers. Despite the claims of a positive nature from some channelers and walk-ins, multiple testimonies of terrifying alien abductions increasingly highlight the fear that cute little E.T. may in fact be a monster.

Although rumors fly at the speed of UFOs, conclusive evidence on both the existence and designs of extraterrestrials among us is not available to most. Our universe is certainly mysterious and vast enough to hold varieties of intelligent forces. The "visitations" captivating so much human interest may indeed be from far away. There is also speculation that at least some of these visitations are actually energetic phenomenon arising from our own Mother Earth: earth vibrations that release moving balls of light and affect unusually sensitive humans in equally unusual ways. The energies of the earth's lay lines, power spots and even the paramagnetic granite used to build the ancient pyramids are known to induce strange states and visions. But as with God, salvation, messiahs and spirit itself, we give UFOs and alleged aliens importance partly because we believe they come from far and unattainable realms. The mysteries within us and near us don't seem to hold enough glamor when compared to those that dwell in other galaxies.

In addition to channeling or wondering about aliens, the New Age movement also gives a great deal of energy and attention to the issue of reincarnation. Many people who believe in this phenomenon are certain their current attributes and the shape of their present lives have been markedly influenced by their past lives. Some believers integrate "past-life" impressions or visions into their lives in a fairly balanced way, similar to a person in counseling who integrates psychological insights from her childhood. Others become obsessed, basing their present and future actions on myriad past-life readings, seeking their past-life lovers and family in every face, searching for clues of past connections to every new landscape they come upon. The extremists are not possessed by outside spirits, but rather by the past itself.

There is no clean slate at birth for one who believes in reincarnation; there is only another dot on the endless time-space continuum. The issue of individual freedom of choice is debated. Some believers contend knowledge of their past lives gives them more awareness of the dynamics operating in their present incarnation, and therefore widens the scope of conscious choice. Others feel the wheel of karma was set in motion so long ago that we are merely actors in a preordained drama, and anyone who believes in free choice is simply deluded. Although the philosophy of karma may seem Eastern or New Age to mainstream Christians, if they look to their own theology of the inescapable human destiny of original sin, perhaps the concept of karma may seem less foreign.

New Age seekers are excited about the possibilities of direct contact with spiritual forces. Many communities now have ongoing women's and men's spirituality groups which may include drumming, meditation, rituals and other activities. There are numerous urban and rural spirituality centers where a variety of classes are offered. New Age book stores carry magazines listing spirituality workshops and retreats. Avenues for spiritual action and knowledge are multiplying. In itself, the interest in spiritual experience is healthy. The excitement alone is more satisfying than the atheistic, existential emptiness and nausea that bohemians and philosophers were experiencing a few decades ago. However, the new enthusiasm needs to be tempered with caution and knowledge. Many seekers tend to think all spiritual energies are positive and they open themselves indiscriminately to a variety of spiritual forces. This is just as naive a stance as to assume all humans will necessarily act in our best interests simply because they are our fellow human beings: a pleasant fantasy but not always a worldly reality.

Most shamans and other spiritual adepts learn to discern the effects and intentions of various forces throughout their training and development. And they learn to take protective or even offensive measures against forces that may be hostile to them. Western spirituality students would be better off doing likewise. "Will it be good for me too?" is the question they must answer as they begin to open themselves to spiritual energies. Only adequate training, experience and a strong spiritual will can answer this question.

I don't bring up negative possibilities to provoke spiritual hysteria and irrational fears in the reader. Nor do I want spiritually open readers to become so terrorized by potential evil possession, or so skeptical of anything new, that they entirely abandon the spiritual quest. The point is preparedness and wisdom. The ability to make conscious choices is part of what defines a human being, and the ability to make educated choices is part of what defines human wisdom. And so I encourage discernment and personal responsibility in one's spiritual development. Responsibility is the ability to choose one's responses, and is fostered through awareness and knowledge. It is acting consciously rather than being acted upon. If we are to be spiritually active and responsible, we need to understand the broad scope of spiritual energies and prepare ourselves to interact with them—with knowledge and power.

Some say the best offense is a good defense. In our preparations for responsible spiritual interactions, this philosophy is worth adopting. Whether or not we ever encounter evil energies, it is always practical to be in a position of power. This means taking care of ourselves, strengthening the will, gathering power and avoiding participation in dark or foolish spiritual activities—such as dabbling in satanism—that would tend to draw unwanted energies. And it means knowing ourselves. We are capable of unconsciously drawing negative human and nonhuman external forces when there is unconscious negativity within us. Awareness of our weaknesses decreases the chance we will draw outer reflections of them, and increases our ability to protect ourselves. And the more clearly we see those weaknesses, the greater our choices for either banishing them or converting them into strengths. As we reduce the possibility of being possessed by outer demons that reflect the inner ones, we arrive at spiritual responsibility and power.

We often carry some of the worse demons within us and in fact have helped create and nourish them. Just as these monsters can drive us toward destructive actions against ourselves and others, so can they drive others to be their own worst enemies or ours. Some of these tormenting demons are irrational fear, jealousy, greed, hatred, despair and self-doubt. To ignore them or pretend they don't exist does not make them go away, but rather turns us into victims of their hidden manipulations. One of the best strategies for demolishing the demons of our own psyches—or at the least rendering them less effective—is to bring them into the light of awareness.

DEALING WITH OUR DEMONS

We all know that darkness is banished by light, but how do we go about hauling these invisible monsters out from their hiding places and bring them into the light, see them for what they are and reduce their power over us?

One effective means for accomplishing these goals is to give them each a visible, tangible form. Try to identify every inner demon that makes you miserable. Call it by its true name (fear, greed, etc.) or give it a nickname—humorous ones work especially well. Then choose the first "entity" you want to deal with and draw or paint a picture of it, make a clay representation or carve a wooden image. Let yourself become deeply involved in the process, and be as imaginative and creative as you'd like.

Once you've finished the representation to your satisfaction, place it on a flat surface. Then put four candles around it, one in each direction. Light your candles with the intention of bringing the monster out of the darkness and into the light of awareness. As you scrutinize it, begin to talk to it. Tell it you see it, describe its attributes and their effect on your well being. Then ask it where it came from. As you listen within yourself, perhaps images will unfold of the initial event or events that created this energy within you. Or you may hear voices describing the events or simply begin to know what they were without seeing or hearing them. Give yourself plenty of time to explore this terrain. You are a detective or tracker seeking clues that will illuminate you from within. If emotions come up in the process, allow them their existence and continue in your search.

When you have all the information you feel you're going to get in this session, describe it out loud to your monster. "This is what I know about your origins. . . ."

Once you are done, tell your monster that its power over you is weakening. Then place it in a special area you are going to reserve for it and future representations of your other monsters. A shelf, a corner of the room on the floor, a tabletop, anything will do. Then tell it that the next time it rises up within you, you are going to surround it with candles—with light—and face it once again. You are going to prevent it from remaining hidden. And you are going to look for positive replacements for it until it becomes so weak that it either disappears entirely or has no more power to push you around.

These positive replacements are going to be acts of kindness toward yourself. It is a good tactic to replace anything negative with something positive rather than leaving an empty space within yourself. And acts of kindness toward self foster increased self-love, which is powerful protection against many varieties of demons. You can either write up a list of possible acts of kindness to take in the future or simply respond spontaneously with whatever suits the purpose of a given moment. Do at least one such act after every dialogue with one of your monsters. Over time you may decide that a daily act of kindness toward yourself might make a positive addition to your spiritual practices. And you don't need to limit yourself—even more than one a day is allowed!

Every time I offer a spirituality workshop, I witness students' struggles with their demons. Sometimes these inner tyrants cause students to feel unworthy of profound spiritual experiences. Other times, students doubt their ability to accomplish the feats of will that I assure them they are quite capable of with practice. Demons of distraction are also very common, the kind that lead students into doing everything except their spiritual practices and rob them of the satisfaction they might otherwise attain. "These are your enemies!" I tell my workshop participants again and again. "Don't let them possess and dominate you. See your enemies for what they are. Remember the treasures of spirit are your birthright—if you want them, go claim them!"

Beyond the images and inner realities of tormenting demons that we have dealt with throughout history, are there outer entities of ultimate evil that are capable of possessing us and destroying our ability to choose our actions? Theologians have been speculating on this for centuries. The image of the archetypal villains—Satan and his minions—is certainly a compelling one. But is the image compelling because it is based on reality or because we created it in keeping with our tendency to externalize great spiritual power—whether it be benevolent or malevolent? Whatever the answer, human choice exists side by side with both good and evil. Spiritual responsibility includes facing the possibility of evil—as well as light and goodness—and making choices about how we will deal with it. Pretending ignorance and playing ostrich do not make evil go away. In fact, such tactics have allowed tyrants such as Hitler and others to more easily sway—or possess—the masses. The antidotes of knowledge and awareness are exactly what we need to increase our choices for wise actions against evil and to reduce the possibility of becoming helpless victims of circumstance.

Should we be concerned about evil coming from nature

herself? There are certainly forces of nature which can endanger human life, such as hurricanes, lightning and rattlesnakes. Nature's alcohol and drugs also can be dangerous when used or overused unwisely. But these dangers don't come from the malicious intent of nature. When such intent does occur, it seems to originate primarily in humans or occasionally in animals trained by humans. This doesn't signify that we humans are inherently evil even though we are capable of evil. Evil intentions and actions are usually a result of the unvanquished inner demons of fear and self-doubt. When people refuse to deal with their own inner negativity, they tend to increasingly see others as a threat. The evil is all outside of them. From these projections then come the justifications for their own dark attitudes and reactions: racism, war, tyranny and oppression of all varieties.

Throughout this book humans have been described as semipermeable energy fields that are affected by external energies. We are gregarious beings and are thus regularly affected by other humans' energies, even though we may not always be conscious of this fact. Most people desire group acceptance and sometimes this desire supersedes the desire to see clearly the influences and motivations of those around them. We can allow ourselves to be literally carried away by a group's energy, without questioning its goals, if our need for acceptance is greater than our personal responsibility. When we abdicate responsibility in this way, we are possessed by the group spirit. And if the most powerful leader or leaders of the group have dark intentions, then we are possessed by evil. But we have in fact chosen evil by refusing to exercise or acknowledge our perceptions. We have chosen to become possessed.

If the human race is to move forward in its developmental stage toward greater maturity, then each of us needs to do what we can to mature individually. Taking responsibility for our lives on all levels is spiritual action, because it requires exercising the spiritual gifts of awareness, will and the ability to learn and make educated choices. Strengthening these attributes helps us stay out of the trap of always blaming others for our problems. During this millennial period of great change and unlimited potentials, I especially urge women to stay clear of the blaming trap. Without discounting real sexist discrimination and oppression, women need to know they have a great deal of power and can use their power for effective change. Simply blaming men for all our problems is not only unjust but shifts our psyches to a stance of helplessness, from which powerful and responsible actions can't take place. We all need to mature—men and women alike. We need to claim our innate strengths, own our weaknesses and support one another in being the unique, powerful individuals we are. The stronger and more empowered we each become, the more confident we will grow in our ability to act and effect positive change. And the less we will wait for someone or something else to fix everything.

To Be or Not to Be

By now the reader may be wondering if she is up to the challenge of being responsible for herself on so many levels day in and day out. Maybe she is wondering if there is an appropriate time or way to let other people or forces be temporarily in control, so she can relax her grip on the reins of her life. And what about setting aside ego or personal preferences and turning our lives over to a Higher Power? Is the author going to call that being irresponsible?

I say we are people with enormous potential, including the ability to make choices about our lives. If this book has helped remind you of that fact and has expanded the range of possible choices you will consider in the future, if it has inspired you to remind others of their potentials and choices and encourage them to exercise those choices, then this book has accomplished a great deal of its purpose. And yes, there *are* times when it is fine to choose to step aside and let other people or forces affect aspects of your life.

For example, at work there may be times when another person has an idea or a way of doing things that is more productive than your own. You can table your own thoughts and methods in exchange for theirs. If you are married or involved in some other kind of extended friendship, there will undoubtedly be times where compromises are called for. One person or the other will decide that acting in a different way than he or she might ordinarily prefer is a worthwhile tradeoff for the benefits derived from sustaining the relationship.

As another example, when you take a class or workshop in which the ideas expressed may be new and even quite foreign to your usual way of doing things, you can decide to set aside your old ways and try something new on for size. If you find it fits you, keep the new perspective and integrate it into your life. At other times, you may choose to temporarily or permanently enter some kind of spiritual retreat or community. If following the community's rules supports you in your goals of spiritual focus, even if it means letting go of some of your secular habits and patterns of personality, you can choose to follow those rules in exchange for the spiritual rewards.

And then there is sex. Sex with someone we trust and care for is a wonderful opportunity for taking turns at the role of control. We can indulge in both nurturing and being nurtured, being more active and then more passive, inciting passion and then allowing ourselves to be overwhelmed by passion. All of us need the chance to periodically let down our defenses, to relax, and even to let the boundaries of personal identity melt into that ephemeral merging with the energies of another human being. And choosing sex with an affectionate and trusted partner is an ideal way for many of us to experience this temporary abandon.

Some people feel we are such imperfect beings that we'd be better off permanently abandoning body, mind, heart and soul to the will of God, and following what I call the "urge to merge" to its ultimate conclusion—Divine possession. I have experienced such sentiments myself. Years ago there were times I was so distressed by aspects of my personality, my ego and those of my fellow human beings that I felt the only solution to all our problems was for each of us to completely step aside, empty ourselves and become perfect channels of Creator's power and glory. To that end I went through periods of intense fasting, meditation and fervent prayers that "I" might be dissolved and thus become such a perfect vessel.

These endeavors had various purifying and strengthening benefits for my body, mind and spirit, and were often deep and transformative. And yet the essential me remained, a clearly present reminder that I hadn't reached my fantasy of perfect and permanent union with God. Yes, I confess. I desired to be totally possessed by the Divine. And I finally arrived at a new perspective as a result of my many efforts in that direction and a great deal of contemplation on the subject of human limitations. What I concluded was that who and how I was—including my ability to grow and learn and change—was already the expression of Creator's will for me. It seemed God didn't really want me to be a mindless zombie with no personality, but rather a human being with appreciation and goals for the many qualities I'd been imbued with at birth. Nor was it appropriate for me to deny the body I'd been given. My body was a perfect vehicle for experiencing myself as a distinct entity with boundaries. It was also the abode of my spirit and by taking care of it I not only provided my spirit with a good home but also gave it the strength to go on journeys away from home. And finally, after all my efforts to serve Creator by emptying myself, I understood the old adage "God helps those who help themselves" in a new way. A spark of the supreme power was already within me. If I developed my gifts and expressed my uniqueness toward the highest goals I could conceive of, Divine action would in fact be supporting and moving through my life and into the world.

As a result of these personal insights and conclusions, I am no longer waiting for Creator to descend from the heavens and save me—or the rest of humanity—as I once did. I am not waiting to be possessed by extraterrestrials, no matter how enlightened, or by any other external source of salvation. And since I already know that the kingdom of heaven—the light of spirit—is within, if Jesus decided to visit us once again with that eternally appropriate message, I would enjoy the reminder but I don't need to wait for it.

I need to experience the kingdom within. Rather than pining for divine intervention, I try more and more to live my life with as much awareness as possible, to act in ways that allow me to be as creative, conscious and vital as I can be. And most days I spend some time in meditation, setting aside thoughts and emotions. This helps me place my focus on the inner mystery within me, the energies that are my spiritual identity and connection with the rest of the mysterious universe.

This book is both a result and a part of my own journey of awareness and of spiritual action. I hope it will be a useful companion and guide for you. The Divine—the power and the glory I've experienced—shines from within every atom of creation. It sings to us in the winds, it dances through our dreams, it reaches out from our cells to claim our loving attention. Its beauty is in the eyes of the beholder. May our eyes behold that beauty, and may our lives become the return of spirit in action.

Bibliography

Balch, James F., M.D. and Phyllis, C.N.C.. *Prescription for Nutritional Healing*. Garden City Park, New York: Avery Publishing Group, Inc., 1990.

Brown, Stephen and Takahashi, Masaru. *Qigong for Health*. New York and Tokyo: Japan Publications, 1986.

Chia, Mantak and Maneewan Chia. *Bone Marrow Nei Kung*. Boston: Charles E. Tuttle Company, 1989.

_____. *Cultivating Female Sexual Energy*. Huntington, New York: Healing Tao Books, 1986.

Choudhury, Bikram. *Bikram's Beginning Yoga Class*. Los Angeles: Jeremy P. Tarcher, Inc., 1978.

Chuen, Master Lain Kam. *The Way of Energy*. New York: Simon and Schuster, 1991.

Daly, Mary. *Gyn/ecology*. Boston: Beacon Press, 1990.

Davis, Patricia. *A Change for the Better*. Woodstock, New York: Beekman Publishers, 1993.

Friedan, Betty. *The Fountain of Age*. New York: Simon and Schuster, 1993.

Gittleman, Ann Louise. *Super Nutrition for Menopause*. New York: Pocket Books, 1993.

Greenwood, Sadja, M.D. *Menopause, Naturally, Updated*. San Francisco: Volcano Press, 1992.

Greer, Germaine. *The Change*. New York: Alfred A. Knopf, 1992.

Hover-Kramer, Dorothea. *Healing Touch: A Resource for Health Care Professionals*. Albany, New York: Del Mar, 1996.

Jwing-Ming, Dr. Yang. *The Essence of Tai Chi Chi Kung*. Jamaica Plain, Massachusetts: Y.M.A.A. Publication Center, Inc., 1990.

——————————. *The Root of Chinese Chi Kung*. Jamaica Plain, Massachusetts: Y.M.A.A. Publication Center, Inc., 1989.

Krieger, Dolores. *Accepting Your Power to Heal: The Personal Practice of Therapy*. Santa Fe: Bear & Co., 1993.

Krippner, Stanley and Villoldo, Alberto. *Healing States*. New York: Simon and Schuster, 1987.

MacMahon, Alice T. *Women and Hormones: An Essential Guide to Being Female*. Maitland, Florida: Family Publications, 1992.

Mendelsohn, Robert S., M.D. *MalePractice: How Doctors Manipulate Women*. Chicago: Contemporary Books, Inc., 1982.

Norman, Laura. *Feet First: A Guide to Foot Reflexology*. New York: Simon and Schuster, 1988.

Perls, Fritz. *Gestalt Therapy: Excitement and Growth in the Human Personality*. Highland, New York: Gestalt Journal Press, 1994.

Ray, Sondra. *Rebirthing in the New Age*. Berkeley, California: Celestial Arts Publishing Company, 1995.

Roth, Gabrielle. *Maps to Ecstasy*. San Rafael, California: New World Library, 1989.

Ryneveld, Edna C. *Secrets of a Natural Menopause*. St. Paul, Minnesota: Llewellyn, 1994.

Sheehy, Gail. *The Silent Passage: Menopause*. New York: Random House, 1992.

Stepanich, Kisma. *Sister Moon Lodge: The Power and Mystery of Menstruation*. St. Paul, Minnesota: Llewellyn, 1992.

Sumrall, Amber C. and Taylor, Dena. *Women of the 14th Moon: Writings on Menopause*. Watsonville, California: Crossing Press, 1991.

Takahashi, Masaru and Stephen Brown. *Quigong for Health: Chinese Traditional Exercise for Cure & Prevention*. New York: Japan Pubns. (U.S.A.), Inc., 1986.

Tierra, Michael. *The Way of Herbs*. New York: Pocket Books, 1990.

Walker, Alice. *Possessing the Secret of Joy*. Orlando, Florida: Harcourt, Brace & Co., 1992.

Weed, Susan. *The Menopausal Years*. Woodstock, New York: Ash Tree Publications, 1992.

About the Author

Josie RavenWing, B.A. in dance movement therapy and M.A. in clinical and humanistic psychology, had her first visionary experience when she was about 10 months old, and this set her on a lifelong journey of spiritual exploration and discovery.

In the early 1970s, she began her work in the field of human development as an innovative pioneer of dance therapy and holistic healing. She also started exploring shamanistic traditions, which she has incorporated in her work since that time. At Antioch University in Seattle, she developed and taught courses in the first Holistic Health graduate program in the U.S. During that same period, her growing concern about women's issues and self-esteem inspired her to organize one of Seattle's first women's support groups and later led her to create a variety of workshops and retreats to meet women's needs for spiritual exploration and growth.

Josie continued to expand her work. Throughout several decades as a psychotherapist, she has integrated Western theory with spiritual, shamanistic and hands-on healing practices of many cultures. She applies her grounded, ongoing synthesis in counseling work with individuals and as an accomplished seminar leader. She has lectured at college campuses and offered her "Awakening" seminars in the United States and abroad for over a decade.

RavenWing's creativity also expresses itself in her songwriting, poetry, ceremonial leadership and spiritual dance choreography. She is currently writing her third book and developing retreats for writers and other professionals seeking spiritual and creative renewal. RavenWing continuously explores ways to inspire people toward awareness, beauty and spiritual fulfillment.

For information on her music tapes, to be on her mailing list for lectures and workshops in your area and for her "Desert Visions" Southwest retreats, or if you would like to sponsor a workshop in your area, please send your request and a self-addressed stamped envelope to Josie RavenWing, c/o The Awakening Seminars, 7990 N.W. 37th St., Ankeny, IA 50021.

Share the Magic of Chicken Soup

Chicken Soup for the Soul™
101 Stories to Open the Heart and Rekindle the Spirit

The #1 *New York Times* bestseller and ABBY award-winning inspirational book that has touched the lives of millions. Whether you buy it for yourself or as a gift to others, you're sure to enrich the lives of everyone around you with this affordable treasure.

Code 262X: Paperback $12.95
Code 2913: Hardcover $24.00
Code 3812: Large print $16.95

A 2nd Helping of Chicken Soup for the Soul™
101 More Stories to Open the Heart and Rekindle the Spirit

This rare sequel accomplishes the impossible—it is as tasty as the original, and still fat-free. If you enjoyed the first *Chicken Soup for the Soul,* be warned: it was merely the first course in an uplifting grand buffet. These stories will leave you satisfied and full of self-esteem, love and compassion.

Code 3316: Paperback $12.95
Code 3324: Hardcover $24.00
Code 3820: Large print $16.95

A 3rd Serving of Chicken Soup for the Soul™
101 More Stories to Open the Heart and Rekindle the Spirit

The latest addition to the *Chicken Soup for the Soul* series is guaranteed to put a smile in your heart. Learn through others the important lessons of love, parenting, forgiveness, hope and perseverance. This tasty literary stew will stay with you long after you've put the book down.

Code 3790: Paperback. $12.95
Code 3804: Hardcover. $24.00
Code 4002: Large print $16.95

Available at your favorite bookstore or call
1-800-441-5569 for Visa or MasterCard orders. Prices do not include shipping and handling. Your response code is HCI.

Extra Helpings of Chicken Soup

Chicken Soup for the Soul™ Cookbook
101 Stories with Recipes from the Heart

Here authors Jack Canfield and Mark Victor Hansen have teamed up with award-winning cookbook author Diana von Welanetz Wentworth and dished up a delightful collection of stories accompanied by mouthwatering recipes.

Code 3545: Paperback $16.95
Code 3634: Hardcover $29.95

Sopa de pollo para el alma
(Spanish Language Version)
Relatos que conmueven el corazón y ponen fuego en el espíritu

The national bestseller and 1995 ABBY Award winner *Chicken Soup for the Soul* is now available in a lovingly prepared Spanish language edition. The stories found in *Sopa de pollo para el alma* are as rich as mole sauce and as robust and invigorating as café Cubano.

Code 3537: Paperback $12.95

Chicken Soup for the Surviving Soul
101 Inspirational Stories to Comfort Cancer Patients and Their Loved Ones

For years, the uplifting stories in the *Chicken Soup for the Soul* series have empowered individuals who have serious illnesses. Now Jack Canfield and Mark Victor Hansen have joined with Patty Aubery and Nancy Mitchell for a special batch of *Chicken Soup* devoted to stories of people beating cancer and finding renewed meaning in their lives.

Code 4029: Paperback $12.95
Code 4037: Hardcover $24.00

Available at your favorite bookstore or call 1-800-441-5569 for Visa or MasterCard orders. Prices do not include shipping and handling. Your response code is HCI.

Lift Your Spirits with Chicken Soup for the Soul™ Audiotapes

The Best of the Original Chicken Soup for the Soul™ Audiotape

This single 90-minute cassette contains the very best stories from the ABBY Award-winning *Chicken Soup for the Soul*. You will be enlightened and entertained by the masterful storytelling of Jack, Mark and friends.

Code 3723: One 90-minute cassette $9.95

Chicken Soup for the Soul™ Audio Gift Set

This six-tape set includes the entire audio collection of stories from *Chicken Soup for the Soul*—over seven hours of listening pleasure. It makes wonderful gift for friends, loved ones or yourself.

Code 3103:
Six cassettes—Seven hours of inspiration $29.95

A 2nd Helping of Chicken Soup for the Soul™ Abridged Version Audiotape

This two-tape volume brings you the authors' favorite stories from *A 2nd Helping of Chicken Soup for the Soul*. Now you can listen to the second batch in your car or in the comfort of your own home.

Code 3766: Two 90-minute cassettes $14.95

The Best of A 3rd Serving of Chicken Soup for the Soul™ Audiotape

The newest *Chicken Soup* stories on this delightful audio book will uplift and entertain you with their empowering messages of love, hope and perseverance. This scrumptious collection is guaranteed to brighten your day.

Code 4045: One 90-minute cassette $9.95

Available at your favorite bookstore or call 1-800-441-5569 for Visa or MasterCard orders. Prices do not include shipping and handling. Your response code is HCI.

Famous Women Discuss Their Spiritual Experiences

Embracing Our Essence
Spiritual Conversations with Prominent Women
Susan Skog

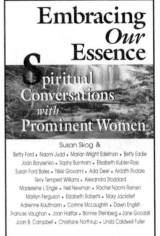

In the first shining collection of its kind, 29 prominent women of our time intimately share with you the philosophies, practices, touchstones and struggles that shape their lush interiors. They discuss the source of the pulsing spirituality sweeping our country and why it's our only hope for personal fulfillment and evolution as a society. The powerful messages shared in this book invite women to discover their own spiritual essence: the intuitiveness, wisdom and compassion that have the power to transform the world. *Embracing Our Essence* is also valuable solace to women and men discovering their own spiritual strength.

Code 3596 paperback $11.95
Code 3782 hardcover $22.00

Includes interviews with:

Betty Ford ♦ Naomi Judd ♦ Marian Wright Edelman
Betty Eadie ♦ Joan Borysenko ♦ Sophy Burnham
Elisabeth Kubler-Ross ♦ Susan Ford Bales ♦ Nikki Giovanni ♦ Ada Deer
Ardath Rodale ♦ Jane Goodall ♦ Linda Caldwell Fuller
Terry Tempest Williams ♦ Alexandra Stoddard ♦ Madeleine L'Engle
Nell Newman ♦ Rachel Naomi Remen ♦ Marilyn Ferguson
Elizabeth Roberts ♦ Mary Jacksteit ♦ Adrienne Kaufmann
Corinne McLaughlin ♦ Dawn English
Frances Vaughan ♦ Joan Halifax ♦ Bonnie Steinberg
Joan B. Campbell ♦ Christiane Northrup